Fodor's InFocus

FLORIDA
KEYS

P9-DHM-782

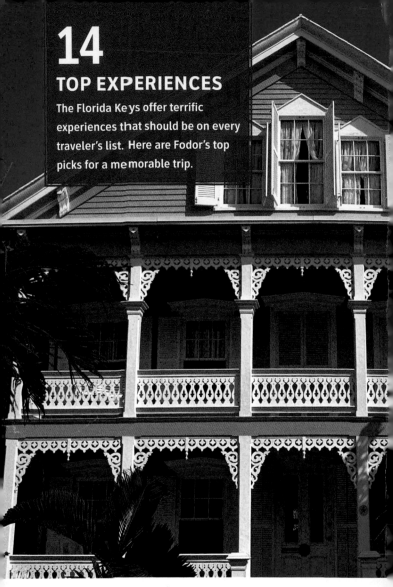

14
TOP EXPERIENCES
The Florida Keys offer terrific experiences that should be on every traveler's list. Here are Fodor's top picks for a memorable trip.

1 Key West Architecture
Built on stilts to keep things cool, Key West's clapboard Conch houses feature porches with gingerbread trim. Many have been converted into atmospheric bed-and-breakfasts. *(Ch. 5)*

2 Kayaking and Canoeing

Whether you prefer sea kayaking, canoeing through calm and wildlife-rich mangrove waters, or stand-up paddleboarding, the Keys provide the setting and the perfect outfitters. *(Ch. 2)*

3 Key Lime Pie

You're going to need a lot of time and appetite, because key lime pie is everywhere, and everyone claims to make the best. *(Ch. 5)*

4 Dolphin Adventures

From watching them in the wild or captivity, to getting in the water to swim and interact with them, experiencing dolphins is a classic Keys adventure. *(Ch. 2)*

5 The Cuba Connection

Cuba looms large in Key West, which was settled by cigar-making immigrants. El Meson Pepe and El Siboney are two restaurants that serve Cuban delicacies. *(Ch. 5)*

6 Duval Street

Do the Duval Crawl in Key West. There are no rules: stop for a drink, simply wander, or shop instead of drink. But you aren't allowed to go fun-free. *(Ch. 5)*

7 Key Largo's Christ of the Deep

Just outside of John Pennecamp Coral Reef State Park on Key Largo, this submerged 9-foot-tall statue makes a divine underwater sight. *(Ch. 2)*

8 Ernest Hemingway's Home

You'll see his name all over Key West, but the best place to start is his historic home, where descendants of his six-toed cats still prowl. *(Ch. 5)*

9 Highway 1

Despite the traffic, the Overseas Highway (aka U.S. 1) is an engineering marvel and the only way to reach the southernmost point in the U.S. *(Ch. 2)*

10 Beaches

Keys beaches, including Bahia Honda State Park, Marathon's Sombrero Beach, and Key West's Fort Zachary Taylor Historic State Park, can be beautiful. *(Ch. 4, 3, 5)*

11 The Dry Tortugas

Seaplanes and fast ferries deliver you to Dry Tortugas National Park, known for its birding, snorkeling, and historic Fort Jefferson. *(Ch. 5)*

12 Fresh Seafood

You don't have to catch your own to relish the lobster, yellowtail snapper, hogfish, and mahi-mahi that are signatures of the Florida Keys. You'll find fresh seafood everywhere. *(Ch. 3)*

13 Fishing

Jump on a party or charter boat for offshore or back-bay fishing. Or cast a line from one of the Keys' many bridges. *(Ch. 4)*

14 Sunset at Key West's Mallory Square

Not only does the setting sun put on a fabulous show, but local musicians, magicians, and performance artists also join the act every evening. *(Ch. 5)*

CONTENTS

ABOUT THIS GUIDE

Fodor's Ratings

Everything in this guide is worth doing—we don't cover what isn't—but exceptional sights, hotels, and restaurants are recognized with additional accolades. **Fodor's Choice ★** indicates our top recommendations; highlights places we deem highly recommended. Care to nominate a new place? Visit Fodors.com/contact-us.

Trip Costs

We list prices wherever possible to help you budget well. Hotel and restaurant price categories from **$** to **$$$$** are noted alongside each recommendation. For hotels, we include the lowest cost of a standard double room in high season. For restaurants, we cite the average price of a main course at dinner or, if dinner isn't served, at lunch. For attractions, we always list adult admission fees; discounts are usually available for children, students, and senior citizens.

Hotels

Our local writers vet every hotel to recommend the best overnights in each price category, from budget to expensive. Unless otherwise specified, you can expect private bath, phone, and TV in your room. For expanded hotel reviews, visit Fodors.com.

Restaurants

Unless we state otherwise, restaurants are open for lunch and dinner daily. We mention dress code only when there's a specific requirement and reservations only when they're essential or not accepted.

Credit Cards

The hotels and restaurants in this guide typically accept credit cards. If not, we'll say so.

Top Picks

★ Fodor's Choice

Listings

- ✉ Address
- 📨 Branch address
- 📫 Mailing address
- ☎ Telephone
- 📠 Fax
- 🌐 Website
- 📧 E-mail
- 🎟 Admission fee
- ⏲ Open/closed times
- [M] Subway
- ✥ Directions or Map coordinates

Hotels & Restaurants

- 🏨 Hotel
- 🛏 Number of rooms
- 🍽 Meal plans
- ✕ Restaurant
- ✍ Reservations
- 👔 Dress code
- 💳 No credit cards
- [$] Price

Other

- ⇨ See also
- ☞ Take note
- ⛳ Golf facilities

EXPERIENCE THE FLORIDA KEYS

WHAT'S WHERE

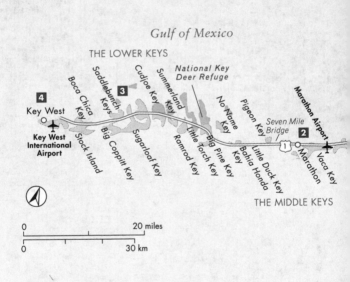

The Upper Keys. As the doorstep to the islands' coral reefs and blithe spirit, the Upper Keys introduce all that is sporting and sea-oriented about the Keys. They stretch from Key Largo to the Long Key Channel (MM 106–65).

The Middle Keys. Centered around the town of Marathon, the Middle Keys hold most of the chain's historic and natural attractions outside of Key West. They go from Conch (pronounced *konk*) Key through Marathon to the south side of the Seven Mile Bridge, including Pigeon Key (MM 65–40).

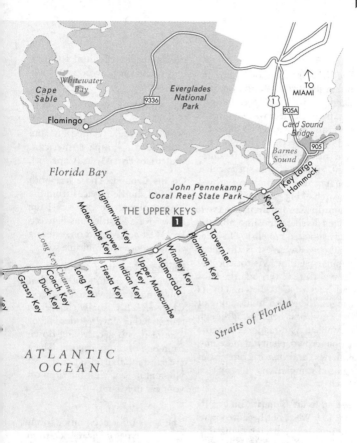

3 The Lower Keys. Pressure drops another notch in this laid-back part of the region, where wildlife and the fishing lifestyle peak. The Lower Keys go from Little Duck Key south through Big Coppitt Key (MM 40–9).

4 Key West. The ultimate in Florida Keys craziness, party town Key West isn't the place for those seeking a quiet retreat. The Key West area encompasses MM 9–0.

FLORIDA KEYS PLANNER

Activities

The Keys are all about being on and in the water. **Diving** in particular draws water-sports enthusiasts to explore the clear waters, vibrant reefs, and sea life. Dive shops up and down Overseas Highway sell dive trips, instruction, and equipment. **Fishing,** too, is spectacular, bringing the rod-and-reel crowd in search of big game such as marlin, tarpon, and mahimahi as well as flats dwellers, most notably the easily spooked bonefish. On land, exploring **Key West** is the most popular pastime. Visitors do the "Duval Crawl" through the pubs and bars of Old Town. On its fringes, the island holds some of the Keys' best beaches, although they are all man-made. For a more serious crowd, plenty of museums, galleries, and historic sites offer cultural stimulation.

Logistics

Getting to the Islands: You can fly into Key West, but because flights are few, many prefer flying into Miami International Airport (MIA) and driving the 110-mile Overseas Highway (aka U.S. 1). Marathon has an airport, but it's served only by charter flights. There's also ferry service from Marco Island and Fort Myers Beach.

Hassle Factor: Medium to high, depending on how far you have to drive.

Nonstops: You can fly nonstop to Key West from Atlanta (Delta), Fort Lauderdale (United), Miami (American), Tampa (American, United), or Fort Myers (Cape Air).

On the Ground: There are both bus and shuttle services from the Miami airport to the Keys; the Lower Keys Shuttle runs between Key West and Marathon, offering cheap service and multiple stops.

Renting a Car: It's possible to get by without a car in Key West, but you'll need one virtually everywhere else. It's usually cheaper to rent in either Fort Lauderdale or Miami if you are driving down from one of those airports. There are substantial drop-off charges if you rent in Key West but drop off your car in Miami.

Where to Stay

The Keys offer accommodations for every type of vacationer, from fishing lodges to luxury hotels to the famed historic B&Bs of Key West.

Resorts: Name-brand destination resorts such as Hyatt and Marriott take care of guests' every need with swimming pools, beaches, spas, restaurants, and concierges who will arrange tours and activities. Smaller resorts have a mom-and-pop feel—some every bit as luxurious as the big guys, others ultracasual.

B&Bs: Government incentives to turn headed-for-decrepit historic homes into lodgings have led to Key West's abundance of guest-houses and B&Bs. They range from all-male gay properties and little bohemian enclaves to elegantly turned-out mansions with no luxury spared. Other Keys have a few more fine choices away from the Key West crowds and clamor.

Fishing Lodges: It's easy to find a fishing lodge in the Keys, outside of Key West. Some are simple and some more luxurious, with marina facilities on-site or close by.

Hotel and Restaurant Costs

Prices in the restaurant reviews are the average cost of a main course at dinner or, if dinner is not served, at lunch; taxes and service charges are generally included. Prices in the hotel reviews are the lowest cost of a standard double room in high season, excluding taxes, service charges, and meal plans (except at all-inclusives). Prices for rentals are the lowest per-night cost for a one-bedroom unit in high season.

Pick the Right Key

Key Largo is great for diving and luxurious resorts and condo rentals; its proximity to the Everglades also makes it a destination for birders.

Islamorada is known for sportfishing (and at times celebrity spotting, particularly for those celebs who like game fishing).

Big Pine Key is great for fishing on a smaller scale or for kayaking.

Key West is known for cultural attractions, nightlife, dining, and great B&Bs; it's also the most popular gay destination in the Keys.

Marathon is home to Curry Hammock State Park, lots of midrange accommodations, pretty good food, and great access to water sports.

Bahia Honda Key has the best beach in the Keys, hands down.

IF YOU LIKE...

Water Sports

Fishing, snorkeling, scuba diving, and glass-bottom-boat tours top the list of Keys activities, but you'll find all manner of water sports from kayaking and stand-up paddleboarding to swimming and sailing.

Bahia Honda State Park, Bahia Honda Key. Not only does this state park boast the Keys' best white-sand beach, it's also the place to go snorkeling and kayaking.

Dry Tortugas National Park. A fast ferry makes the 2¼-hour trip each way from Key West to the reefs and historic fort on Garden Key. Once there, the snorkeling is fabulous.

Fishing trips. Party boats and charter captains in all the major Keys take you where the fish are biting. You have your choice of back-bay (known by locals as "backcountry") and deep-sea excursions.

John Pennekamp Coral Reef State Park, Key Largo. One of the most popular stops for snorkelers and divers, it also offers glass-bottom-boat tours to the reef that rims it.

Looe Key Reef, Lower Keys. One of the most stunning stretches of reef and marine life in the Keys, it is also the setting for the annual Underwater Music Festival.

Seafood

You don't have to eat seafood in the Keys, but it's so fresh that it's hard to resist, and the many talented chefs know their seafood.

Ambrosia, Key West. The undisputed master of sushi in these parts, it makes the ultimate use of local fresh fish.

B.O.'s Fish Wagon, Key West. It doesn't get any funkier than this broken-down food truck that has grown into a junkyard-chic restaurant.

Chef Michael's, Islamorada. Here is one prime example of how Keys chefs know their way around fine Continental cuisine.

El Meson de Pepe, Key West. Authentic Cuban cuisine is easy to find in Key West, but this spot has the best setting for watching the sunset at Mallory Square.

The Fish House, Key Largo. Dining in a restaurant with no views and no windows might not sound like a Keys experience, but this is the ultimate in seafood served fresh.

If You Like...   > 17

Nightlife

You don't have to wait for nightfall to get started on Key West's celebrated party scene. The other Keys, too, claim their favorite watering holes—usually (and appropriately) on the water.

The Garden of Eden, Key West. Bare it all at this upstairs clothing-optional spot.

Green Parrot Bar, Key West. Another Key West classic—in fact, the town's oldest bar—it hosts live entertainment nightly at MM 0.

La Te Da Bar, Key West. For purely Keys-style entertainment, catch the hilarious drag shows here.

Lorelei Cabana Bar, Islamorada. Teetering at the edge of a marina, its sunset entertainment draws the fishing and party crowds.

Sloppy Joe's, Key West. The first name in nightlife in Old Town, it jams day and night with live music.

Snapper's, Key Largo. Live bands play daily at this marina-side spot, where the food is as good as the cocktails.

Culture

Don't discount the Keys' serious side. The islands offer both history and arts in the most surprising places.

Ernest Hemingway Home and Museum, Key West. The unofficial patron saint of Key West, Nobel Prize–winning author Ernest Hemingway lived, fished, and wrote in Key West for more than 10 years—one of several celebrated writers who migrated here.

History of Diving Museum, Islamorada. It peeks into the development of scuba diving with 13 galleries of hands-on exhibits.

Key West Forts. Explore Fort Zachary Taylor Historic State Park and East and West Martello Towers to learn about Key West's military importance in times past.

Key West Museum of Art and History, Key West. Housed in the late-19th-century customhouse, the museum hosts changing art exhibits and permanent displays about island bygones.

Pigeon Key, Marathon. Take a ferryboat to this 5-acre key that once held the Keys' railroading operations and housed its workers. Check out the railroad museum and Bahamian architecture.

WHEN TO GO

In high season, from mid-December through mid-April, traffic is inevitably heavy. From November to mid-December, crowds are thinner, the weather is superlative, and hotels and shops drastically reduce their prices. Summer is a second high season, especially among families, Europeans, bargain seekers, and lobster divers.

Florida is rightly called the Sunshine State, but it could also be dubbed the "Humidity State." From June through September, 90% humidity levels are not uncommon. Thankfully, the weather in the Keys is more moderate than in mainland Florida. Temperatures can be 10°F cooler during the summer and up to 10°F warmer during the winter. The Keys also get substantially less rain than mainland Florida, mostly in quick downpours on summer afternoons. In hurricane season, June through November, the Keys get their fair share of warnings; pay heed, and evacuate earlier rather than later, when flights and automobile traffic get backed up.

Festivals and Events

Fishing tournaments start in December with the **Islamorada Fishing Club Sailfish Tournament** in the so-called Sportsfishing Capital of the World. Come spring and summer, different target fish inspire the **Islamorada All-Tackle Spring Bonefish Tournament** in April and **Big Pine & Lower Keys Dolphin Tournament** in June. (Mahimahi is the catch of the latter.)

Key Largo celebrates Easter Keys-style during its **Underwater Easter Egg Hunt** followed in July by another signature below-the-surface tradition, the **Underwater Music Festival** on Looe Key Reef.

Next in importance comes seafood. Four biggies take place during the winter season, starting in late January with the **Key West Wine and Food Festival** and the **Florida Keys Seafood Festival** in Key West, as well as the **Key Largo Stone Crab & Seafood Festival**. In March, the **Original Marathon Seafood Festival** has been happening since the 1970s. To celebrate lobster season, Key West throws its **Lobsterfest** each August.

Finally, the islands celebrate their culture and heritage at such hallmark events as **Sculpture Key West,** a winter-long outdoor exhibition; Marathon's annual **Pigeon Key Art Festival** in February; and the 10-day **Conch Republic Independence Celebration** in Key West every April. Two of Key West's most publicized events include the **Hemingway Days** in July, with its highly competitive Hemingway look-alike contest, and October's manic **Fantasy Fest.**

KIDS AND FAMILIES

Families who love beaches, snorkeling, kayaking, and sea creatures will revel in the Keys. Although many smaller resorts and B&Bs discourage children, plenty of family resorts have kids' programs and activities. Key West's wild party scene may seem the least attractive to families, yet it, too, boasts family resorts, beaches, and age-appropriate attractions.

Upper Keys

The **Playa Largo Resort** and **Marriott's Key Largo Bay Beach Resort** offer the best family amenities in a beachfront destination resort setting with planned activities. **John Pennekamp Coral Reef Resort** also provides snorkel and glass-bottom-boat tours, kayak rentals, and safe beaches. In Islamorada to the south, the atmosphere is more upscale, but **Cheeca Lodge** has always been a family favorite, given its private beach and eco-educational Camp Cheeca.

Take the kids to **Robbie's Marina** in Islamorada, and have lunch at **Hungry Tarpon** before you feed sardines to the truly hungry tarpon. **Theater of the Sea** entails more marine-life interaction, including rays, dolphins, and sea lions.

Middle Keys

Hawks Cay, north of Marathon, is a perfect match for families with its villas, pirate-themed pool, kids'

program, and dolphin encounters. For more dolphin interactions, check out **Dolphin Research Center** or **Dolphin Cove.** Families will also feel at home at **Tranquility Bay** in Marathon, where they can play on the beach and spread out in a town house behind picket fences. Don't miss **Crane Point Museum, Nature Center, and Historic Site,** and **Pigeon Key** for easy-to-absorb lessons in history and the environment.

Lower Keys and Key West

Budget at least a half day to spend beaching, snorkeling, kayaking, and hiking at **Bahia Honda State Park.** It's also a good place to rent a cabin (if you reserve early). Go in the morning or evening to try to spot the tiny deer at **National Key Deer Refuge** on Big Pine Key. In Key West, family lodging choices include the **Casa Marina resort, Hyatt Key West Resort, Southernmost Beach Resort,** and **The Reach resort**—all boast beach access and distance from the Duval Street hubbub. Casual seafood restaurants such as the **Half Shell Raw Bar** welcome children, and the **Key West Butterfly and Nature Conservatory, Key West Aquarium, Conch Tour Train, beaches,** and **Eco-Discovery Center** give families many days' worth of entertainment and enlightenment.

BEST BEACHES

Long Key State Park
The beach at Long Key State Park at MM 67.5 is a typical Upper Keys beach. Rather than a sandy beach, what you see are more like sand flats, where low tide reveals the coral bedrock of the ecosystem. If you're willing to camp, you can be lulled to sleep by the sound of the gentle sea waves—there are no hotel rooms or cabins at the park. (The beach is accessible only to day-trippers and campers.)

Sombrero Beach
Something of a local hangout, Sombrero Beach in Marathon is worth getting off-the-beaten-Overseas-Highway path for (exit at MM 50 onto Sombrero Beach Road). Families will find much to do on the man-made coved beach and its green, manicured lawn, playground area, and clear, calm waters. Separate sections also accommodate boaters and windsurfers.

Bahia Honda State Park
This state park at MM 37 holds three beaches, considered the best beaches in all of the Keys. Sandspur Beach is the most removed from crowds, with long stretches of powdery sand and a campground. Loggerhead Beach is closer to the park's concession area, where you can rent snorkel equipment and kayaks. Like Sandspur, it faces the Atlantic Ocean, but waves are typically wimpy. Near Loggerhead, Calusa Beach on the gulf side near the marina is popular with families, offering a small and safe swimming area, picnic facilities, and camping.

Higgs Beach
This beach on Atlantic Boulevard in Key West is as urban as beaches in the Keys get, with lots of amenities, activities, and distractions. Visitors can check out a historic site, eat at a popular beachfront Italian restaurant, rent a kayak, play volleyball or tennis, or let their children loose at the playground—all within walking distance of the long sweep of man-made beach and sparkling-clear, shallow, calm water.

Fort Zachary Taylor Historic State Park
This man-made beach is part of a Civil War–era fort complex and arguably the best beach in Key West, with its typically small waves, swaying Australian pines, water-sports equipment rentals, and shaded picnic grounds. From mid-January through mid-April, it also hosts an alfresco collection of oversize art called Sculpture Key West, which showcases artists from across the country.

1

GREAT ITINERARIES

If You Have 3 Days

Spend your first morning diving or snorkeling at John Pennekamp Coral Reef State Park in **Key Largo.** Celebrate sunset with dinner at a waterside restaurant. On Day 2 savor the breathtaking views on the two-hour drive to Key West. Along the way, stop at Crane Point Museum, Nature Center and Historic Site in **Marathon.** Another worthwhile detour is Bahia Honda Key State Park on **Bahia Honda Key,** where you can stretch your legs on a nature trail or snorkel on an off-shore reef. Once you arrive in **Key West,** watch the sunset at the Mallory Square celebration. The next day, take a trolley tour of Old Town, stroll Duval Street and visit a museum or two, or spend some beach time at Fort Zachary Taylor Historic State Park.

If You Have 7 Days

Spend your first day as you would in the above itinerary, but stay both the second and third nights in **Islamorada,** fitting in some fishing, boating, or kayaking excursions from Robbie's Marina and a visit to Theater of the Sea. On the fourth morning head to **Marathon.** Visit Crane Point Museum, Nature Center and Historic Site and walk out on the Old Seven Mile Bridge or take the ferry to Pigeon Key. Spend the night and head the next morning to Bahia

Honda State Park on **Bahia Honda Key** for snorkeling, kayaking, fishing, hiking, and beaching. Spend the night in a waterfront cabin or in the campground. On your sixth day, continue to **Key West,** and get in a little sightseeing before watching the sun set at Mallory Square, and spend the night and your last day visiting the sites, shops, restaurants, and bars in one of America's most lauded vacation spots.

If You Have 10 Days

To the seven-day itinerary add a few hours on Sombrero Beach in **Marathon** on Day 4, and spend the night in a local resort. Devote Day 6 to either snorkeling or diving at Looe Key Reef and a visit to the National Key Deer Refuge on **Big Pine Key.** Spend the night in the Lower Keys before heading to **Key West.** On Day 7, take a break from driving at Fort Zachary Taylor Historic State Park beach. Explore the fort and nearby Eco-Discovery Center. Book ferry passage to **Dry Tortugas National Park** for Day 8 to snorkel and explore the fort. Spend the remaining couple of nights and days sampling Key West's attractions and nightlife.

THE UPPER KEYS

Updated by Jill Martin

DIVING AND SNORKELING RULE IN the Upper Keys, thanks to North America's only living coral barrier reef that runs a few miles off the Atlantic coast. Divers of all skill levels benefit from accessible dive sites and an established tourism infrastructure. Fishing is another huge draw, especially around Islamorada, known for its sportfishing in both deep offshore waters and in the backcountry. Offshore islands accessible only by boat are popular destinations for kayakers. In short, if you don't like the water you might get bored here.

But true nature lovers won't feel shortchanged. Within 1½ miles of the bay coast lie the mangrove trees and sandy shores of Everglades National Park, where naturalists lead tours of one of the world's few saltwater forests. Here you'll see endangered manatees, curious dolphins, and other marine creatures. Although the number of birds has dwindled since John James Audubon captured their beauty on canvas, bird-watchers will find plenty to see, including the rare Everglades snail kite, bald eagles, ospreys, and a colorful array of egrets and herons. At sunset flocks take flight as they gather to find their night's roost, adding a swirl of activity to an otherwise quiet time of day.

ORIENTATION AND PLANNING

GETTING ORIENTED

The best way to explore this stretch, or any stretch, of the Florida Keys is by boat. As soon as possible you should jump on any seaworthy vessel to see the view of and from the water. And make sure you veer off the main drag of U.S. 1. Head toward the water, where you'll often find the kind of laid-back restaurants and hotels that define the Keys. John Pennekamp Coral Reef State Park is the region's most popular destination, but it's certainly not the only place to get in touch with nature.

PLANNING

Greyhound (about $25 per person), Keys Transportation ($49 per person), and Keys Shuttle (about $70 per person) all offer shared-ride transportation to the Keys with various stops. SuperShuttle charges about $280 for up to 10 passengers for nonstop trips from Miami International Airport to the Upper Keys. Shared-ride trips are also available. For

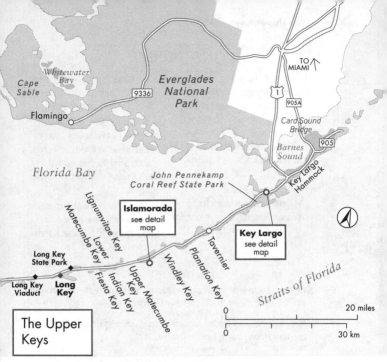

The Upper Keys

trips to the airport, place your request 24 hours in advance. *See Air Travel in Travel Smart for details.*

In the Upper Keys the accommodations are as varied as they are plentiful. Most lodgings are in small, narrow, waterfront complexes with efficiencies and one- or two-bedroom units. These places offer dockage and often arrange boating, diving, and fishing excursions. There are also full-scale resorts with every type of activity imaginable and smaller boutique hotels where the attraction is personalized service. Depending on which way the wind blows and how close the property is to the highway, there may be some noise from U.S. 1. If this is an annoyance for you, ask for a room as far away from the traffic as possible. Some properties require two- or three-day minimum stays during holiday and high-season weekends. Conversely, discounts apply for midweek, weekly, and monthly stays.

The Upper Keys are full of low-key eateries, where the owner is also the chef and the food is tasty and never too fussy. The one exception is Islamorada, where you'll find more upscale restaurants, but Key Largo has a few that can compete plate-for-plate. Restaurants may close for a

TOP REASONS TO GO

■ **Snorkeling.** The best snorkeling spots in these parts are to be found around the awe-inspiring *Christ of the Deep*, east of John Pennekamp Coral Reef State Park in the Florida Keys National Marine Sanctuary.

■ **Sunsets.** Find a comfortable place to watch the sunset, keeping an eye out for the elusive green flash.

■ **Aquatic Mammals.** Get up close and personal with sea life at Theater of the Sea.

■ **Boating.** Start with a visit to Robbie's Marina on Lower Matecumbe Key in Islamorada, a salty spot to find everything from fishing charters to kayak rentals.

■ **Nightlife.** It's not a disco, but you can dance the night away to music by local bands at Lorelei's Cabana Bar.

two- to four-week vacation during the slow season between early September and mid-November.

Restaurant and hotel reviews have been shortened. For full information, visit Fodors.com.

WHAT IT COSTS				
	$	**$$**	**$$$**	**$$$$**
Restaurants	under $15	$15–$20	$21–$30	over $30
Hotels	under $200	$200–$300	$301–$400	over $400

Prices in the restaurant reviews are the average cost of a main course at dinner or, if dinner isn't served, at lunch. Prices in the hotel reviews are the lowest cost of a standard double room in high season.

KEY LARGO

56 miles south of Miami International Airport.

The first of the Upper Keys reachable by car, 30-mile-long Key Largo is the largest island in the chain. Key Largo—named Cayo Largo (Long Key) by the Spanish—makes a great introduction to the region. This is the gateway to the Keys, and an evening of fresh seafood and views of the sunset on the water will get you in the right state of mind.

The history of Largo reads much like that of the rest of the Keys: a succession of native people, pirates, wreckers, and developers. The first settlement on Key Largo was named

Planter, back in the days of pineapple, and later, key lime plantations. For a time it was a convenient shipping port, but when the railroad arrived Planter died on the vine. Today, three communities—North Key Largo and Key Largo as well as the separately incorporated city of Tavernier—make up the whole of Key Largo.

What's there to do on Key Largo besides gaze at the sunset? Not much if you're not into diving or snorkeling. Nobody comes to Key Largo without visiting John Pennekamp Coral Reef State Park, one of the jewels of the state park system. Water-sports enthusiasts head to the adjacent Key Largo National Marine Sanctuary, which encompasses about 190 square miles of coral reefs, sea-grass beds, and mangrove estuaries. If you've never tried diving, Key Largo is the perfect place to learn. Dozens of companies will be more than happy to show you the ropes.

Fishing is the other big draw, and world records are broken regularly in the waters around the Upper Keys. There are plenty of charter companies to help you find the big ones, and teach you how to hook the elusive bonefish, sometimes known as the ghost fish.

On land, Key Largo provides all the conveniences of a major resort town, including restaurants that will cook your catch or prepare their own creations with inimitable style. Keep a lookout on menus for local specialties like cracked conch, spiny lobster, and stone crab. Don't pass up a chance to try key lime pie.

Most businesses are lined up along U.S. 1, the four-lane highway that runs down the middle of the island. Cars whiz past at all hours—something to remember when you're booking a room. Most lodgings are on the highway, so you'll want to be as far back as possible. At MM 95, look for the mural painted in 2011 to commemorate the 100th anniversary of the railroad to the Keys.

GETTING HERE AND AROUND

Key Largo is 56 miles south of Miami International Airport, with its mile markers ranging from 106 to 91. The island runs northeast–southwest, with the Overseas Highway, divided by a median most of the way, running down the center. If the highway is your only glimpse of the island, you're likely to feel barraged by its tacky commercial side. Make a point of driving Route 905 in North Key Largo and down side streets to get a better feel for it.

VISITOR INFORMATION

In addition to traditional tourist information, many divers will be interested in the Florida Keys National Marine Sanctuary, which has an office in Key Largo.

Contacts Florida Keys National Marine Sanctuary. ✉ *MM 95.23 BS* ☎ *305/809–4700* ⊕ *floridakeys.noaa.gov.* **Key Largo Chamber of Commerce.** ✉ *MM 106 BS, 10600 Overseas Hwy., Key Largo* ☎ *305/451–4747, 800/822–1088* ⊕ *www.keylargochamber.org.*

EXPLORING

FAMILY **Dagny Johnson Key Largo Hammock Botanical State Park.** American crocodiles, mangrove cuckoos, white-crowned pigeons, Schaus swallowtail butterflies, mahogany mistletoe, wild cotton, and 100 other rare critters and plants inhabit these 2,400 acres, sandwiched between Crocodile Lake National Wildlife Refuge and the waters of Pennekamp Coral Reef State Park. The park is also a user-friendly place to explore the largest remaining stand of the vast West Indian tropical hardwood hammock and mangrove wetland that once covered most of the Keys. Interpretive signs describe many of the tropical tree species along a wide, 1-mile, paved road (2 miles round-trip) that invites walking and biking. A new, unpaved, extended loop trail can add 1–2 miles to your walk. There are also more than 6 additional miles of nature trails, most of which are accessible to both bikes and wheelchairs with a permit, easily obtainable from John Pennekamp State Park. Pets are welcome if on a leash no longer than 6 feet. You'll also find restrooms, information kiosks, and picnic tables. ■ TIP→ **Rangers recommend not visiting when it's raining as the trees can drip poisonous sap.** ✉ *Rte. 905 OS, ½ mile north of Overseas Hwy., North Key Largo* ☎ *305/451–1202* ⊕ *www. floridastateparks.org/parks-and-trails/dagny-johnson-key-largo-hammock-botanical-state-park* 🖭 *$2.50 (exact change needed for the honor box).*

FAMILY **Dolphins Plus Bayside.** This educational program begins with a get-acquainted session beneath a tiki hut. After that, you slip into the water for some frolicking with your new dolphin pals. Options range from a shallow-water swim to a hands-on structured swim with a dolphin. You can also spend the day shadowing a trainer—it's $350 for a half day or a hefty $630 for a full day. ✉ *MM 101.9 BS, 101900 Overseas Hwy., Key Largo* ☎ *305/451–4060, 866/860–7946* ⊕ *www.dolphinsplus.com* 🖭 *$10 admission only; interactive programs from $150.*

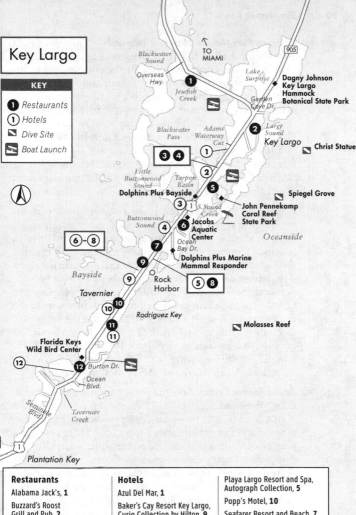

Key Largo

KEY

1 *Restaurants*
① *Hotels*
◤ *Dive Site*
⛴ *Boat Launch*

Blackwater
Sound

*Overseas
Hwy.*

TO
MIAMI

905

*Jewfish
Creek*

Lake
Surprise

**Dagny Johnson
Key Largo
Hammock
Botanical State Park**

*Garden
Cove Dr.*

*Blackwater
Pass*

*Adams
Waterway
Cut*

2

Large
Sound
Key Largo

◤ Christ Statue

*Little
Buttonwood
Sound*

3 4

1

2

*Tarpon
Basin*

5

Dolphins Plus Bayside

◤ Spiegel Grove

3 1

*S. Sound
Creek*

**John Pennekamp
Coral Reef
State Park**

*Buttonwood
Sound*

4 6

**Jacobs
Aquatic
Center**

Oceanside

6 - 8

7

*Ocean
Bay Dr.*

**Dolphins Plus Marine
Mammal Responder**

9

Bayside

9

5 8

**Rock
Harbor**

Tavernier

10 10

Rodriguez Key

◤ Molasses Reef

11

11

**Florida Keys
Wild Bird Center**

12

12 *Burton Dr.*

⛴

*Ocean
Blvd.*

*Seminole
Blvd.*

*Tavernier
Creek*

⛴

1

Plantation Key

Restaurants

Alabama Jack's, **1**

Buzzard's Roost
Grill and Pub, **2**

Chad's Deli & Bakery, **12**

The Fish House, **5**

Harriette's Restaurant, **10**

Jimmy Johnson's Big Chill, **4**

Key Largo Conch House, **6**

Mrs. Mac's Kitchen, **7**

Sal's Ballyhoo's, **9**

Snapper's, **11**

Sol By the Sea, **8**

Sundowners, **3**

Hotels

Azul Del Mar, **1**

Baker's Cay Resort Key Largo,
Curio Collection by Hilton, **9**

Coconut Bay Resort & Bay
Harbor Lodge, **6**

Coconut Palm Inn, **12**

Kona Kai Resort, Gallery &
Botanic Gardens, **8**

Largo, a Private Sanctuary, **3**

MB Resort at Key Largo, **11**

Marriott's Key Largo Bay
Beach Resort, **2**

The Pelican, **4**

Playa Largo Resort and Spa,
Autograph Collection, **5**

Popp's Motel, **10**

Seafarer Resort and Beach, **7**

FAMILY **Dolphins Plus Marine Mammal Responder.** This nonprofit focuses on marine mammal conservation, and you can help it by participating in one of the educational offerings. One popular option is the Splash and Wade, a shallow-water program that begins with a one-hour briefing, after which you enter the water up to your waist to interact with the dolphins. Prefer to stay mostly dry? Opt to paint with a dolphin, or get a dolphin "kiss." For tactile interaction (fin tows, for example), sign up for the Interactive Swim, which is more expensive. ⌂ *MM 99, 31 Corrine Pl., Key Largo* ☎ *305/453–4321* ⊕ *www.dpmmr. org* ▭ *Programs from $125.*

FAMILY **Florida Keys Wild Bird Center.** Have a nose-to-beak encounter with ospreys, hawks, herons, and other unreleasable birds at this bird rehabilitation center. The birds live in spacious screened enclosures along a boardwalk running through some of the best waterfront real estate in the Keys. Rehabilitated birds are set free, but about 30 have become permanent residents. Free birds—especially pelicans and egrets—come to visit every day for a free lunch from the center's staff. A short nature trail runs into the mangrove forest (bring bug spray May to October). Be sure to visit its interactive education center about 1½ miles south. ⌂ *MM 93.6 BS, 93600 Overseas Hwy., Tavernier* ☎ *305/852–4486* ⊕ *www.keepthemflying.org* ▭ *Free, donations accepted.*

FAMILY **Jacobs Aquatic Center.** Take the plunge at one of three swimming pools: an eight-lane, 25-meter lap pool with two diving boards; a 3- to 4-foot-deep pool accessible to people with mobility challenges; and an interactive children's play pool with a waterslide, pirate ship, waterfall, and sloping zero entry instead of steps. Because so few of the motels in Key Largo have pools, it remains a popular destination for visiting families. ⌂ *Key Largo Community Park, 320 Laguna Ave., at St. Croix Pl., Key Largo* ☎ *305/453–7946* ⊕ *www.jacobsaquaticcenter.org* ▭ *$12 ($2 discount weekdays).*

BEACHES

★ **Fodor's Choice John Pennekamp Coral Reef State Park.** This state
FAMILY park is on everyone's list for easy access to the best diving and snorkeling in Florida. The underwater treasure encompasses 78 nautical square miles of coral reefs and sea-grass beds. It lies adjacent to the Florida Keys National Marine Sanctuary, which contains 40 of the 52 species of coral in

the Atlantic Reef System and nearly 600 varieties of fish, from the colorful parrotfish to the demure cocoa damselfish. Whatever you do, get in the water. Snorkeling and diving trips ($30 and $75, respectively; equipment extra) and glass-bottom-boat rides to the reef ($24) are available, weather permitting. One of the most popular snorkel trips is to see *Christ of the Deep,* the 2-ton underwater statue of Jesus. The park also has nature trails, two man-made beaches, picnic shelters, a snack bar, and a campground. **Amenities:** food and drink; parking (fee); showers; toilets; water sports. **Best for:** snorkeling; swimming. ✉ *MM 102.5 OS, 102601 Overseas Hwy., Key Largo* ☎ *305/451–1202 for park, 305/451–6300 for excursions* 🌐 *pennekamppark.com* 🎟 *$4 for 1 person in vehicle, $8 for 2–8 people, $2 for pedestrians and cyclists or extra people (plus a 50¢ per-person county surcharge).*

WHERE TO EAT

$ ✕ **Alabama Jack's.** *Seafood.* Calories be damned—the conch fritters here are heaven on a plate. Don't expect the traditional, golf-ball-size spheres of dough; these are unusual, mountainous, free-form creations of fried, loaded-with-flavor perfection. **Known for:** heavenly conch fritters; unique setting; live music. [$] *Average main: $11* ✉ *58000 Card Sound Rd., Key Largo* ☎ *305/248–8741.*

★ $$$ **Fodor's Choice** ✕ **Buzzard's Roost Grill and Pub.** *Seafood.* The views are nice at this waterfront restaurant but the food is what gets your attention. Burgers, fish tacos, and seafood baskets are lunch faves. **Known for:** marina views; daily chef's specials; Sunday brunch with live steel drums. [$] *Average main: $21* ✉ *Garden Cove Marina, 21 Garden Cove Dr., Key Largo* ☎ *305/453–3746* 🌐 *www.buzzardsroostkeylargo.com.*

$ ✕ **Chad's Deli & Bakery.** *American.* It's a deli! It's a bakery! It's a pasta place! It's also where the locals go. **Known for:** homemade soups and chowders; eight varieties of supersized homemade cookies; huge portions. [$] *Average main: $10* ✉ *MM 92.3 BS, 92330 Overseas Hwy., Tavernier* ☎ *305/853–5566* 🌐 *www.chadsdeli.com.*

$$$ ✕ **The Fish House.** *Seafood.* Restaurants not on the water have to produce the highest-quality food to survive in the Keys. Try fish Matecumbe style—baked with tomatoes, capers, olive oil, and lemon juice, or the buttery pan sautéed. **Known for:** smoked fish chunks and dip; excellent key lime pie; fresh-as-can-be seafood served fast. [$] *Average main:*

$21 ✉ MM 102.4 OS, 102341 Overseas Hwy., Key Largo ☎ 305/451–4665 🌐 www.fishhouse.com ⏲ Closed Sept.

$ 🍴 **Harriette's Restaurant.** *American.* If you're looking for comfort food—like melt-in-your-mouth biscuits the size of a salad plate or old-fashioned hotcakes with sausage or bacon—try this refreshing throwback for a hearty breakfast. At lunch, Harriette's shines in the burger department, and all the soups—from garlic tomato to chili—are homemade. **Known for:** always a wait but worth it; best muffins in Key Largo; tight dining space. [$] *Average main: $8 ✉ MM 95.7 BS, 95710 Overseas Hwy., Key Largo ☎ 305/852–8689 ⏲ No dinner ☞ American Express not accepted.*

$$ 🍴 **Jimmy Johnson's Big Chill.** *Seafood.* Owned by former NFL coach Jimmy Johnson, this waterfront establishment offers three entertaining experiences: the best sports bar in the Upper Keys; a main restaurant with all-glass dining room and a waterfront deck; and an enormous outdoor tiki bar with entertainment seven nights a week. There's even a pool and cabanas where (for an entrance fee) you can spend the day sunning. **Known for:** the place to watch a game; fantastic bay views; brick oven chicken wings with rosemary. [$] *Average main: $20 ✉ MM 104 BS, 104000 Overseas Hwy., Key Largo ☎ 305/453–9066 🌐 www.jjsbigchill.com.*

$$ 🍴 **Key Largo Conch House.** *American.* This family-owned restaurant in a Victorian-style home tucked into the trees is worth seeking out. Seven varieties of Benedicts, including conch, are brunch favorites, while lunch and dinner menus highlight local seafood like lionfish (when available) and yellowtail snapper. **Known for:** shrimp and grits; all-season outside dining; seafood tacos. [$] *Average main: $16 ✉ MM 100.2, 100211 Overseas Hwy., Key Largo ☎ 305/453–4844 🌐 www.keylargoconchhouse.com.*

$$ FAMILY 🍴 **Mrs. Mac's Kitchen.** *Seafood.* Locals pack the counters and booths at this tiny eatery where license plates decorate the walls, to dine on everything from blackened prime rib to crab cakes. Every night is themed including Meatloaf Monday, Italian Wednesday, and Seafood Sensation (offered Friday and Saturday). **Known for:** a second location ½ mile south with a full liquor bar; champagne breakfast; being a stop on the Florida Keys Food Tour. [$] *Average main: $17 ✉ MM 99.4 BS, 99336 Overseas Hwy., Key Largo ☎ 305/451–3722, 305/451–6227 🌐 www.mrsmacskitchen.com ⏲ Closed Sun.*

$$$ 🍴 **Sal's Ballyhoo's.** *Seafood.* Occupying a 1930s Conch house with outdoor seating right alongside U.S. 1 under the seagrape trees, this local favorite is all about the fish: yellowtail

snapper, tuna, and mahimahi. Choose your favorite, then choose your preparation, such as the Hemingway, with a Parmesan crust, crabmeat, and key lime butter. **Known for:** spicy corn muffins; fish and fried-tomato sandwich; grilled avocado appetizer. Ⓢ *Average main: $24* ✉ *MM 97.8 median, 97800 Overseas Hwy., Key Largo* ☎ *305/852–0822* ⊕ *www.ballyhoosrestaurant.com.*

$$ ✕ **Snapper's.** *Seafood.* In a lively, mangrove-ringed, waterfront setting, Snapper's has live music, Sunday brunch (including a build-your-own Bloody Mary bar), killer rum drinks, and seating alongside the fishing dock. "You hook 'em, we cook 'em" is the motto here but you have to clean your own fish and dinner is $14 for a single diner, $15 per person family-style meal with a mix of preparations when you provide the fish. **Known for:** grouper Oscar-style; fun and happening vibe; local crowd. Ⓢ *Average main: $17* ✉ *MM 94.5 OS, 139 Seaside Ave., Key Largo* ☎ *305/852–5956* ⊕ *www.snapperskeylargo.com.*

$$$ ✕ **Sol By The Sea.** *Caribbean.* This is the spot you might imagine when you think of dining by the water in the Keys. The Caribbean-influenced menu includes things like octopus *a la plancha,* crispy lobster (the presentation is a photo op), and guava-glazed grouper. **Known for:** picturesque spot; unique key lime dessert; Caribbean-influenced seafood. Ⓢ *Average main: $25* ✉ *Playa Largo Resort, MM 97 BS, 97540 Overseas Hwy., Key Largo* ☎ *305/853–1001* ⊕ *www.playalargoresort.com.*

$$$ ✕ **Sundowners.** *American.* If it's a clear night and you can snag a reservation, this restaurant will treat you to a sherbet-hue sunset over Florida Bay. The food is also excellent: try the key lime seafood, a happy combo of sautéed shrimp, lobster, and crabmeat swimming in a tangy sauce spiked with Tabasco served over penne or rice. **Known for:** prime rib every Wednesday and Friday; Friday-night fish fry; choose your fish, choose your prepation. Ⓢ *Average main: $29* ✉ *MM 104 BS, 103900 Overseas Hwy., Key Largo* ☎ *305/451–4502* ⊕ *sundownerskeylargo.com.*

WHERE TO STAY

$$ ▧ **Azul del Mar.** *B&B/Inn.* The dock points the way to many beautiful sunsets at this no-smoking, adults-only boutique hotel, which Karol Marsden (an ad exec) and her husband Dominic (a travel photographer) have transformed from a run-down mom-and-pop place into a waterfront gem. **Pros:** quality bed linens and towels; good location;

sophisticated design. **Cons:** small beach; high prices; minimum stays during holidays. $ *Rooms from: $299* ✉ *MM 104.3 BS, 104300 Overseas Hwy., Key Largo* ☎ *305/451–0337, 888/253–2985* 🌐 *www.azulkeylargo.com* 🛏 *6 units* 🍴 *No meals.*

★ $$$ FAMILY **Fodor's Choice** 🏨 **Baker's Cay Resort Key Largo, Curio Collection by Hilton.** *Resort.* Nestled within a "hardwood hammock" (localese for uplands habitat where hardwood trees such as live oak grow) near the southern border of Everglades National Park, this sparkling new, sprawling 13-acre resort is not to be missed. **Pros:** you never have to leave the resort; pretty pools with waterfalls; 21-slip marina for all your boating needs. **Cons:** some rooms overlook the parking lot; pools near the highway; expensive per-night resort fee. $ *Rooms from: $399* ✉ *MM 97 BS, 97000 Overseas Hwy., Key Largo* ☎ *305/852–5553, 888/871–3437* 🌐 *www.keylargoresort.com* 🛏 *200 rooms* 🍴 *No meals.*

$ 🏨 **Coconut Bay Resort & Bay Harbor Lodge.** *Resort.* Some 200 feet of waterfront is the main attraction at these side-by-side sister properties that offer a choice between smaller rooms and larger separate cottages. **Pros:** temperature-controlled pool; owner Peg's homemade, amazing scones; free use of kayaks, paddleboat, and paddleboards. **Cons:** a bit dated; small sea-walled sand beach; bring your own charcoal for the barbecue grills. $ *Rooms from: $195* ✉ *MM 97.7 BS, 97702 Overseas Hwy., Key Largo* ☎ *305/852–1625, 800/385–0986* 🌐 *www.bayharborkeylargo.com* 🛏 *21 units* 🍴 *Free Breakfast.*

$$ 🏨 **Coconut Palm Inn.** *B&B/Inn.* You'd never find this waterfront haven unless someone told you it was there, as it's tucked into a residential neighborhood beneath towering palms and native gumbo limbos. **Pros:** secluded and quiet; 100% smoke-free resort; sophisticated feel. **Cons:** front desk closes early each evening; no access to ice machine when staff leave; breakfast is ho-hum. $ *Rooms from: $299* ✉ *MM 92 BS, 198 Harborview Dr., via Jo-Jean Way off Overseas Hwy., Tavernier* ☎ *305/852–3017* 🌐 *www.coconutpalminn.com* 🛏 *20 rooms* 🍴 *Free Breakfast.*

★ $$ **Fodor's Choice** 🏨 **Kona Kai Resort, Gallery & Botanic Gardens.** *Resort.* Brilliantly colored bougainvillea, coconut palm, and guava trees—and a botanical garden of other rare species—make this 2-acre adult hideaway one of the prettiest places to stay in the Keys. **Pros:** friendly staff; free use of sports equipment; spa-like pool area. **Cons:** expensive; some rooms are very close together. $ *Rooms from: $299* ✉ *MM 97.8 BS, 97802 Overseas Hwy., Key Largo*

☎ *305/852–7200, 800/365–7829* 🌐 *www.konakairesort.com* 🛏 *13 rooms* 🍴 *Free Breakfast.*

$$$$ 🏨 **Largo, a Private Sanctuary.** *Resort.* Paradise and serenity await behind the 10-foot-tall, dark-wood Kong gates. **Pros:** privacy like few places can offer; complimentary kayaks and paddleboards; weekday special rates. **Cons:** no food or drinks on-site for purchase; not within walking distance of sights; quietude isn't for everyone. [$] *Rooms from: $500* ✉ *MM 101.7 BS, 101740 Overseas Hwy., Key Largo* ☎ *305/451–0424* 🌐 *www.largoresort.com* 🛏 *6 bungalows* 🍴 *No meals.*

$$$ FAMILY 🏨 **Marriott's Key Largo Bay Beach Resort.** *Resort.* This 17-acre bay-side resort has plenty of diversions, from diving to a day spa. **Pros:** lots of activities; free covered parking; dive shop on property; free Wi-Fi. **Cons:** rooms facing highway can be noisy; thin walls; starting to show wear. [$] *Rooms from: $359* ✉ *MM 103.8 BS, 103800 Overseas Hwy., Key Largo* ☎ *305/453–0000, 866/849–3753* 🌐 *www.marriottkeylargo.com* 🛏 *153 rooms* 🍴 *No meals.*

$$ 🏨 **MB Resort at Key Largo.** *B&B/Inn.* With its sherbet-hue rooms and plantation-style furnishings, these tropical-style units range in size from simple lodge rooms to luxury two-bedroom suites. **Pros:** luxurious rooms; 10% discount to Snapper's restaurant next door; discounted ecotours from the dock. **Cons:** no beach; some find the music from next door bothersome; office closes at 8 pm. [$] *Rooms from: $269* ✉ *MM 94.5 OS, 147 Seaside Ave., Key Largo* ☎ *305/852–6200, 800/401–0057* 🌐 *www.mbatkeylargo.com* 🛏 *14 rooms* 🍴 *Free Breakfast.*

$ 🏨 **The Pelican.** *Hotel.* This 1950s throwback is reminiscent of the days when parents packed the kids into the station wagon and headed to no-frills seaside motels, complete with old-fashioned fishing off the dock. **Pros:** free use of kayaks and a canoe; well-maintained dock; reasonable rates. **Cons:** some rooms are small; basic accommodations and amenities; road noise with some units. [$] *Rooms from: $159* ✉ *MM 99.3, 99340 Overseas Hwy., Key Largo* ☎ *305/451–3576, 877/451–3576* 🌐 *www.hungrypelican.com* 🛏 *21 units* 🍴 *Free Breakfast.*

★ Fodor's Choice 🏨 **Playa Largo Resort and Spa, Autograph Collection.**
$$$ *Resort.* At this luxurious 14-acre bay-front retreat, you'll find one of the nicest beaches in the Keys, as well as water sports galore, bocce, tennis, basketball, and a fitness center with inspiring pool views. **Pros:** comfortable rooms, most with balconies; excellent service; Playa Largo Kids Club. **Cons:** $41.93 per night resort fee; minimum stays

may be required; luxury will cost you. $ *Rooms from: $399* ✉ *97450 Overseas Hwy., Key Largo* ☎ *305/853–1001* 🌐 *playalargoresort.com* ⇌ *178 units* 🍴 *No meals* 💳 *No credit cards.*

$ 🏨 **Popp's Motel.** *Hotel.* Stylized metal herons mark the entrance to this 67-year-old family-run motel. **Pros:** great beach; intimate feel; full kitchen in each unit. **Cons:** limited amenities; minimum stays in season; limited dock space. $ *Rooms from: $149* ✉ *MM 95.5 BS, 95500 Overseas Hwy., Key Largo* ☎ *305/852–5201, 877/852–5201* 🌐 *www.poppsmotel.com* ⇌ *9 units* 🍴 *No meals.*

$ 🏨 **Seafarer Resort and Beach.** *Hotel.* If you're looking for modern and updated, this very basic, budget lodging isn't for you—this place is all about staying on the water for a song. **Pros:** kitchen units available; complimentary kayak use; cheap rates. **Cons:** can hear road noise in some rooms; some complaints about cleanliness. $ *Rooms from: $149* ✉ *MM 97.6 BS, 97684 Overseas Hwy., Key Largo* ☎ *305/852–5349* 🌐 *www.seafarerkeylargo.com* ⇌ *15 units* 🍴 *Free Breakfast.*
FAMILY

NIGHTLIFE

The semiweekly *Keynoter* (Wednesday and Saturday), the weekly *Reporter* (Thursday), and Friday-through-Sunday editions of the *Miami Herald* are the best sources of information on entertainment and nightlife. Daiquiri bars, tiki huts, and seaside shacks pretty well summarize Key Largo's bar scene.

Breezers Tiki Bar & Grille. Mingle with locals over cocktails and catch amazing sunsets from the comfort of an enclosed, air-conditioned bar. Floor-to-ceiling doors can be opened on cool days and closed on hot days. It's located at Marriott's Key Largo Bay Beach Resort. ✉ *Marriott's Key Largo Bay Beach Resort, 103800 Overseas Hwy., Key Largo* ☎ *305/453–0000.*

Caribbean Club. Walls plastered with Bogart memorabilia remind customers that the classic 1948 Bogart–Bacall flick *Key Largo* has a connection with this worn watering hole. Although no food is served and the floors are bare concrete, this landmark draws boaters, curious visitors, and local barflies to its humble bar stools and pool tables. But the real magic is around back, where you can grab a seat on the deck and catch a postcard-perfect sunset. Live music draws revelers Thursday through Sunday. ✉ *MM 104 BS, 104080 Overseas Hwy., Key Largo* ☎ *305/451–4466* 🌐 *caribbeanclubkl.com.*

Corks & Curds. While it's only open till 9 pm, it's still the new place to see and be seen. It's dark and a little mysterious, and the wine, cheese pairings, meats, and fondues are five-star worthy. Sit at the bar, on a couch, or at a high top, and be transported to somewhere other than a typical, tropical Keys venue. Check the calendar for wine tastings and cooking classes. ✉ *99201 Overseas Hwy., Key Largo* ☎ *305/451–0995* ⊕ *www.corksandcurdsfl.com.*

FAMILY **Skipper's Dockside.** There's a fun, new place in the heart of Key Largo, and marina views are just one of its many charms. Sit outside under the tiki, or in a brightly colored Adirondack chair by the fire pits, or inside amid driftwood walls and prize catches. No matter: what you'll remember is the fresh, everything-made-in-house food. To familiar faves like conch fritters and fish sandwiches, the chef adds captivating tropical twists, like a toasted coconut bun for your mahimahi. The wall of TVs makes this a great place to catch a game, and daily live music enhances the laid-back Keys atmosphere. Happy hour is weekdays 3–6 pm and includes food specials and an extensive kids' menu. ✉ *MM 100 OS, 528 Caribbean Dr., Key Largo* ☎ *305/453–9794* ⊕ *www.skippersdockside.com.*

SHOPPING

For the most part, shopping is sporadic in Key Largo, with a couple of shopping centers and fewer galleries than you find on the other big islands. If you're looking to buy scuba or snorkel equipment, you'll have plenty of choices.

★ Fodor'sChoice **Key Largo Chocolates.** Specializing in key lime
FAMILY truffles made with quality Belgian chocolate, this is the only chocolate factory in the Florida Keys. But you'll find much more than just the finest white-, milk-, and dark-chocolate truffles; try the cupcakes, ice cream, and famous "chocodiles." The salted turtles, a fan favorite, are worth every calorie. Chocolate classes are also available for kids and adults, and a small gift area showcases local art, jewelry, hot sauces, and other goodies. Look for the bright-green-and-pink building. ✉ *MM 100 BS, 100471 Overseas Hwy., Key Largo* ☎ *305/453–6613* ⊕ *www.keylargochocolates.com.*

Key Lime Products. Go into olfactory overload—you'll find yourself sniffing every single bar of soap and scented candle inside this key lime treasure trove. Take home some key lime juice (supereasy pie-making directions are right on the bottle), marmalade, candies, sauces, even key lime shampoo. Outside, you'll find a huge selection of wood carvings, pottery, unique patio furniture, and artwork. The fresh fish sandwiches and conch fritters served at the on-site Key Lime Cafe are alone worth the stop. ✉ *MM 95.2 BS, 95231 Overseas Hwy., Key Largo* ☎ *305/853–0378, 800/870–1780* ⊕ *www.keylimeproducts.com.*

★ Fodor'sChoice **Old Road Gallery.** This shop is filled with treasures like functional and imaginative ceramics, bronze castings, realistic copper creations, and jewelry, all created by local artists—but it's the secret sculpture garden that gives this place its unique atmosphere. Stroll the winding paths and discover cypress furniture, whimsical gnomes, glass gazing globes, and a working pottery and copper studio. Peacocks may greet you on the path, as might locals who come with their lunch and linger beneath the shade of the native hardwood trees (all labeled with ceramic nameplates). Owner-artists Cindy and Dwayne King are sensational hosts and genuinely embody the joyful spirit of the Florida Keys. ✉ *88888 Old Hwy., in the median between Overseas Hwy. and Old Hwy., Tavernier* ☎ *305/852–8935* ⊕ *www.oldroadgallery.com.*

Randy's Florida Keys Gift Co. Since 1989, Randy's has been *the* place for unique gifts. Owner Randy and his wife Lisa aren't only fantastic at stocking the store with a plethora of items, they're also well respected in the community for their generosity and dedication. Stop in and say hello, then browse the aisles and loaded shelves filled with key lime candles, books, wood carvings, jewelry, clothing, T-shirts, and eclectic, tropical decor items. This friendly shop prides itself on carrying wares from local craftsmen, and there's something for every budget. ✉ *102421 Overseas Hwy., Key Largo* ✛ *On U.S. 1, next to the Sandal Factory Outlet* ☎ *305/453–9229* ⊕ *www.keysmermaid.com.*

Shell World. You can find lots of shops in the Keys that sell cheesy souvenirs—snow globes, alligator hats, and shell-encrusted anything. This is the granddaddy of them all. But this sprawling building in the median of Overseas Highway contains much more than the usual tourist trinkets—you'll find high-end clothing, jewelry, housewares, artwork, and a wide selection of keepsakes, from delightfully tacky to tasteful. ✉ *MM 97.5, 97600 Overseas Hwy., Key Largo* ☎ *305/852–8245, 888/398–6233* ⊕ *www.shell-worldflkeys.com.*

SPORTS AND THE OUTDOORS

BIKING

Not as big a pursuit as on other islands, biking can be a little dangerous along Key Largo's main drag. Parts of the still-developing Florida Keys Overseas Heritage Trail take you off Highway 1 along Old Highway.

Bubba's. Bubba's organizes one-week custom biking tours through the Keys along the heritage trail. A van accompanies tours to carry luggage and tired riders. Former police officer Bubba Barron also hosts an annual one-week ride down the length of the Keys every November. Riders can opt for tent camping or motel-room accommodations. Meals are included, but bike rentals are extra. ⊠ *Key Largo* ☎ *321/759–3433* ⊕ *www.bubbaspamperedpedalers.com* ⊠ *From $1,210 per person, double occupancy.*

BOATING

FAMILY **Everglades Eco-Tours.** For over 30 years, Captain Sterling has operated Everglades and Florida Bay ecology tours and more expensive sunset cruises. With his expert guidance, you can see dolphins, manatees, and birds from the casual comfort of his pontoon boat, equipped with PVC chairs. Bring your own food and drinks; each tour has a maximum of six people. ⊠ *Sundowners Restaurant, MM 104 BS , 103900 Overseas Hwy., Key Largo* ☎ *305/853–5161, 888/224–6044* ⊕ *www.captainsterling.com* ⊠ *From $59.*

FAMILY **M.V. *Key Largo Princess.*** Two-hour glass-bottom-boat trips and more expensive sunset cruises on a luxury 70-foot motor yacht with a 280-square-foot glass viewing area depart from the Holiday Inn docks three times a day. ■TIP→ **Purchase tickets online to save big.** ⊠ *Holiday Inn, MM 100 OS, 99701 Overseas Hwy., Key Largo* ☎ *305/451–4655, 877/648–8129* ⊕ *www.keylargoprincess.com* ⊠ *$30.*

CANOEING AND KAYAKING

Sea kayaking continues to gain popularity in the Keys. You can paddle for a few hours or the whole day, on your own or with a guide. Some outfitters even offer overnight trips. The **Florida Keys Overseas Paddling Trail,** part of a statewide system, runs from Key Largo to Key West. You can paddle the entire distance, 110 miles on the Atlantic side, which takes 9 to 10 days. The trail also runs the chain's length on the bay side, which is a longer route.

Coral Reef Park Co. At John Pennekamp Coral Reef State Park, this operator has a fleet of canoes and kayaks for gliding around the 2½-mile mangrove trail or along the coast. Powerboat rentals are also available. ⊠ *MM 102.5 OS, 102601 Overseas Hwy., Key Largo* ☎ *305/451–6300* ⊕ *www.pennekamppark.com* ⊒ *Rentals from $20 per hr.*

Florida Bay Outfitters. Rent canoes, sea kayaks, or Hobie Eclipses (the newest craze) from this company, which sets up self-guided trips on the Florida Keys Paddling Trail, helps with trip planning, and matches equipment to your skill level. It also runs myriad guided tours around Key Largo. Take a full-moon paddle or a one- to seven-day kayak tour to the Everglades, Lignumvitae Key, or Indian Key. ⊠ *MM 104 BS, 104050 Overseas Hwy., Key Largo* ☎ *305/451–3018* ⊕ *www.paddlefloridakeys.com* ⊒ *From $15.*

DOLPHIN INTERACTION PROGRAMS

The Keys have a number of places where visitors can interact with dolphins. Some people, especially children, love learning about the dolphins and seeing them up close, while others bristle at seeing the animals kept in captivity to serve public whims. If you're among the latter, you'll want to avoid these programs and perhaps opt for a dolphin-spotting tour in the wild (but even these are questioned by some environmentalists if the tour operators do anything to attract the dolphins to the boat). Feeding them is strictly taboo, but some tour operators slap the side of the boat and circle around the spotted dolphin. For listings of businesses that are recognized as dolphin-friendly by the National Oceanic and Atmospheric Administration (NOAA), visit ⊕ *www.dolphinsmart.org.*

FISHING

Private charters and big "head" boats (so named because they charge "by the head") are great for anglers who don't have their own vessel.

Sailors Choice. Fishing excursions depart twice daily (half-day trips are cash only), but the company also does private charters. The 65-foot boat leaves from the Holiday Inn docks. Rods, bait, and license are included. ⊠ *Holiday Inn Resort & Marina, MM 100 OS, 99701 Overseas Hwy., Key Largo* ☎ *305/451–1802, 305/451–0041* ⊕ *www.sailorschoicefishingboat.com* ⊒ *From $45.*

SCUBA DIVING AND SNORKELING

Much of what makes the Upper Keys a singular dive destination is variety. Places like Molasses Reef, which begins 3 feet below the surface and descends to 55 feet, have something for everyone from novice snorkelers to experienced divers. The *Spiegel Grove*, a 510-foot vessel, lies in 130 feet of water, but its upper regions are only 60 feet below the surface. On rough days, Key Largo Undersea Park's Emerald Lagoon is a popular spot. Expect to pay about $80 to $85 for a two-tank, two-site dive trip with tanks and weights, or $35 to $40 for a two-site snorkel outing. Get big discounts by booking multiple trips.

Amy Slate's Amoray Dive Resort. This outfit makes diving easy. Stroll down to the full-service dive shop (PADI, TDI, and BSAC certified), then onto a 45-foot catamaran. Certification courses are also offered. ⊠ *MM 104.2 BS, 104250 Overseas Hwy., Key Largo* ☎ *305/451–3595, 800/426–6729* ⊕ *www.amoray.com* ☜ *From $85.*

Conch Republic Divers. Book diving instruction as well as scuba and snorkeling tours of all the wrecks and reefs of the Upper Keys. Two-location dives are the standard, and you'll pay an extra $20 for tank and weights. ⊠ *MM 90.8 BS, 90800 Overseas Hwy., Key Largo* ☎ *305/852–1655, 800/274–3483* ⊕ *www.conchrepublicdivers.com* ☜ *From $80.*

Coral Reef Park Co. At John Pennekamp Coral Reef State Park, this company gives 3½-hour scuba and 2½-hour snorkeling tours of the park. In addition to the great location and the dependability it's also suited for water adventurers of all levels. ⊠ *MM 102.5 OS, 102601 Overseas Hwy., Key Largo* ☎ *305/451–6300* ⊕ *www.pennekamppark.com* ☜ *From $30.*

Horizon Divers. The company has customized diving and snorkeling trips that depart daily aboard a 45-foot catamaran. ⊠ *105800 Overseas Hwy., Key Largo* ☎ *305/453–3535, 800/984–3483* ⊕ *www.horizondivers.com* ☜ *From $50 for snorkeling, from $85 for diving.*

Island Ventures. If you like dry, British humor and no crowds, this is the operator for you. It specializes in small groups for snorkeling or dive trips, no more than 10 people per boat. Scuba trips are two tanks, two locations, and include tanks and weights; ride-alongs pay just $35. Choose morning or afternoon. ⊠ *Jules Undersea Lodge, 51 Shoreland*

Dr., Key Largo ☎ *305/451–4957* ⊕ *www.islandventure.com*
⊠ *Snorkel trips $45, diving $85.*

★ **Fodor's**Choice **Quiescence Diving Services.** This operator sets
itself apart in two ways: it limits groups to six to ensure
personal attention and offers both two-dive day and night
dives, as well as twilight dives when sea creatures are most
active. There are also organized snorkeling excursions.
⊠ *MM 103.5 BS, 103680 Overseas Hwy., Key Largo*
☎ *305/451–2440* ⊕ *www.quiescence.com* ⊠ *Snorkel trips
$55, diving from $89.*

Rainbow Reef Dive Center. The PADI five-star facility has
been around since 1975 and offers day and night dives,
a range of courses, and dive-lodging packages. Two-tank
reef dives include tank and weight rental. There are also
organized snorkeling trips with equipment. Two location to
choose from. ⊠ *MM 100 OS, 522 Caribbean Dr., Key Largo*
☎ *305/451–1113, 800/451–1113* ⊕ *www.oceandivers.com*
⊠ *Snorkel trips from $35, diving from $80.*

ISLAMORADA

Islamorada is between MM 90.5 and 70.

Early settlers named this key after their schooner, *Island
Home,* but to make it sound more romantic they trans-
lated it into Spanish: *Isla Morada.* The Chamber of Commerce prefers to use its literal translation, "Purple Island,"
which refers either to a purple-shelled snail that once inhabited these shores or to the brilliantly colored orchids and
bougainvilleas.

Early maps show Islamorada as encompassing only Upper
Matecumbe Key. But the incorporated "Village of Islands"
is made up of a string of islands that the Overseas Highway crosses, including Plantation Key, Windley Key, Upper
Matecumbe Key, Lower Matecumbe Key, Craig Key, and
Fiesta Key. In addition, two state-park islands accessible
only by boat—Indian Key and Lignumvitae Key—belong
to the group.

Islamorada (locals pronounce it *"eye*-la-mor- *ah*-da") is
one of the world's top fishing destinations. For nearly
100 years, seasoned anglers have fished these clear, warm
waters teeming with trophy-worthy fish. There are numerous options for those in search of the big ones, including
chartering a boat with its own crew or heading out on a

2

vessel rented from one of the plethora of marinas along this 20-mile stretch of the Overseas Highway. More than 150 backcountry guides and 400 offshore captains are at your service.

GETTING HERE AND AROUND

Most visitors arrive in Islamorada by car. If you're flying in to Miami International Airport or Key West International Airport, you can easily rent a car (reserve in advance) to make the drive.

TOURS

Contact **Florida Keys Food Tours.** ☎ 305/393–9183 ⊕ www. flkeysfoodtours.com.

VISITOR INFORMATION

Contact **Islamorada Chamber of Commerce & Visitors Center.** ✉ MM 87.1 BS, 87100 Overseas Hwy., Islamorada ☎ 305/664–4503, 800/322–5397 ⊕ www.islamoradachamber.com.

EXPLORING

TOP ATTRACTIONS

Florida Keys Memorial / Hurricane Monument. On Monday, September 2, 1935, more than 400 people perished when the most intense hurricane to make landfall in the United States swept through this area of the Keys. Two years later, the Florida Keys Memorial was dedicated in their honor. Native coral rock, known as keystone, covers the 18-foot obelisk monument that marks the remains of more than 300 storm victims. A sculpted plaque of bending palms and waves graces the front (although many are bothered that the palms are bending in the wrong direction). In 1995, the memorial was placed on the National Register of Historic Places. ✉ MM 81.8, *in front of the public library, 81831 Old State Hwy. 4A, Upper Matecumbe Key* ⊹ *Just south of the Cheeca Lodge entrance* 🖾 *Free.*

History of Diving Museum. Adding to the region's reputation for world-class diving, this museum plunges into the history of man's thirst for undersea exploration. Among its 13 galleries of interactive and other interesting displays are a submarine and helmet re-created from the film *20,000 Leagues Under the Sea.* Vintage U.S. Navy equipment, diving helmets from around the world, and early scuba gear explore 4,000 years of diving history. For the grand finale, spend $3 for a mouthpiece and sing your favorite tune at

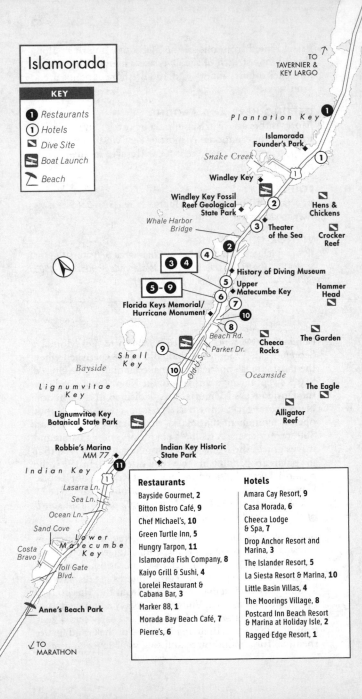

Islamorada

KEY

- **1** Restaurants
- ① Hotels
- Dive Site
- Boat Launch
- Beach

TO TAVERNIER & KEY LARGO

Plantation Key

1

Islamorada Founder's Park

①

Snake Creek

Windley Key

2

Windley Key Fossil Reef Geological State Park

Whale Harbor Bridge

3 Theater of the Sea

2

4

3 **4**

History of Diving Museum

5 Upper Matecumbe Key

6

5–9

7

10

Florida Keys Memorial/ Hurricane Monument

8

Beach Rd.

Parker Dr.

Cheeca Rocks

⑨

Shell Key

Bayside

⑩

Old U.S. 1

Oceanside

Lignumvitae Key

Lignumvitae Key Botanical State Park

Robbie's Marina MM 77

11

Indian Key

Indian Key Historic State Park

Lasarra Ln.

Sea Ln.

Ocean Ln.

Sand Cove

Costa Bravo

Lower Matecumbe Key

Toll Gate Blvd.

Anne's Beach Park

TO MARATHON

Hens & Chickens

Crocker Reef

Hammer Head

The Garden

The Eagle

Alligator Reef

Restaurants

Bayside Gourmet, **2**

Bitton Bistro Café, **9**

Chef Michael's, **10**

Green Turtle Inn, **5**

Hungry Tarpon, **11**

Islamorada Fish Company, **8**

Kaiyo Grill & Sushi, **4**

Lorelei Restaurant & Cabana Bar, **3**

Marker 88, **1**

Morada Bay Beach Café, **7**

Pierre's, **6**

Hotels

Amara Cay Resort, **9**

Casa Morada, **6**

Cheeca Lodge & Spa, **7**

Drop Anchor Resort and Marina, **3**

The Islander Resort, **5**

La Siesta Resort & Marina, **10**

Little Basin Villas, **4**

The Moorings Village, **8**

Postcard Inn Beach Resort & Marina at Holiday Isle, **2**

Ragged Edge Resort, **1**

the helium bar. There are extended hours (until 6:45 pm) on the third Wednesday of every month. ⊠ *MM 83 BS, 82990 Overseas Hwy., Upper Matecumbe Key* ☎ *305/664–9737* ⊕ *www.divingmuseum.org* ☎ *$12.*

FAMILY **Robbie's Marina.** Huge, prehistoric-looking denizens of the not-so-deep, silver-sided tarpon congregate around the docks at this marina on Lower Matecumbe Key. Children—and lots of adults—pay $4 for a bucket of sardines to feed them and $2.25 each for dock admission. Spend some time hanging out at this authentic Keys community, where you can grab a bite to eat indoors or out, shop at a slew of artisans' booths, or charter a boat, kayak, or other watercraft. ⊠ *MM 77.5 BS, 77522 Overseas Hwy., Lower Matecumbe Key* ☎ *305/664–8070, 877/664–8498* ⊕ *www. robbies.com* ☎ *Dock access $1.*

FAMILY **Theater of the Sea.** The second-oldest marine-mammal center in the world doesn't attempt to compete with more modern, more expensive parks. Even so, it's among the better attractions north of Key West, especially if you have kids in tow. In addition to marine-life exhibits and shows, you can make reservations for up-close-and-personal encounters like a swim with a dolphin or sea lion, or stingray and turtle feedings (which include general admission; reservations required). These are popular, so reserve in advance. Ride a "bottomless" boat to see what's below the waves and take a guided tour of the marine-life exhibits. Nonstop animal shows highlight conservation issues. You can stop for lunch at the grill, shop in the extensive gift shop, or sunbathe and swim at the private beach. This easily could be an all-day attraction. ⊠ *MM 84.5 OS, 84721 Overseas Hwy., Windley Key, Islamorada* ☎ *305/664–2431* ⊕ *www.theaterofthesea. com* ☎ *$35.95; interaction programs $45–$199.*

WORTH NOTING

Indian Key Historic State Park. Mystery surrounds 10-acre Indian Key, on the ocean side of the Matecumbe islands. Before it became one of the first European settlements outside Key West, it was inhabited by American Indians for several thousand years. The islet served as a base for 19th-century shipwreck salvagers until an Indian attack wiped out the settlement in 1840. Dr. Henry Perrine, a noted botanist, was killed in the raid. Today his plants grow in the town's ruins. Most people kayak or canoe here from Indian Key Fill or take a boat from Robbie's Marina to tour the nature trails and the town ruins or to snorkel.

There are no restrooms or picnic facilities on Indian Key. ✉ *Indian Key, Islamorada* ☎ *305/664–2540 park* ⊕ *www. floridastateparks.org/parks-and-trails/indian-key-historic- state-park* ✆ *Free.*

FAMILY **Islamorada Founder's Park.** This public park is the gem of Islamorada and boasts a palm-shaded beach, swimming pool, marina, skate park, tennis, and plenty of other facilities. If you want to rent a boat or learn to sail, businesses here can help you. If you're staying in Islamorada, admission is free. Those staying elsewhere pay $8 (cash only) to enter the park. Either way, you pay an additional $3 to use the Olympic-size pool. A spiffy amphitheater hosts concerts, plays, and shows. The shallow-water beach is ideal for swimming and for families with little ones. Showers and bathrooms are beachside. ✉ *MM 87 BS, 87000 Overseas Hwy., Plantation Key* ☎ *305/853–1685* ⊕ *www. islamorada.fl.us/departments/parks_and_recreation/found- ers_park.php.*

Lignumvitae Key Botanical State Park. On the National Register of Historic Places, this 280-acre bay-side island is the site of a virgin hardwood forest and the 1919 home of chemical magnate William Matheson. His caretaker's cottage serves as the park's visitor center. Access is by boat—your own, a rented vessel, or a tour operated from Robbie's Marina. The tour leaves at 8:30 am Friday through Sunday and takes in both Lignumvitae and Indian Keys (reservations required). Paddling here from Indian Key Fill, at MM 78.5, is a popular pastime. The only way to do the trails is by a guided ranger walk, offered seasonally December through April at 10 am and 2 pm Friday to Sunday. Wear long sleeves and pants, and bring mosquito repellent. On the first Saturday in December is the Lignumvitae Christmas Celebration, when the historic home is decorated 1930s-style. ✉ *Islamorada* ☎ *305/664–2540 park, 305/664–8070 boat tours* ⊕ *www. floridastateparks.org/parks-and-trails/lignumvitae-key-bo- tanical-state-park* ✆ *$2.50; $35 for boat tours.*

Upper Matecumbe Key. This was one of the first of the Upper Keys to be permanently settled. Early homesteaders were so successful at growing pineapples in the rocky soil that at one time the island yielded the country's largest annual crop. However, foreign competition and the hurricane of 1935 killed the industry. Today, life centers on fishing and tourism, and the island is filled with everything from bait shops and charter boats to eclectic galleries and fusion restaurants. ⊠ *MM 84–79, Islamorada.*

Windley Key. This is the highest point in the Keys, though at 16 feet above sea level it's not likely to give anyone altitude sickness. Originally two islets, this area was first inhabited by American Indians, who left behind a few traces of their dwellings, and then by farmers and fishermen who built their homes here in the mid-1800s. Henry Flagler bought the land from homesteaders in 1908 for his Florida East Coast Railway, filling in the inlet between what were then called the Umbrella Keys. His workers quarried coral rock for the rail bed and bridge approaches—the same rock used in many historic South Florida structures, including Miami's Vizcaya and the Hurricane Monument on Upper Matecumbe. Although the Quarry Station was destroyed by the 1935 hurricane, quarrying continued until the 1960s. Today, this is where you'll find Theater of the Sea, the famous Holiday Isle (now Postcard Inn), and Windley Key Fossil Reef Geological State Park. ⊠ *MM 86–84, Islamorada.*

FAMILY **Windley Key Fossil Reef Geological State Park.** The fossilized-coral reef, dating back about 125,000 years, demonstrates that the Florida Keys were once beneath the ocean. Excavation of Windley Key's limestone bed by the Florida East Coast Railway exposed the petrified reef, full of beautifully fossilized brain coral and sea ferns. Visitors can see the fossils along a 300-foot quarry wall when hiking the park's three trails. There are guided (Friday, Saturday, and Sunday only) and self-guided tours along the trails, which lead to the railway's old quarrying equipment and cutting pits, where you can make rubbings of the quarry walls. The **Alison Fahrer Environmental Education Center** holds historic, biological, and geological displays about the area, including videos. The first Saturday in March is Windley Key Day, when the park sells native plants and hosts environmental exhibits. ⊠ *MM 84.9 BS, Windley Key, Islamorada* ☎ *305/664–2540* ⊕ *www.floridastateparks.org/parks-and-trails/windley-key-fossil-reef-geological-state-park* ☜ *$2.50; additional $2 for guided tours (self-guided free)* ⊗ *Closed Tues. and Wed.*

WHERE TO EAT

$$ 🍴**Bayside Gourmet.** *Italian.* This tiny counter-service restaurant is the best-kept secret in Islamorada, with the tastiest and most affordable ($10) grouper Reuben sandwich in the Keys. It's a small place—with six tables inside, a bar overlooking the kitchen, and an outdoor patio—and most diners are locals. **Known for:** excellent key lime pie; microbrews; seafood omelets. [$] *Average main: $17* ✉ *MM 82.7 BS, 82758 Overseas Hwy., Islamorada* ☎ *305/735–4471* 🌐 *baysidegourmet.com.*
FAMILY

$ 🍴**Bitton Bistro Cafe.** *French.* Authentic French food is on the menu at this supercasual eatery run by chef-owner Michel Bitton. The gelatos and wide selection of homemade French pastries might be famous, but don't miss the opportunity to savor his daily quiches, fresh salads with Dijon vinaigrette, humongous crepes, rustic soups, and French baguette sandwiches. **Known for:** oversize crepes; freshly made gelato; wide assortment of macarons. [$] *Average main: $10* ✉ *MM 82 OS, 82245 Overseas Hwy., Islamorada* ☎ *305/396–7481* 💳 *No credit cards.*

★ **Fodor's Choice** 🍴**Chef Michael's.** *Seafood.* This local favorite whose motto is "Peace. Love. Hogfish." has been making big waves since its opening in 2011 with chef Michael Ledwith at the helm. Seafood is selected fresh daily, then elegantly prepared with a splash of tropical flair. **Known for:** watermelon mint sangria; fresh catch "Juliette" with shrimp and scallops; intimate tropical dining. [$] *Average main: $30* ✉ *MM 81.7, 81671 Overseas Hwy., Upper Matecumbe Key* ☎ *305/664–0640* 🌐 *www.foodtotalkabout.com* 🕒 *No lunch Mon.–Sat.*
$$$

$$$ 🍴**Green Turtle Inn.** *Seafood.* This circa-1947 landmark inn and its vintage neon sign is a slice of Florida Keys history. Period photographs decorate the wood-paneled walls. **Known for:** excellent conch chowder; a piece of Florida Keys history; huge homemade sticky buns. [$] *Average main: $24* ✉ *MM 81.2 OS, 81219 Overseas Hwy., Upper Matecumbe Key* ☎ *305/664–2006* 🌐 *www.greenturtlekeys.com* 🕒 *Closed Mon.*

$$ 🍴**Hungry Tarpon.** *Seafood.* As part of the colorful, bustling Old Florida scene at Robbie's Marina, you know that the seafood here is fresh and top quality. The extensive menu seems as if it's bigger than the dining space, which consists of a few tables and counter seating indoors, plus tables out back under the mangrove trees. **Known for:** insanely good Bloody Marys with a beefstick straw; heart-of-the-action

location; biscuits and gravy. $ *Average main: $19* ✉ *MM 77.5 BS, 77522 Overseas Hwy., Lower Matecumbe Key* ☎ *305/664–0535* 🌐 *www.hungrytarpon.com.*

$$ 🍴 **Islamorada Fish Company.** *Seafood.* When a restaurant is
FAMILY owned by Bass Pro Shops, you know the seafood should be as fresh as you can get it. The restaurant, housed in an open-air, oversize tiki hut on Florida Bay, is the quintessential Keys experience, with menu highlights that include cracked conch beaten 'til tender and fried crispy, and fresh catch Portofino blackened perfectly and topped with Key West shrimp and a brandied lobster sauce. **Known for:** tourist hot spot; great views; afternoon fish and shark feedings in its private lagoon. $ *Average main: $18* ✉ *MM 81.5 BS, 81532 Overseas Hwy., Windley Key* ☎ *305/664–9271* 🌐 *restaurants.basspro.com/fishcompany/Islamorada.*

$$$$ 🍴 **Kaiyo Grill & Sushi.** *Japanese.* The decor—an inviting setting that includes colorful abstract mosaics and upholstered banquettes—almost steals the show, but the food is equally interesting. The menu, a fusion of East and West, offers sushi rolls that combine local ingredients with traditional Japanese tastes. **Known for:** drunken scallops; showstopping decor; dessert cupcakes that look like sushi. $ *Average main: $35* ✉ *MM 81.5 OS, 81701 Overseas Hwy., Upper Matecumbe Key* ☎ *305/664–5556* ⏲ *Closed Sun. and Mon. No lunch.*

$$ 🍴 **Lorelei Restaurant & Cabana Bar.** *American.* While local anglers gather here for breakfast, lunch and dinner bring a mix of islanders and visitors for straightforward food and front-row seats to the sunset. Live music seven nights a week ensures a lively nighttime scene, and the menu staves off inebriation with burgers, barbecued baby back ribs, and Parmesan-crusted snapper. **Known for:** amazing sunset views; you catch it, they'll cook it; excellent tuna nachos. $ *Average main: $15* ✉ *MM 82 BS, 81924 Overseas Hwy., Upper Matecumbe Key* ☎ *305/664–2692* 🌐 *www.loreleicabanabar.com.*

$$$$ 🍴 **Marker 88.** *Seafood.* A few yards from Florida Bay, on one of the Keys only natural beaches, this popular seafood restaurant has large picture windows that offer great sunset views, but most choose to dine outside on the sand. Chef Bobby Stoky serves such irresistible entrées as onion-crusted mahimahi and house-smoked sea-salt-and-black-pepper-encrusted rib eye. **Known for:** a gathering place for locals and visitors; fantastic fresh fish sandwich; extensive wine list. $ *Average main: $34* ✉ *MM 88 BS, 88000 Overseas Hwy., Plantation Key* ☎ *305/852–9315* 🌐 *www.marker88.info.*

2

$$$ 🍴 **Morada Bay Beach Café.** *Eclectic.* This bay-front restaurant
FAMILY wins high marks for its surprisingly stellar cuisine, tables in the sand, and tiki torches that bathe the evening in romance. Seafood takes center stage, but you can always get roasted organic chicken or prime rib. **Known for:** feet-in-the-sand dining; full-moon parties; intoxicating sunset views. [$] *Average main: $27* ✉ *MM 81 BS, 81600 Overseas Hwy., Upper Matecumbe Key* ☎ *305/664–0604* 🌐 *www.moradabay.com.*

★ **Fodor's Choice** 🍴 **Pierre's.** *French.* One of the Keys' most elegant
$$$$ restaurants, Pierre's marries colonial style with modern food trends and lets you taste the world from its romantic verandas. French chocolate, Australian lamb, Hawaiian fish, Florida lobster—whatever is fresh and in season will be masterfully prepared and beautifully served. **Known for:** romantic spot for that special night out; seasonally changing menu; full-moon parties. [$] *Average main: $43* ✉ *MM 81.5 BS, 81600 Overseas Hwy., Upper Matecumbe Key* ☎ *305/664–3225* 🌐 *www.moradabay.com* ⏲ *No lunch.*

WHERE TO STAY

$$ 🏨 **Amara Cay Resort.** *Resort.* Simple yet chic, Islamorada's newest resort is an oceanfront gem. **Pros:** free shuttle to local attractions; free use of kayaks, bikes, paddleboards; oceanfront zero-entry pool. **Cons:** pricey $30 daily resort fee; living areas of rooms lack seating. [$] *Rooms from: $299* ✉ *MM 80 OS, 80001 Overseas Hwy., Islamorada* ☎ *305/664–0073* 🌐 *www.amaracayresort.com* 🛏 *110 rooms* 🍽 *No meals.*

★ **Fodor's Choice** 🏨 **Casa Morada.** *B&B/Inn.* This relic from the
$$$$ 1950s has been restyled into a suave, design-forward, all-suites property with outdoor showers and Jacuzzis in some of the suites. **Pros:** private island connected by footbridge; adults only; complimentary use of bikes, kayaks, paddleboards, and snorkel gear. **Cons:** dinner off property; beach is small and inconsequential; minimum two-night stay on weekends. [$] *Rooms from: $400* ✉ *MM 82 BS, 136 Madeira Rd., Upper Matecumbe Key* ☎ *305/664–0044, 888/881–3030* 🌐 *www.casamorada.com* 🛏 *16 suites* 🍽 *Free Breakfast.*

★ **Fodor's Choice** 🏨 **Cheeca Lodge & Spa.** *Resort.* While Chee-
$$$$ ca's 27 acres took a beating during Hurricane Irma, the grounds are looking better every month, and this legendary resort still packs in more amenities than any other we can think of. **Pros:** everything you need is on-site; new designer rooms; water-sports center on property. **Cons:** expensive

rates; expensive resort fee; very busy. $ *Rooms from: $410* ⊠ *MM 82 OS, 81801 Overseas Hwy., Upper Matecumbe Key* ☎ *305/664–4651, 800/327–2888* ⊕ *www.cheeca.com* ⇨ *123 rooms* ❖*No meals.*

$$ ☒ **Drop Anchor Resort and Marina.** *Hotel.* Immaculately maintained, this place has the feel of an old friend's beach house, even though it's been completely redone since Hurricane Irma blew through town. **Pros:** bright and colorful; very clean; laid-back charm. **Cons:** noise from the highway; beach is for fishing not swimming; simplicity isn't for everyone. $ *Rooms from: $200* ⊠ *MM 85 OS, 84959 Overseas Hwy., Windley Key* ☎ *305/664–4863, 888/664–4863* ⊕ *www.dropanchorresort.com* ⇨ *18 suites* ❖*No meals.*

$$ ☒ **The Islander Resort.** *Resort.* Guests here get to choose between a self-sufficient town home on the bay side or an oceanfront resort with on-site restaurants and oodles of amenities. **Pros:** spacious rooms; nice kitchens; eye-popping views. **Cons:** pricey; ocean side not open till January 2019; no dining at bay-side location. $ *Rooms from: $300* ⊠ *MM 82.1 OS, 82200 Overseas Hwy., Upper Matecumbe Key* ☎ *305/664–0082* ⊕ *www.islanderfloridakeys.com* ⇨ *25 town homes at the bay-side property* ❖*No meals.*

$$$$ ☒ **La Siesta Resort & Marina.** *Resort.* With 6 acres of oceanfront property, a range of accommodations from studio
FAMILY units to a glamorous three-bedroom waterfront home, and a staff who go the extra mile, this resort has everything a visitor to the Keys could want. **Pros:** free use of kayaks, paddleboards, bicycles, and fishing rods; free Wi-Fi; access to sister properties. **Cons:** $30-per-night resort fee; bar-café only open till 5 pm; not a swimming beach. $ *Rooms from: $413* ⊠ *MM 80.2 OS, 80241 Overseas Hwy., Islamorada* ☎ *305/664–2132, 855/335–1078 reservations* ⊕ *www.lasiestaresort.com* ⇨ *53 rooms* ❖*Free Breakfast.*

$$$$ ☒ **Little Basin Villas.** *Rental.* These two-story, state-of-the-art,
FAMILY 1,600-square-foot villas could easily be the set for a *Coastal Living* magazine shoot. **Pros:** great location; nice pool and tiki huts; floating dock for launching kayaks. **Cons:** no office on-site; mangroves block full water views. $ *Rooms from: $550* ⊠ *MM 81.8 BS, 84 Johnson Rd., Islamorada* ✛ *Next to the Islamorada Public Library* ☎ *305/363–8999* ⊕ *littlebasinvillas.com* ⇨ *9 villas* ❖*No meals.*

★ **Fodor's**Choice ☒ **The Moorings Village.** *Hotel.* This tropical
$$$$ retreat is everything you imagine when you envision the laid-back Keys—from hammocks swaying between towering trees to manicured sand lapped by aqua-green waves. **Pros:** romantic setting; good dining options with room-

charging privileges; beautiful views. **Cons:** no room service; $25 daily resort fee for activities; must cross the highway to walk or drive to its restaurants. $ *Rooms from: $800* ✉ *MM 81.6 OS, 123 Beach Rd., Upper Matecumbe Key* ☎ *305/664–4708* 🌐 *www.themooringsvillage.com* 🛏 *17 cottages* 🍴 *No meals.*

$$ 🏨 **Postcard Inn Beach Resort & Marina at Holiday Isle.** *Resort.* After an $11 million renovation that encompassed updating everything from the rooms to the public spaces, this iconic property (formerly known as the Holiday Isle Beach Resort) has found new life. **Pros:** large private beach; heated pools; on-site restaurants including Ciao Hound Italian Kitchen & Bar. **Cons:** rooms near tiki bar are noisy; minimum stay required during peak times; rooms without an oceanfront view overlook a parking lot. $ *Rooms from: $267* ✉ *MM 84 OS, 84001 Overseas Hwy., Plantation Key* ☎ *305/664–2321* 🌐 *www.holidayisle.com* 🛏 *145 rooms* 🍴 *No meals.*

$$ 🏨 **Ragged Edge Resort.** *Hotel.* Nicely tucked away in a res-
FAMILY idential area at the ocean's edge, this family-owned hotel draws returning guests who'd rather fish off the dock and grill up dinner than loll around in Egyptian cotton sheets. **Pros:** oceanfront setting; boat docks and ramp; cheap rates for Islamorada. **Cons:** dated decor; off the beaten path; not within walking distance to anything. $ *Rooms from: $209* ✉ *MM 86.5 OS, 243 Treasure Harbor Rd., Plantation Key* ☎ *305/852–5389, 800/436–2023* 🌐 *www.ragged-edge.com* 🛏 *10 units* 🍴 *No meals.*

NIGHTLIFE

Islamorada is not known for its raging nightlife, but for local fun. Lorelei's is legendary, as is the Postcard Inn at Holiday Isle. Others cater to the town's sophisticated clientele and fishing fervor.

Hog Heaven. Come by boat or car to this oceanfront restaurant and sports bar where you can soak in the views dockside or relax in the air-conditioning. Munch on fresh fish sandwiches or barbecue dishes while you shoot pool, catch the big game on large flat screens, or dance to a live band or DJ. Late night can get a bit wild and loud. ✉ *MM 85.3 OS, 85361 Overseas Hwy., Islamorada* ☎ *305/664–9669* 🌐 *www.hogheavensportsbar.com.*

Lorelei Restaurant & Cabana Bar. A larger-than-life mermaid guides you to the kind of place you fantasize about during those long, cold winters up north. It's all about good drinks, tasty pub grub, and beautiful sunsets set to live bands playing island tunes and light rock nightly. Dining is all outdoors, on a deck or under the trees. Service is slow, sometime even nonexistent. ✉ *MM 82 BS, 81924 Overseas Hwy., Upper Matecumbe Key* ☎ *305/664–2692* ⊕ *www. loreleicabanabar.com.*

Zane Grey Long Key Lounge. On the second floor of World Wide Sportsman, Zane Grey Long Key Lounge was created to honor writer Zane Grey, one of the most famous members of the Long Key Fishing Club. The lounge displays the author's furniture, photographs, books, and memorabilia. It's a low-key place to listen to live blues, jazz, and Motown. The wide veranda invites sunset watching, but don't miss the Brunswick mahogany back bar from the late 1800s. A full menu is available indoors and out. ✉ *MM 81.5 BS, 81576 Overseas Hwy., Upper Matecumbe Key* ☎ *305/664– 4615* ⊕ *restaurants.basspro.com/ZaneGreyLounge.*

Ziggie & Mad Dog's. The area's glam celebrity hangout, Ziggie & Mad Dog's serves appetizers with its happy-hour drink specials. Its wine list and outrageous steaks have become legendary. ✉ *MM 83 BS, 83000 Overseas Hwy., Upper Matecumbe Key* ☎ *305/664–3391* ⊕ *www.ziggie- andmaddogs.com.*

SHOPPING

Art galleries, upscale gift shops, and the mammoth World Wide Sportsman (if you want to look the part of a local fisherman, you must wear a shirt from here) make up the variety and superior style of Islamorada shopping.

BOOKS
Hooked on Books. Among the best buys in town are the used best sellers at this bookstore, which also sells new titles, audiobooks, and CDs. The Florida book collection is noteworthy. ✉ *MM 81.9 OS, 81909 Overseas Hwy., Upper Matecumbe Key* ☎ *305/517–2602* ⊕ *www.hooke- donbooksfloridakeys.com.*

GALLERIES
Pasta Pantaleo's Signature Gallery. Roberto Pantaleo, better known as "Pasta," is one of the Keys' best-known (and wildly collected) artists. His depictions of sea life must be seen, from vibrant turtles to subtle seas and mangroves. His work can also be seen in the new Roberto Russell Galleries. ✉ *81599 Old*

Hwy., Islamorada ⊹ Downtown Islamorada in the Morada Way Art District ☎ 305/619–9924 ⊕ www.artbypasta.com.

Rain Barrel Artisan Village. This is a natural and unhurried shopping showplace. Set in a tropical garden of shady trees, native shrubs, and orchids, the crafts village has shops selling the work of local and national artists as well as resident artists who sell work from their own studios. Take a selfie with "Betsy," the giant Florida lobster, roadside. ⊠ *MM 86.7 BS, 86700 Overseas Hwy., Plantation Key* ☎ 305/852–3084.

Redbone Gallery. This gallery stocks hand-stitched clothing, giftware, and jewelry, in addition to works of art by watercolorists C. D. Clarke, Christine Black, and Julie Joyce; and painters David Hall, Steven Left, Tim Borski, and Jorge Martinez. Proceeds benefit cystic fibrosis research. Find them in the Morada Way Arts and Cultural District. ⊠ *MM 81.5 OS, 200 Morada Way, Upper Matecumbe Key* ☎ 305/664–2002 ⊕ www.redbone.org.

GIFTS

Banyan Tree Garden and Boutique. Stroll and shop among the colorful orchids and lush plants at this outdoor garden and indoor boutique known for its tropical splendor, unique gifts, and free-spirited clothing. There is nothing quite like it in the area. ⊠ *MM 81.2 OS, 81197 Overseas Hwy., Upper Matecumbe Key* ☎ 305/664–3433 ⊕ www. banyantreeboutique.com.

Ocean Gardens. Warning: you could spend hours in here, and drop some serious cash on the one-of-a-kind home-decor pieces and marine antiques. It's more than a shop, it's a showroom of all things upscale nautical. Come browse and be amazed. ⊠ *MM 82.2 OS, 82237 Overseas Hwy., Islamorada* ☎ 305/664–2793 ⊕ www.oceangardensandgifts.com.

JEWELRY

Blue Marlin Jewelers. For more than 20 years, this family-owned and -operated jeweler has been providing unique sparkle and shine to the lives of visitors and locals alike. At the premier jeweler in the Keys, you will find a gorgeous selection of nautical- and tropical-themed jewelry as well as high-end pens, pocket knives, and money clips that are functional art. Looking for a Rolex? You'll find it here. Blue Marlin is a member of the American Gem Society and all sales staff boast AGS credentials. This is the place to find yourself some bling with a flavor of the islands. ⊠ *MM 81.5 OS, 81549 Old Hwy., Islamorada* ☎ 305/664–8004 ⊕ www.bluemarlinjewelry.com.

SHOPPING CENTERS

Casa Mar Village. Change is good, and in this case, it's fantastic. What was once a row of worn-down buildings is now a merry blend of gift shops and galleries with the added bonus of a place selling fresh-roasted coffee. By day, these colorful shops glisten at their canal-front location; by nightfall, they're lit up like a lovely Christmas town. The offerings include What The Fish Rolls & More restaurant; Casa Mar Seafood fish market; and Paddle The Florida Keys, where you can rent paddleboards and kayaks. ⊠ *MM 90 OS, 90775 Old Hwy., Upper Matecumbe Key* ⊕ *www. casamarvillage.com.*

Village Square at the Trading Post. This shopping village has garden alcoves, picnic tables, and fun shops with everything from trendy clothing and artwork to home decor. There's even yoga in the garden Monday and Friday at 9:45 am. Grab a bite at Bad Boy Burrito where the fish tacos are almost legendary. ⊠ *MM 81.8 BS, 81868 Overseas Hwy., Islamorada* ☎ *305/440–3951* ⊕ *www.villagesquareislamorada.com.*

SPORTING GOODS

World Wide Sportsman. This two-level retail center sells upscale and everyday fishing equipment, resort clothing, sportfishing art, and other gifts. When you're tired of shopping, relax at the Zane Grey Long Key Lounge, located on the second level—but not before you step up and into *Pilar,* a replica of Hemingway's boat. ⊠ *MM 81.5 BS, 81576 Overseas Hwy., Upper Matecumbe Key* ☎ *305/664–4615, 800/327–2880.*

SPORTS AND THE OUTDOORS

BOATING

Early Bird Fishing Charters. Captain Ross knows these waters well and he'll hook you up with whatever is in season—mahimahi, sailfish, tuna, and wahoo, to name a few—while you cruise on a comfy and stylish 43-foot custom Willis charter boat. The salon is air-conditioned for those hot summer days, and everything but booze and food is included. ⊠ *Bud and Mary's Marina, MM 79.8 OS, 79851 Overseas Hwy., Islamorada* ☎ *305/942–3618* ⊕ *www.fishearlybird. com* ⌖ *4 hrs $850; 6 hrs $1,100; 8 hrs $1,300.*

Keys Boat Rental. You can rent both fishing and deck boats here (from 18 to 29 feet) by the day or the week. Free local delivery with seven-day rentals from each of its locations is available. ⊠ *MM 85.9 BS and 99.7 OS, 85920 Overseas Hwy., Upper*

Matecumbe Key ☎ *305/664–9404, 877/453–9463* ⊕ *www.keysboatrental.com* ⊜ *Rentals from $240 per day.*

Nauti-Limo. Captain Joe Fox has converted the design of a 1983 pink Caddy stretch limo into a less-than-luxurious but certainly curious watercraft. The seaworthy hybrid—complete with wheels—can sail with the top down if you're in the mood. Only in the Keys! One-hour and longer tours are available. New to the fleet is a 40-foot pirate ship, complete with plastic swords, that can hold about 14 people, available for two-hour rides. ⊠ *Lorelei Restaurant & Yacht Club, MM 82 BS, 96 Madeira Rd., Upper Matecumbe Key* ☎ *305/942–3793* ⊕ *www.nautilimo.com* ⊜ *From $90.*

Robbie's Boat Rentals. This full-service company will even give you a crash course on how not to crash your boat. The rental fleet includes an 18-foot skiff with a 90-horsepower outboard to a 21-foot deck boat with a 130-horsepower engine. Robbie's also rents snorkeling gear (there's good snorkeling nearby) and sells bait, drinks, and snacks. Want to hire a guide who knows the local waters and where the fish lurk? Robbie's offers offshore-fishing trips, patch-reef trips, and party-boat fishing. Backcountry flats trips are a specialty. ⊠ *MM 77.5 BS, 77522 Overseas Hwy., Lower Matecumbe Key* ☎ *305/664–9814, 877/664–8498* ⊕ *www.robbies.com* ⊜ *From $185 per day.*

FISHING

Here in the self-proclaimed "Sportfishing Capital of the World," sailfish is the prime catch in the winter and mahi-mahi in the summer. Buchanan Bank just south of Islamorada is a good spot to try for tarpon in the spring. Blackfin tuna and amberjack are generally plentiful in the area, too. ■TIP→ **The Hump at Islamorada ranks highest among anglers' favorite fishing spots in Florida (declared Florida Monthly magazine's best for seven years in a row) due to the incredible offshore marine life.**

★ **Fodor'sChoice Bamboo Charters.** Captain Matt is not only a world-class fisherman and guide, but he also studied to be a marine biologist. He knows his stuff and can put you on the fish, whether you want a calm day in the shallow waters of the backcountry or a day at the reef catching snapper, grouper, or anything else with fins. At the marina, you'll have access to a bathroom and shower, and parking is hassle-free. ⊠ *Angler House Marina, 80500 Overseas Hwy., Islamorada* ☎ *305/394–0000* ⊕ *www.bamboocharters.com.*

Captain Ted Wilson. Go into the backcountry for bonefish, tarpon, redfish, snook, and shark aboard a 17-foot boat that accommodates up to three anglers. Choose half-day (four hours), three-quarter-day (six hours), or full-day (eight hours) trips, or evening tarpon fishing excursions. Rates are for one or two anglers. There's a $75 charge for an additional person. ⊠ *Bud N' Mary's Marina, MM 79.9 OS, 79851 Overseas Hwy., Upper Matecumbe Key* ☎ *305/942–5224* ⊕ *www.captaintedwilson.com* ⊛ *Half-day and evening trips from $450.*

Florida Keys Fly Fish. Like other top fly-fishing and light-tackle guides, Captain Geoff Colmes helps his clients land trophy fish in the waters around the Keys, from Islamorada to Flamingo in the Everglades. ⊠ *105 Palm La., Upper Matecumbe Key* ☎ *305/393–1245* ⊕ *www.floridakeysflyfish. com* ⊛ *From $550.*

Florida Keys Outfitters. Long before fly-fishing became popular, Sandy Moret was fishing the Keys for bonefish, tarpon, and redfish. Now he attracts anglers from around the world on a quest for the big catch. His weekend fly-fishing classes include classroom instruction, equipment, and daily lunch. Guided fishing trips can be done for a half day or full day. Packages combining fishing and accommodations at Islander Resort are available. ⊠ *Green Turtle, MM 81.2, 81219 Overseas Hwy., Upper Matecumbe Key* ☎ *305/664–5423* ⊕ *www.floridakeysoutfitters.com* ⊛ *Half-day trips from $550.*

Miss Islamorada. This 65-foot party boat offers full-day trips. Bring your lunch or buy one from the dockside deli. ⊠ *Bud N' Mary's Marina, MM 79.8 OS, 79851 Overseas Hwy., Upper Matecumbe Key* ☎ *305/664–2461, 800/742–7945* ⊕ *www.budnmarys.com* ⊛ *$70.*

SCUBA DIVING AND SNORKELING

Florida Keys Dive Center. Dive from John Pennekamp Coral Reef State Park to Alligator Reef with this outfitter. The center has two 46-foot Coast Guard–approved dive boats, offers scuba training, and is one of the few Keys dive centers to offer nitrox and trimix (mixed-gas) diving. ⊠ *MM 90.5 OS, 90451 Overseas Hwy., Plantation Key* ☎ *305/852–4599, 800/433–8946* ⊕ *www.floridakeysdivectr. com* ⊛ *Snorkeling from $38, diving from $84.*

Islamorada Dive Center. This one-stop dive shop has a resort, pool, restaurant, lessons, and twice-daily dive and snorkel trips and the newest fleet in the Keys. You can take a day trip with a two-tank dive or a one-tank night trip with their equipment or yours. Snorkel and spearfishing trips are also available. ⊠ *MM 84 OS, 84001 Overseas Hwy., Windley Key* ☎ *305/664–3483, 800/327–7070* ⊕ *www.islamoradadivecenter.com* ⊴ *Snorkel trips from $45, diving from $85.*

San Pedro Underwater Archaeological Preserve State Park. About 1¼ nautical miles south of Indian Key is the San Pedro Underwater Archaeological Preserve State Park, which includes the remains of a Spanish treasure-fleet ship that sank in 1733. The state of Florida protects the site for divers; no spearfishing or souvenir collecting is allowed. Seven replica cannons and a plaque enhance what basically amounts to a 90-foot-long pile of ballast stones. Resting in only 18 feet of water, its ruins are visible to snorkelers as well as divers and attract a colorful array of fish. ⊠ *MM 85.5 OS, Islamorada* ☎ *305/664–2540* ⊕ *www.floridastateparks.org/parks-and-trails/san-pedro-underwater-archaeological-preserve-state-park.*

TENNIS

Islamorada Tennis Club. Not all Keys recreation is on the water. Play tennis and pickleball year-round at a well-run facility with four clay and two hard courts (all lighted), same-day racket stringing, ball machines, private lessons, and a full-service pro shop. ⊠ *MM 76.8 BS, 76800 Overseas Hwy., Upper Matecumbe Key* ☎ *305/664–5341* ⊕ *islamoradatennisclub.com* ⊴ *From $25.*

WATER SPORTS

The Kayak Shack. You can rent kayaks for trips to Indian (about 20 minutes one-way) and Lignumvitae (about 45 minutes one-way) Keys, two favorite destinations for paddlers. Kayaks can be rented for a half day (and you'll need plenty of time to explore those mangrove canopies). The company also offers guided two-hour Jet Ski tours, including a snorkel trip to Indian Key or backcountry ecotours. It also rents stand-up paddleboards, including instruction, and canoes. ⊠ *Robbie's Marina, MM 77.5 BS, 77522 Overseas Hwy., Lower Matecumbe Key* ☎ *305/664–4878* ⊕ *www.kayakthefloridakeys.com* ⊴ *From $40 for single, $55 for double; guided trips from $45.*

LONG KEY

MM 70–65.5.

Long Key isn't a tourist hot spot, making it a favorite destination for those looking to avoid the masses and enjoy some natural history.

EXPLORING

Layton Nature Trail. Up the road about ½ mile from Long Key State Park, beginning at a close-to-the-ground marker, is a free trail that leads through a tropical-hardwood forest to a rocky Florida Bay shoreline overlooking shallow grass flats. It takes about 20 minutes to walk the ¼-mile trail. The mangroves and vegetation took a hard hit in the hurricane, but the trail is still open. ⊠ *MM 67.7 BS, Long Key.*

Long Key State Park. Come here for solitude, hiking, and fishing. On the ocean side, the 1.1-mile Golden Orb Trail leads to a boardwalk that cuts through the mangroves (may require some wading) and alongside a lagoon where waterfowl congregate (as do mosquitoes, so be prepared). A 1¼-mile canoe trail leads through a tidal lagoon, and a broad expanse of shallow grass flats is perfect for bone-fishing. Bring a mask and snorkel to observe the marine life in the shallow water. In summer, no-see-ums (biting sand flies) also love the beach, so again—be prepared. The picnic area is on the water, too, but lacks a beach. Canoes rent for $10 per day, and kayak rentals start at $17.50 for a single for two hours, $21.50 for a double. Rangers lead tours every Wednesday and Thursday at 10 on birding, boating, or beachcombing. Camping is indefinitely unavailable due to severe hurricane damage. ⊠ *MM 67.5 OS, 67400 Overseas Hwy., Long Key* ☎ *305/664–4815* ⊕ *www.floridastateparks.org/park/Long-Key* ⊠ *$4.50 for 1 person, $5.50 for 2 people, and 50¢ for each additional person in the group.*

Long Key Viaduct. As you cross Long Key Channel, look beside you at the old viaduct. The second-longest bridge on the former rail line, this 2¼-mile-long structure has 222 reinforced-concrete arches. The old bridge is popular with cyclists and joggers. Anglers fish off the sides day and night. ⊠ *Long Key.*

BEACHES

Long Key State Park Beach. Camping, snorkeling, and bonefishing are the favored activities along this narrow strip of natural, rocky shoreline and its shallow, sea-grass-bottom waters. It lines the park's campground, open only to registered campers, but currently still closed due to Hurricane Irma. The day area offers a nice respite, although those expecting a wide, sandy beach will be disappointed. If you're seeking a spot by the shoreline, this could be your place in the sun. **Amenities:** showers; toilets. **Best for:** snorkeling; swimming; walking. ✉ *MM 67.5 OS, 67400 Overseas Hwy., Long Key* ☎ *305/664–4815* 🌐 *www.floridastateparks.org/park/Long-Key* 🎟 *$4.50 for 1 person, $5.50 for 2 people, and 50¢ for each additional person in the group.*

WHERE TO STAY

$$ 🏨 **Lime Tree Bay Resort.** *Resort.* Easy on the eye and the wallet, this 2½-acre resort on Florida Bay offers simple accommodations that are far from the hustle and bustle of the larger islands. **Pros:** great views; friendly staff; close to Long Key State Park. **Cons:** limited dock space; shared balconies; $25 daily resort fee. [$] *Rooms from: $210* ✉ *MM 68.5 BS, 68500 Overseas Hwy., Layton* ☎ *305/664–4740, 800/723–4519* 🌐 *www.limetreebayresort.com* 🛏 *48 units* 🍴 *Free Breakfast.*

3

THE MIDDLE KEYS

Visit Fodors.com for advice, updates, and bookings

Updated
by Jill
Martin

MOST OF THE ACTIVITY IN the Middle Keys revolves around the town of Marathon, the region's third-largest metropolitan area. On either end of it, smaller keys hold resorts, wildlife research and rehab facilities, a historic village, and a state park. The Middle Keys make a fitting transition from the Upper Keys to the Lower Keys not only geographically but also mentally. Crossing Seven Mile Bridge prepares you for the slow pace and don't-give-a-damn attitude you'll find a little farther down the highway. Fishing is one of the main attractions—in fact, the region's commercial fishing industry was founded here in the early 1800s. Diving is another popular pastime. There are also beaches and natural areas to enjoy in the Middle Keys, where mainland stress becomes an ever more distant memory.

ORIENTATION AND PLANNING

GETTING ORIENTED

If you get bridge fever—the heebie-jeebies when driving over long stretches of water—you may need a pair of blinders (or a couple of tranquilizers) before tackling the Middle Keys. Stretching from Conch Key to the far side of the Seven Mile Bridge, this zone is home to the region's two longest bridges: Long Key Viaduct and Seven Mile Bridge, both historic landmarks.

PLANNING

To get to the Middle Keys you can fly into either Miami International Airport or Key West International Airport. Key West is closer, but there are far fewer flights coming in and going out. Rental cars are available at both airports. In addition, there is bus service from the Key West airport, $4 one-way with Key West Transit. SuperShuttle charges $300 for up to 11 passengers from Miami International Airport (MIA) to Big Pine Key. Keys Shuttle charges $70 per passenger from MIA to Marathon. You can also take an Uber from MIA to Marathon for about $140.

U.S. 1 takes you from one end of the region to the other in a direct line that takes in most of the sights, but you'll find some interesting resorts and restaurants off the main drag. *See Air Travel: Ground Transportation and Bus Travel in Travel Smart.*

TOP REASONS TO GO

■ **Crane Point.** Visit 63-acre Crane Point Museum, Nature Center and Historic Site in Marathon for a primer on local natural and social history.

■ **A Beach for the Whole Family.** Sun, swim, and play with abandon at Marathon's family-oriented Sombrero Beach.

■ **Pigeon Key.** Step into the era of railroad building with a ferry ride to Pigeon Key's historic village, which was once a residential camp for workers on Henry M. Flagler's Overseas Railroad.

■ **Dolphins.** Kiss a dolphin, and maybe even watch one paint, at Dolphin Research Center, which was begun by the maker of the movie *Flipper.*

■ **Fishing.** Anglers will be happy to hear that the deep-water fishing off Marathon is superb in both the bay and the ocean.

3

From quaint old cottages to newly built town-house communities, the Middle Keys have it all, often with prices that are more affordable than at the chain's extremes. Hawks Cay has the region's best selection of lodgings.

Hope you're not tired of seafood, because the run of fish houses continues in the Middle Keys. In fact, Marathon boasts some of the best. Several are not so easy to find, but worth the search because of their local color and water views. Expect casual and friendly service with a side of sass. Restaurants may close for two to four weeks during the slow season between September and mid-November, so call ahead if you have a particular place in mind.

Restaurant and hotel reviews have been shortened. For full information, visit Fodors.com.

WHAT IT COSTS				
	$	$$	$$$	$$$$
Restaurants	under $15	$15–$20	$21–$30	over $30
Hotels	under $200	$200–$300	$301–$400	over $400

Prices in the restaurant reviews are the average cost of a main course at dinner or, if dinner isn't served, at lunch. Prices in the hotel reviews are the lowest cost of a standard double room in high season.

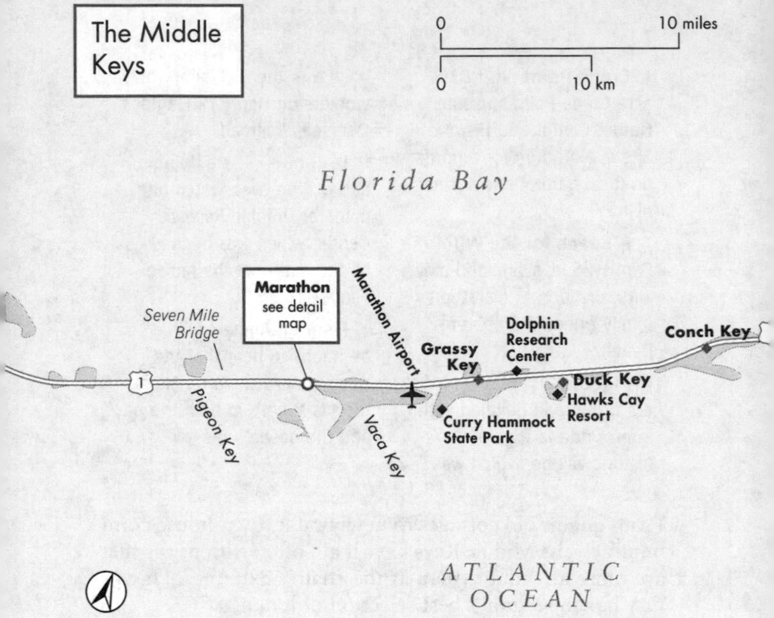
The Middle Keys
0
10 miles
0
10 km
Florida Bay
Marathon
see detail map
Marathon Airport
Seven Mile Bridge
Dolphin Research Center
Conch Key
Grassy Key
Duck Key
Hawks Cay Resort
1
Pigeon Key
Vaca Key
Curry Hammock State Park
ATLANTIC OCEAN

CONCH KEY

MM 63–60.

This stretch of islands ranges from rustic fishing village to boating elite. Fishing dominates the economy, and many residents are descendants of immigrants from the mainland South. Across a causeway from the tiny fishing village of Conch Key is Duck Key, home to a more upscale community. There are a few lodging options here for those exploring Marathon or taking advantage of the water sports on Duck Key.

WHERE TO STAY

$$$$ 🏨 **Little Conch Key.** *Rental.* The colorful one-bedroom cottages that dotted the beach here before Hurricane Irma are gone, but the two-bedroom villas now enjoy unobstructed ocean and beach views—and the resort pool all to themselves. **Pros:** far from traffic noise; sandy beach; some units have gourmet kitchens. **Cons:** far from restaurants; minimum stay required; privacy comes at a price. [$] *Rooms from: $400* ✉ *MM 62.3 OS, 62250 Overseas Hwy., Conch Key* ☎ *305/289–1377* 🛏 *4 villas* 🍴 *Free Breakfast.*

DUCK KEY

MM 61.

Duck Key holds one of the region's nicest marina resorts, Hawks Cay, plus a boating-oriented residential community.

WHERE TO EAT

$$$ FAMILY 🍴 **Angler and Ale.** *Seafood.* If you're a fan of vibrant coastal decor and fresh local seafood, you'll gush over this restaurant and bar overlooking the water and Hawks Cay Marina. The menu is diverse and the drinks are served in mason jars. **Known for:** locally sourced seafood like grouper cheeks and Key West pink shrimp; pricey menu; family-friendly. [$] *Average main: $30* ✉ *Hawks Cay Resort, 540 Duck Key Dr., Duck Key* ☎ *305/209–9991* 🌐 *www.hawkscay.com.*

$$$$ 🍴 **Sixty-One Prime.** *American.* This fine-dining restaurant in Hawks Cay Resort serves steaks and seafood in an elegant setting. Chefs work with local farmers and fishermen to find what's fresh and in season, then create a menu that will wow your palate (and your wallet). **Known for:** naturally raised certified Black Angus beef; nightly changing menu; attentive service. [$] *Average main: $36* ✉ *Hawks Cay Resort, 61 Hawks Cay Blvd., Duck Key* ☎ *305/743–7000, 888/432–2242* 🌐 *www.hawkscay.com* ⏲ *No lunch.*

WHERE TO STAY

★ $$$ FAMILY **Fodor's Choice** 🏨 **Hawks Cay Resort.** *Resort.* The 60-acre, Caribbean-style retreat with a full-service spa and two restaurants has plenty to keep the kids occupied (and adults happy). **Pros:** huge rooms; restful spa; full-service marina and dive shop. **Cons:** no real beach; far from Marathon's attractions; tram gets busy so either wait or walk far. [$] *Rooms from: $315* ✉ *MM 61 OS, 61 Hawks Cay Blvd., Duck Key* ☎ *305/743–7000, 888/432–2242* 🌐 *www.hawkscay.com* 🔑 *431 units* 🍽 *No meals.*

SPORTS AND THE OUTDOORS

DOLPHIN INTERACTION

Dolphin Connection. Hawks Cay Resort's Dolphin Connection offers three programs, including Dockside Dolphins, a 30-minute encounter from the dry training docks; Dolphin Discovery, an in-water program that lasts about 45 minutes and lets you kiss, touch, and feed the dolphins; and Trainer for a Day, a three-hour session with the animal training team. ⊠ *Hawks Cay Resort, MM 61 OS, 61 Hawks Cay Blvd., Duck Key* ☎ *305/289–9975* ⊕ *www.dolphinconnection.com* ⊠ *From $69.*

SCUBA DIVING AND SNORKELING

Dive Duck Key. Dive Duck Key is a full-service dive shop offering rentals, charters, lessons, and certification courses. Scuba trips are offered with and without gear. Basic open-water certification courses are also available, but these require four days of your time; a shorter resort course can be finished in a day. There's also Snuba, a snorkel-scuba hybrid where your tanks float on the surface rather than being attached to your back. ⊠ *Hawks Cay Resort, MM 61 OS, 61 Hawks Cay Blvd., Duck Key* ☎ *305/289–4931, 877/386–3483* ⊕ *www.diveduckkey.com* ⊠ *Diving from $65, Snuba excursions from $115.*

WATER SPORTS

Sundance Watersports. Snorkel the beautiful reefs of the Florida Keys (using your own equipment or theirs) or spend a memorable evening on a sunset cruise with Sundance Watersports. ⊠ *Robbie's MM 77.5 OS, 77522 Overseas Hwy., Lower Matecumbe Key* ☎ *305/743–0145, 305/664–9510 for reservations* ⊕ *www.sundancewatersports.org or robbies.com* ⊠ *From $42.*

GRASSY KEY

MM 60–57.

Local lore has it that this sleepy little key was named not for its vegetation—mostly native trees and shrubs—but for an early settler by the name of Grassy. A few families operating small fishing camps and roadside motels primarily inhabit the key. There's no marked definition between it and Marathon, so it feels sort of like a suburb of its much larger neighbor to the south. Grassy Key's sights tend toward the natural, including a worthwhile dolphin attraction and a small state park.

GETTING HERE AND AROUND

Most visitors arriving by air drive to this destination either from Miami International Airport or Key West International Airport. Rental cars are readily available at both, and in the long run, are the most convenient means of transportation for getting here and touring around the Keys.

EXPLORING

Curry Hammock State Park. Looking for a slice of the Keys that's far removed from tiki bars? On the ocean and bay sides of Overseas Highway are 260 acres of upland hammock, wetlands, and mangroves. On the bay side, there's a trail through thick hardwoods to a rocky shoreline. The ocean side is more developed, with a sandy beach, a clean bathhouse, picnic tables, a playground, grills, and a 28-site campground, each with electric and water. Locals consider the paddling trails under canopies of arching mangroves one of the best kayaking spots in the Keys. Manatees frequent the area, and it's a great spot for bird-watching. Herons, egrets, ibis, plovers, and sanderlings are commonly spotted. Raptors are often seen in the park, especially during migration periods. ⊠ *MM 57 OS, 56200 Overseas Hwy., Little Crawl Key* ☎ *305/289–2690* ⊕ *www.floridastateparks.org/parks-and-trails/curry-hammock-state-park* 🖾 *$4.50 for 1 person, $6 for 2, $0.50 per additional person* ⚲ *Campsites are $43 per night.*

FAMILY **Dolphin Research Center.** The 1963 movie *Flipper* popularized the notion of humans interacting with dolphins, and Milton Santini, the film's creator, also opened this center, which is home to a colony of dolphins and sea lions. The nonprofit center has educational sessions and programs that allow you to greet the dolphins from dry land or play with them in their watery habitat. You can even paint a T-shirt with a dolphin—you pick the paint, the dolphin "designs" your shirt. The center also offers five-day programs for children and adults with disabilities. ⊠ *MM 59 BS, 58901 Overseas Hwy., Grassy Key* ☎ *305/289–1121 information, 305/289–0002 reservations* ⊕ *www.dolphins.org* 🖾 *$28.*

WHERE TO EAT

$$$ ✕**Hideaway Café.** *American.* It's easy to miss this café tucked between Grassy Key and Marathon, but when you find it (upstairs at Rainbow Bend Resort), you'll discover a favorite of locals who appreciate a well-planned menu, lovely ocean view, and quiet evening away from the crowds. For starters, dig into escargots à la Edison (sautéed with vegetables, pepper, cognac, and cream) before feasting on several specialties, such as a rarely found chateaubriand for one, or the seafood medley combining the catch of the day with scallops and shrimp. **Known for:** seclusion and quiet; amazing escargot; hand-cut steaks and fresh fish.

$ *Average main: $30* ✉ *Rainbow Bend Resort, MM 58 OS, 57784 Overseas Hwy., Grassy Key* ☎ *305/289–1554* 🌐 *www.hideawaycafe.com* ⊘ *No lunch.*

WHERE TO STAY

$ 🏨 **Gulf View Waterfront Resort.** *Resort.* With tropical birds and a a tortoise on the property, this homey duplex on the water is part resort, part menagerie. **Pros:** parklike setting; sandy area with hammocks and tikis; close to restaurants. **Cons:** no elevator to office and second-story accommodations; some traffic noise; not a swimming beach. $ *Rooms from: $182* ✉ *MM 58.7 BS, 58743 Overseas Hwy., Grassy Key* ☎ *305/289–1414, 877/289–0111* 🌐 *www.gulfviewwaterfrontresort.com* 🛏 *11 units* 🍴 *No meals.*

MARATHON

MM 53–47.5.

New Englanders founded this former fishing village in the early 1800s. The community on Vaca Key subsequently served as a base for pirates, salvagers (also known as "wreckers"), spongers, and, later, Bahamian farmers who eked out a living growing cotton and other crops. More Bahamians arrived in the hope of finding work building the railroad. According to local lore, Marathon was renamed when a worker commented that it was a marathon task to position the tracks across the 6-mile-long island.

During the building of the railroad, Marathon developed a reputation for lawlessness that rivaled that of the Old West. It is said that to keep the rowdy workers from descending on Key West for their off-hours endeavors, residents would send boatloads of liquor up to Marathon. Needless to say, things have quieted down considerably since then.

Still, Marathon is a bustling town, at least compared to other communities in the Keys. As it leaves something to be desired in the charm department, Marathon may not be your first choice of places to stay, but water-sports types will find plenty to enjoy, and its historic and natural attractions merit a visit. Surprisingly good dining options abound, so you'll definitely want to stop for a bite even if you're just passing through on the way to Key West.

Throughout the year, Marathon hosts fishing tournaments (practically monthly), a huge seafood festival in March, and lighted boat parades around the holidays.

GETTING HERE AND AROUND

SuperShuttle charges $190 per passenger for trips from Miami International Airport to the Upper Keys. To go farther into the Keys, you must book an entire 11-person van, which costs about $300 to Marathon. For a trip to the airport, place your request 24 hours in advance.

Miami-Dade Transit provides daily bus service from MM 50 in Marathon to the Florida City Wal-Mart Supercenter on the mainland. The bus stops at major shopping centers as well as on demand anywhere along the route during daily round-trips on the hour from 6 am to 10 pm. The cost is $2 one-way, exact change required. The Key West Transit bus runs from Marathon to Key West ($4 one-way), with scheduled stops along the way. *For details, see Air Travel: Ground Transportation and Bus Travel.*

VISITOR INFORMATION

Contact Greater Marathon Chamber of Commerce and Visitor Center. ⊠ *MM 53.5 BS, 12222 Overseas Hwy., Marathon* ☎ *305/743–5417, 800/262–7284* ⊕ *www.floridakeysmarathon.com.*

EXPLORING

Grassy Key segues into Marathon with little more than a slight increase in traffic and higher concentration of commercial establishments. Marathon's roots are anchored in fishing and boating, so look for marinas to find local color, fishing charters, and good restaurants. At its north end, Key Colony Beach is an old-fashioned island neighborhood worth a visit for its shops and restaurants. Nature lovers shouldn't miss the Florida Keys Aquarium Encounters and the attractions on Crane Point. Other good places to leave the main road are at Sombrero Beach Road (MM 50), which leads to the beach, and 35th Street (MM 49), which takes you to a funky little marina and restaurant. U.S. 1 hightails through Hog Key and Knight Key before the big leap over Florida Bay and Hawk's Channel via the Seven Mile Bridge.

FAMILY **Crane Point Museum, Nature Center, and Historic Site.** Tucked away from the highway behind a stand of trees, Crane Point—part of a 63-acre tract that contains the last-known undisturbed thatch-palm hammock—is delightfully undeveloped. This multiuse facility includes the **Museum of Natural History of the Florida Keys,** which has displays about local wildlife, a seashell exhibit, and

Marathon

KEY
- 1 Restaurants
- 1 Hotels
- Dive Site
- Boat Launch

Conch Key

Duck Key

Hawks Cay Resort & Sixty-One Prime

TO ISLAMORADA

Dolphin Research Center

Grassy Key

Bamboo Key

Crawl Key

Curry Hammock State Park

Thunderbolt

Greater Marathon Chamber of Commerce

Coco Plum Dr.

125 St. Key Colony Bch.

Golf Course

Florida Keys Aquarium Encounters

117 St.

107 St.

110 St.

Marathon

Dolphin Dr.

100 St.

Marathon Airport
MM 32

183 St.

92 St.

Crane Point Museum, Nature Center, and Historic Site

164 St.

62 St.

The Turtle Hospital
MM 48.5

49 St.

Gulf Terr. Ave.

Vaca Key

39 St.

Sombrero Beach

The American

Boot Key Bridge

17 St.

Boot Key

Old Seven Mile Bridge

Pigeon Key

Seven Mile Bridge

Sombrero Reef

TO LOWER KEYS

Restaurants
Fish Tales Market and Eatery, **1**

Herbie's Bar & Chowder House, **3**

Key Colony Inn, **2**

Keys Fisheries Market & Marina, **4**

Lazy Days South, **6**

The Stuffed Pig, **5**

Sunset Grille & Raw Bar, **7**

Hotels
Glunz Ocean Beach Hotel & Resort, **1**

Tranquility Bay, **2**

a marine-life display that makes you feel like you're at the bottom of the sea. Kids love the replica 17th-century galleon and pirate dress-up room where they can play, and the re-created **Cracker House** filled with insects, sea-turtle exhibits, and children's activities. On the 1-mile indigenous loop trail, visit the **Laura Quinn Wild Bird Center** and the remnants of a Bahamian village, site of the restored **George Adderly House.** It is the oldest surviving example of Bahamian tabby (a concretelike material created from sand and seashells) construction outside Key West. A boardwalk crosses wetlands, rivers, and mangroves before ending at Adderly Village. From November to Easter, docent-led tours are available; bring good walking shoes and bug repellent during warm weather. ⊠ *MM 50.5 BS, 5550 Overseas Hwy., Marathon* ☎ *305/743–9100* ⊕ *www.cranepoint.net* ☎ *$14.95.*

FAMILY **Florida Keys Aquarium Encounters.** This isn't your typical large-city aquarium. It's more hands-on and personal, and it's all outdoors with several tiki huts to house the encounters and provide shade as you explore, rain or shine; plan to spend at least two to three hours here. You'll find a 200,000-gallon aquarium and plenty of marine encounters (extra cost), as well as guided tours, viewing areas, and a predator tank. The Coral Reef encounter ($95 snorkel, $130 regulator) lets you dive in a reef environment without hearing the theme from *Jaws* in your head (although you can see several sharks on the other side of the glass). Touch tanks are great for all ages and even have unique critters like slipper lobsters. Hungry? The on-site Eagle Ray Cafe serves up wings, fish tacos, salads, burgers, and more. Note that general admission is required, even if you're signed up for a marine encounter. ⊠ *MM 53 BS, 11710 Overseas Hwy., Marathon* ☎ *305/407–3262* ⊕ *www.floridakeysaquariumencounters.com* ☎ *$20.*

Pigeon Key. There's much to like about this 5-acre island under the Old Seven Mile Bridge. You might even recognize it from a season finale of the TV show *The Amazing Race.* You can reach it via a ferry that departs from their new gift shop location, a trailer at mile marker 47.5. Once there, tour the island on your own or join a guided tour to explore the buildings that formed the early-20th-century work camp for the Overseas Railroad that linked the mainland to Key West in 1912. Later the island became a fish camp, a state park, and then government-administration headquarters. Exhibits in a small museum recall the history of the Keys, the railroad, and railroad baron Henry M. Flagler. The ferry ride with tour lasts two hours; visitors can self-tour and catch the ferry back in a half hour. ■TIP→ **Bring your own snorkel gear and dive flag and you can snorkel right from the shore.** Pack a picnic lunch, too. ⊠ *MM 47.5 BS, between the Marriott and Hyatt Place, 2010 Overseas Hwy., Pigeon Key* ☎ *305/743–5999* ⊕ *pigeonkey.net* ☎ *$12.*

Seven Mile Bridge. This is one of the most photographed images in the Keys. Actually measuring slightly less than 7 miles, it connects the Middle and Lower Keys and is believed to be the world's longest segmental bridge. It has 39 expansion joints separating its various concrete sections. Each April runners gather in Marathon for the annual Seven Mile Bridge Run. The expanse running parallel to Seven Mile Bridge is what remains of the **Old Seven Mile Bridge,** an engineering and architectural marvel in its day that's now on the National Register of Historic Places. Once proclaimed the Eighth Wonder of the World, it rested on a record 546 concrete piers. No cars are allowed on the old bridge today. ⊠ *Marathon.*

FAMILY **The Turtle Hospital.** More than 100 injured sea turtles check in here every year. The 90-minute guided tours take you into recovery and surgical areas at the world's only state-certified veterinary hospital for sea turtles. In the "hospital bed" tanks, you can see recovering patients and others that are permanent residents due to their injuries. After the tour, you can feed some of the "residents." Call ahead—space is limited and tours are sometimes canceled due to medical emergencies. The turtle ambulance out front makes for a memorable souvenir photo. ⊠ *MM 48.5 BS, 2396 Overseas Hwy., Marathon* ☎ *305/743–2552* ⊕ *www.turtlehospital.org* ☎ *$25.*

BEACHES

FAMILY **Sombrero Beach.** No doubt one of the best beaches in the Keys, here you'll find pleasant, shaded picnic areas that overlook a coconut palm–lined grassy stretch and the Atlantic Ocean. Roped-off areas allow swimmers, boaters, and windsurfers to share the narrow cove. Facilities include barbecue grills, a large playground, a pier, a volleyball court, and a paved, lighted bike path off Overseas Highway. Sunday afternoons draw lots of local families toting coolers. The park is accessible for those with disabilities and allows leashed pets. Turn east at the traffic light in

TURTLE TIME

Five species of threatened and endangered sea turtles frequent the waters of the Florida Keys. The **loggerhead**, the most common, is named for the shape of its noggin. It grows to a heft of 300 pounds. It is the only one of the local turtles listed as threatened rather than endangered.

The vegetarian **green turtle** was once hunted for its meat, which has brought populations to their endangered stage. It can reach an impressive 500 pounds.

Named for the shape of its mouth, the **hawksbill turtle** is a relative lightweight at 150 pounds. It prefers rocks and reefs for habitat. The Keys are the only U.S. breeding site for the endangered critter.

The largest reptile alive, the **leatherback turtle** can weigh in at up to 2,000 pounds, attained from a diet of mainly jellyfish.

The rarest of local sea turtles, the **Kemp's ridley** is named after a Key West fisherman. A carnivore, it grows to 100 pounds.

The biggest threats to sea turtle survival include fibropapilloma tumors, monofilament fishing lines (which can sever their flippers), entanglement in ropes and nets, boat propeller run-ins, swallowing plastic bags (which appear to them as jellyfish), oil spills, and other human and natural impact.

Marathon and follow signs to the end. **Amenities:** showers; toilets. **Best for:** swimming; windsurfing. ✉ *MM 50 OS, Sombrero Beach Rd., Marathon* ☎ *305/743–0033* 🎟 *Free.*

WHERE TO EAT

$ 🍴 Fish Tales Market and Eatery. *Seafood.* This no-frills, roadside eatery has a loyal local following, an unfussy ambience, a couple of outside picnic tables, and friendly service. Signature dishes include snapper on grilled rye with coleslaw and melted Muenster cheese, a fried fish burrito, George's crab cake, and tomato-based conch chowder. **Known for:** luscious lobster bisque; fresh and affordable seafood and meat market; affordable dinner specials. [$] *Average main: $10* ✉ *MM 52.5 OS, 11711 Overseas Hwy., Marathon* ☎ *305/743–9196, 888/662–4822* ⏲ *Closed Sun. No dinner Sat.*

$ 🍴 **Herbie's Bar & Chowder House.** *Seafood.* This shacklike, Old Keys spot has been the go-to for quick and affordable comfort food since the 1940s. You'll find all the local staples—conch, lobster tail, fried oysters, and fresh fish—as well as cheeseburgers, shrimp scampi, and filet mignon. **Known for:** great craft-beer selection; crispy conch fritters; good key lime pie. [$] *Average main: $10* ✉ *MM 50.5, 6350 Overseas Hwy., Marathon* ☎ *305/743–6373* 🌐 *www.herbiesrestaurant.com* ⏲ *Closed Tues. and most of Oct.*

$$ 🍴 **Key Colony Inn.** *Italian.* The inviting aroma of an Italian kitchen pervades this family-owned favorite known for its Sunday brunch, served November through April. For lunch there are fish and steak entrées served with fries, salad, and bread in addition to Italian specialties. **Known for:** friendly and attentive service; Italian specialties; Sunday brunch. [$] *Average main: $20* ✉ *MM 54 OS, 700 W. Ocean Dr., Key Colony Beach* ☎ *305/743–0100* 🌐 *www.kcinn.com.*

$$ FAMILY 🍴 **Keys Fisheries Market & Marina.** *Seafood.* You can't miss the enormous tiki bar on stilts, but the walk-up window on the ground floor is the heart of this warehouse turned restaurant. A huge lobster Reuben served on thick slices of toasted bread is the signature dish, and the adults-only upstairs tiki bar offers a sushi and raw bar for eat-in only. **Known for:** seafood market; marina views; fish-food dispensers (25¢) so you can feed the tarpon. [$] *Average main: $16* ✉ *MM 49 BS, 3390 Gulfview Ave., at the end of 35th St., Marathon* ✣ *Turn onto 35th St. from Overseas Hwy.* ☎ *305/743–4353, 866/743–4353* 🌐 *www.keysfisheries.com.*

★ $$$ **Fodor's Choice** 🍴 **Lazy Days South.** *Seafood.* Tucked into Marathon Marina a half mile north of the Seven Mile Bridge, this restaurant offers views just as spectacular as its highly lauded food. A spin-off of an Islamorada favorite, here you'll find a wide range of daily offerings from fried or sautéed conch and a coconut-fried fish du jour sandwich to seafood pastas and beef tips over rice. **Known for:** water views; delicious seafood entrées; hook and cook. [$] *Average main: $22* ✉ *MM 47.3 OS, 725 11th St., Marathon* ☎ *305/289–0839* 🌐 *www.new.lazydayssouth.com.*

$ 🍴 **The Stuffed Pig.** *Diner.* With only nine tables and a counter inside, this breakfast-and-lunch place is always hopping. The kitchen whips up daily lunch specials like seafood platters or pulled pork with hand-cut fries, but the all-day breakfast is the main draw. **Known for:** pig's breakfast special; daily lunch specials; large portions. [$] *Average main: $9* ✉ *MM 49 BS, 3520 Overseas Hwy., Marathon*

☎ *305/743–4059* 🌐 *www.thestuffedpig.com* 💳 *No credit cards* 🕒 *No dinner.*

$$$ 🍴 **Sunset Grille & Raw Bar.** *Seafood.* Treat yourself to a seafood lunch or dinner at this vaulted tiki hut at the foot of the Seven Mile Bridge. For lunch, try the Voodoo grouper sandwich topped with mango-guava mayo (and wear your swimsuit if you want to take a dip in the pool afterwards). **Known for:** weekend pool parties and barbecues; pricey dinner specials; a swimming pool for patrons. $ *Average main: $22* ✉ *MM 47 OS, 7 Knights Key Blvd., Marathon* ☎ *305/396–7235* 🌐 *www.sunsetgrille7milebridge.com.*

3

WHERE TO STAY

$$ 🏨 **Glunz Ocean Beach Hotel & Resort.** *Rental.* The Glunz family got it right when they purchased this former time-share property and put a whole lot of love into renovating it to its full oceanfront potential. **Pros:** no resort fees, ever; nice private beach; excellent free Wi-Fi. **Cons:** small elevator; no interior corridors; not cheap. $ *Rooms from: $300* ✉ *MM 53.5 OS, 351 E. Ocean Dr., Key Colony Beach* ☎ *305/289–0525* 🌐 *www.GlunzOceanBeachHotel.com* 🛏 *46 units* 🍽 *No meals.*

★ **$$$$** FAMILY **Fodor's Choice** 🏨 **Tranquility Bay.** *Resort.* Ralph Lauren could have designed the rooms at this stylish, luxurious resort on a nice beach. **Pros:** secluded setting; tiki bar on the beach; main pool is nice and big. **Cons:** a bit sterile; no privacy on balconies; cramped building layout. $ *Rooms from: $425* ✉ *MM 48.5 BS, 2600 Overseas Hwy., Marathon* ☎ *305/289–0888, 866/643–5397* 🌐 *www.tranquilitybay.com* 🛏 *102 rooms* 🍽 *No meals.*

SPORTS AND THE OUTDOORS

BIKING

Tooling around on two wheels is a good way to see Marathon. There's easy cycling on a 1-mile off-road path that connects to the 2 miles of the Old Seven Mile Bridge leading to Pigeon Key.

Bike Marathon Bike Rentals. "Have bikes, will deliver" could be the motto of this company, which gets beach cruisers to your hotel door, including a helmet, basket, and lock. It also rents kayaks. There's no physical location, but services are available Monday through Saturday 9–4 and Sunday 9–2. ✉ *Marathon* ☎ *305/743–3204* 🌐 *www.bikemarathonbikerentals.com* 🎫 *$45 per wk.*

BOATING

Sail, motor, or paddle: whatever your mode, boating is what the Keys is all about. Brave the Atlantic waves and reefs or explore the backcountry islands on the gulf side. If you don't have a lot of boating and chart-reading experience, it's a good idea to tap into local knowledge on a charter.

Captain Pip's. This operator rents 18- to 24-foot outboards as well as snorkeling gear. Ask about multiday deals, or try one of the accommodation packages and walk right from your bay-front room to your boat. ✉ *MM 47.5 BS, 1410 Overseas Hwy., Marathon* ☎ *305/743–4403, 800/707–1692* ⊕ *www.captainpips.com* ☜ *Rentals from $199 per day.*

Fish'n Fun. Get out on the water on 19- to 26-foot power-boats. Rentals can be for a half or full day. The company also offers free delivery in the Middle Keys. ✉ *Duck Key Marina, MM 61 OS, 1149 Greenbriar Rd., Marathon* ☎ *305/743–2275, 800/471–3440* ⊕ *www.fishnfunrentals. com* ☜ *From $175.*

FISHING

For recreational anglers, the deepwater fishing is superb in both bay and ocean. Marathon West Hump, one good spot, has depths ranging from 500 to more than 1,000 feet. Locals fish from a half dozen bridges, including Long Key Bridge, the Old Seven Mile Bridge, and both ends of Tom's Harbor. Barracuda, bonefish, and tarpon all frequent local waters. Party boats and private charters are available.

Marathon Lady. Morning, afternoon, and night, fish for mahimahi, grouper, and other tasty catch aboard this 73-footer, which departs on half-day excursions from the Vaca Cut Bridge (MM 53), north of Marathon. Join the crew for night fishing ($55) from 6:30 to midnight from Memorial Day to Labor Day; it's especially beautiful on a full-moon night. ✉ *MM 53 OS, 11711 Overseas Hwy., at 117th St., Marathon* ☎ *305/743–5580* ⊕ *www.marathon-lady.net* ☜ *From $45.*

Sea Dog Charters. Captain Jim Purcell, a deep-sea specialist for ESPN's *The American Outdoorsman*, provides one of the best values in Keys fishing. Next to the Seven Mile Grill, his company offers half- and full-day offshore, reef and wreck, and backcountry fishing trips, as well as fishing and snorkeling trips aboard 30- to 37-foot boats. The per-person cost for a half-day trip is the same regardless of whether your group fills the boat, and includes bait, light tackle, ice, coolers, and fishing licenses. If you prefer an all-day private charter on a 37-foot boat, he offers those, too, for up to six people. A fuel surcharge may apply. ⊠ *MM 47.5 BS, 1248 Overseas Hwy., Marathon* ☎ *305/743–8255* ⊕ *www.seadogcharters.net* ⌨ *From $60.*

GOLF

Key Colony Beach Golf & Tennis. Designed by Wayne Spano and opened in 1973, this 9-holer near Marathon has no reserved tee times, and there's never a rush to hurry up and play through. In fact, you can finish in about 45 minutes even with slow greens as it's an easy, flat course to walk. Just show up any time from 7:30 am to dusk. Regulars say you only need three clubs to play the entire course, making it perfect for beginners or those who can't hit far. A little pro shop meets basic golf needs. Club rentals are only $3 per person, but the choices are a bit worn; pull carts are $2. You'll also have free use of the club's lighted tennis courts. ⊠ *MM 53.5 OS, 460 8th St., Key Colony Beach* ⊕ *www.keycolonybeach.net/ recreation.html* ⌨ *$13 for 9 holes; $8 for each additional 9 holes* ⚐ *9 holes, 972 yards, par 3.*

SCUBA DIVING AND SNORKELING

Local dive operations take you to Sombrero Reef and Lighthouse, the most popular down-under destination in these parts. For a shallow dive and some lobster nabbing, Coffins Patch, off Key Colony Beach, is a good choice. A number of wrecks such as the *Thunderbolt* serve as artificial reefs. Many operations out of this area will also take you to Looe Key Reef.

Hall's Diving Center & Career Institute. The institute has been training divers for more than 40 years. Along with conventional twice-a-day snorkel and two-tank dive trips to the reefs at Sombrero Lighthouse and wrecks like the *Thunderbolt,* the company has more unusual offerings like rebreather, photography, and nitrox courses. ⊠ *MM 48.5 BS, 1994 Overseas Hwy., Marathon* ☎ *305/743–5929, 800/331–4255* ⊕ *www.hallsdiving.com* ⌨ *From $45.*

Spirit Snorkeling. Join regularly scheduled snorkeling excursions to Sombrero Reef and Lighthouse Reef on this company's comfortable catamaran. It also offers sunset cruises and private charters. ⊠ *MM 47.5 BS, 1410 Overseas Hwy., Slip No. 1, Marathon* ☎ *305/289–0614* ⊕ *www.captainpips. com* ⌨ *From $30.*

Tildens Scuba Center. Since the mid-1980s, Tildens Scuba Center has been providing lessons, tours, gear rental, and daily snorkel, scuba, and Snuba adventures. Look for the huge, colorful angelfish sculpture outside the building. ✉ *MM 49.5 BS, 4650 Overseas Hwy., Marathon* ☎ *305/743–7255, 888/728–2235* ✈ *From $60 for snorkel trips; from $70 for dive trips.*

THE LOWER KEYS

Updated
by Jill
Martin

BEGINNING AT BAHIA HONDA KEY, the islands of the Florida Keys become smaller, more clustered, and more numerous, a result of ancient tidal water flowing between the Florida Straits and the gulf. Here you're likely to see more birds and mangroves than other tourists, and more refuges, beaches, and campgrounds than museums, restaurants, and hotels. The islands are made up of two types of limestone, both denser than the highly permeable Key Largo limestone of the Upper Keys. As a result, freshwater forms in pools rather than percolating through the rock, creating watering holes that support alligators, snakes, deer, rabbits, raccoons, and migratory ducks. (Many of these animals can be seen in the National Key Deer Refuge on Big Pine Key.) Nature was generous with her beauty in the Lower Keys, which have both Looe Key Reef, arguably the Keys' most beautiful tract of coral, and Bahia Honda State Park, considered one of the best beaches in the world for its fine sand dunes, clear warm waters, and panoramic vista of bridges, hammocks, and azure sky and sea. Big Pine Key is fishing headquarters for a laid-back community that swells with retirees in the winter. South of it, the dribble of islands can flash by in a blink of an eye if you don't take the time to stop at a roadside eatery or check out tours and charters at the little marinas. They include Little Torch Key, Middle Torch Key, Ramrod Key, Summerland Key, Cudjoe Key, Sugarloaf Keys, and Saddlebunch Key. Lying offshore Little Torch Key, Little Palm Island (scheduled to reopen in the fall of 2019) once welcomed U.S. presidents and other notables to its secluded fishing camp. It was also the location for the movie *PT 109* about John F. Kennedy's celebrated World War II heroism. Today it still offers respite to the upper class in the form of an exclusive getaway resort accessible only by boat or seaplane.

ORIENTATION AND PLANNING

GETTING ORIENTED

In truth, the Lower Keys include Key West, but since it's *covered in its own section and is* as different from the rest of the Lower Keys as peanut butter is from jelly, this section covers just the keys between MM 38.5 and MM 9. The Seven Mile Bridge drops you into the lap of this homey, quiet part of the Keys.

TOP REASONS TO GO

- **Wildlife viewing.** The Lower Keys are populated with all kinds of animals. Watch especially for the Key deer but also other wildlife at the Blue Hole in National Key Deer Refuge.

- **Bahia Honda Key State Park.** Explore the beach and trails, and then camp for the night at this gorgeous state park.

- **Kayaking.** Get out in a kayak to spot birds in the Keys' backcountry wildlife refuges.

- **Snorkeling.** Grab a mask and fins and head to Looe Key Reef to see amazing coral formations and fish so bright and animated they look like cartoons.

- **Fishing.** All kinds of fishing are great in the Lower Keys. Cast from a bridge, boat, or shoreline flats for bonefish, tarpon, and other feisty catches.

4

Heed speed limits in these parts. They may seem incredibly strict, given that the traffic is lightest of anywhere in the Keys, but the purpose is to protect the resident Key deer population, and officers of the law pay strict attention.

PLANNING

To get to the Lower Keys, fly into either Miami International Airport or Key West International Airport. Key West is considerably closer, but there are far fewer flights coming in and going out. Rental cars are available at both airports. In addition, there is bus service from the Key West airport; $4 one-way with Key West Transit. *For detailed information on these services, see Air Travel in Travel Smart.*

Fishing lodges, dive resorts, and campgrounds are the most prevalent type of lodging in this part of the Keys. Rates are generally much lower than on other Keys, especially Key West, which makes this a good place to stay if you're on a budget.

Restaurants are fewer and farther between in the Lower Keys, and you won't find the variety of offerings in eateries closer to Miami and in Key West. Mostly you'll find seafood joints where dinner is fresh off the hook and license plates or dollar bills stuck to the wall count for decor. For a special occasion, hop aboard the ferry at Little Torch Key to experience the globe-trotting cuisine of private Little Palm Island Resort & Spa once it reopens in the fall of 2019. Restau-

The Lower
Keys

Gulf of Mexico

National Key
Deer Refuge

Boca Chica Key
Saddlebunch Keys
Sugarloaf Key
Cudjoe Key
Summerland Key
Ramrod Key
Little Torch Key
Big Pine Key
No Name Key

Key West

Key West
International
Airport

Stock Island
Big Coppitt Key

Looe Key
Reef Resort
& Dive Center

Parmer's
Resort

Little Palm
Island Resort
& Spa

Big Pine Key
Fishing Lodge

Deer Run
Bed &
Breakfast

Bahia Honda
State Park

Bahia Honda Key

*Seven Mile
Bridge*

ATLANTIC
OCEAN

0 ——— 20 miles

0 ——— 30 km

rants may close for a two- to four-week vacation during the
slow season, between mid-September and mid-November.

*Restaurant and hotel reviews have been shortened. For full
information, visit Fodors.com.*

WHAT IT COSTS				
	$	**$$**	**$$$**	**$$$$**
Restaurants	under $15	$15–$20	$21–$30	over $30
Hotels	under $200	$200–$300	$301–$400	Over $400

Prices in the restaurant reviews are the average cost of a main course at dinner or,
if dinner isn't served, at lunch. Prices in the hotel reviews are the lowest cost of a
standard double room in high season.

BAHIA HONDA KEY

MM 38.5–36.

All of Bahia Honda Key is devoted to its eponymous state park, which keeps it in a pristine state. Besides the park's outdoor activities, it offers an up-close view of the original railroad bridge.

GETTING HERE AND AROUND

Bahia Honda Key lies a short distance from the southern terminus of the Seven Mile Bridge. A two-lane road travels its 2-mile length. It is 32 miles north of Key West and served by Key West Transit. *See Bus Travel in Travel Smart.*

4

EXPLORING

TOP ATTRACTIONS

★ FodorsChoice **Bahia Honda State Park.** Most first-time visitors
FAMILY to the region are dismayed by the lack of beaches—but then they discover Bahia Honda Key. The 524-acre park sprawls across both sides of the highway, giving it 2½ miles of fabulous sandy coastline. The snorkeling isn't bad, either; there's underwater life (soft coral, queen conchs, random little fish) just a few hundred feet offshore. Seasonal ranger-led nature programs take place at or depart from the Sand and Sea Nature Center. There are rental cabins, a campground, snack bar, gift shop, 19-slip marina, nature center, and facilities for renting kayaks and arranging snorkeling tours. Get a panoramic view of the island from what's left of the railroad—the Bahia Honda Bridge. ⊠ *MM 37 OS, 36850 Overseas Hwy., Bahia Honda Key* ☎ *305/872-2353* ⊕ *www.floridastateparks.org/park/Bahia-Honda* ☜ *$4.50 for single-occupant vehicle, $8 for vehicle with 2–8 people, plus $0.50 per person up to 8.*

BEACHES

Sandspur Beach. Bahia Honda Key State Beach contains three beaches in all—on both the Atlantic Ocean and the Gulf of Mexico. Schedule to reopen in June 2019 after being devastated by Hurricane Irma, Sandspur Beach, the largest, is regularly declared the best beach in the Florida Keys, and you'll be hard-pressed to argue. The sand is baby-powder soft, and the aqua water is warm, clear, and shallow. With their mild currents, the beaches are great for swimming, even with small fry. **Amenities:** food and drink; showers; toilets; water sports. **Best for:** snorkeling;

swimming. ✉ *MM 37 OS, 36850 Overseas Hwy., Bahia Honda Key* ☎ *305/872–2353* 🌐 *www.floridastateparks.org/park/Bahia-Honda* 🎟 *$4.50 for single-occupant vehicle, $9 for vehicle with 2–8 people.*

WHERE TO STAY

$ 🏨 **Bahia Honda State Park Cabins.** *Rental.* Elsewhere you'd pay big bucks for the wonderful water views available at these cabins on Florida Bay. Each of three cabins has two, two-bedroom units with a full kitchen and bath and air-conditioning (but no television, radio, or phone). **Pros:** great bay-front views; beachfront camping; affordable rates. **Cons:** books up fast; area can be buggy. [$] *Rooms from: $163* ✉ *MM 37 OS, 36850 Overseas Hwy., Bahia Honda Key* ☎ *305/872–2353, 800/326–3521* 🌐 *www.reserveamerica.com* 🛏 *6 cabins* 🍴 *No meals.*

SPORTS AND THE OUTDOORS

SCUBA DIVING AND SNORKELING

Bahia Honda Dive Shop. The concessionaire at Bahia Honda State Park manages a 19-slip marina; rents wet suits, snorkel equipment, and corrective masks; and operates twice-daily offshore-reef snorkel trips. Park visitors looking for other fun can rent kayaks and beach chairs. ✉ *MM 37 OS, 36850 Overseas Hwy., Bahia Honda Key* ☎ *305/872–3210* 🌐 *www.bahiahondapark.com* ☞ *Kayak rentals from $10 per hr; snorkel tours from $30.*

BIG PINE KEY

MM 32–30.

Welcome to the Keys' most natural holdout, where wildlife refuges protect rare and endangered animals. Here you have left behind the commercialism of the Upper Keys for an authentic backcountry atmosphere. How could things get more casual than Key Largo, you might wonder? Find out by exiting U.S. 1 to explore the habitat of the charmingly diminutive Key deer or cast a line from No Name Bridge. Tours explore the expansive waters of National Key Deer Refuge and Great White Heron National Wildlife Refuge, one of the first such refuges in the country. Along with Key West National Wildlife Refuge, it encompasses more than 200,000 acres of water and more than 8,000 acres of land on 49 small islands. Besides its namesake bird, the Great

White Heron National Wildlife Refuge provides habitat for uncounted species of birds and three species of sea turtles. It is the only U.S. breeding site for the endangered hawksbill turtle.

GETTING HERE AND AROUND

Most people rent a car to get to Big Pine Key so they can also explore Key West and other parts of the chain.

VISITOR INFORMATION

Contact Big Pine and the Lower Keys Chamber of Commerce. ✉ *31020 Overseas Hwy., Big Pine Key* ☎ *305/872–2411, 800/872–3722* ⊕ *www.lowerkeyschamber.com.*

4

EXPLORING

TOP ATTRACTIONS

National Key Deer Refuge. This 84,824-acre refuge was established in 1957 to protect the dwindling population of the Key deer, one of more than 22 animals and plants federally classified as endangered or threatened, including five that are found nowhere else on Earth. The Key deer, which stands about 30 inches at the shoulders and is a subspecies of the Virginia white-tailed deer, once roamed throughout the Lower and Middle Keys, but hunting, destruction of their habitat, and a growing human population caused their numbers to decline to 27 by 1957. The deer have made a comeback, increasing their numbers to approximately 750. The best place to see Key deer in the refuge is at the end of Key Deer Boulevard and on No Name Key, a sparsely populated island just east of Big Pine Key. Mornings and evenings are the best time to spot them. Deer may turn up along the road at any time of day, so drive slowly. They wander into nearby yards to nibble tender grass and bougainvillea blossom, but locals do not appreciate tourists driving into their neighborhoods after them. Feeding them is against the law and puts them in danger.

A quarry left over from railroad days, the **Blue Hole** is the largest body of freshwater in the Keys. From the observation platform and nearby walking trail, you might see the resident alligator, turtles, and other wildlife. There are two well-marked trails, recently revamped: the Jack Watson Nature Trail (0.6 mile), named after an environmentalist and the refuge's first warden; and the Fred Mannillo Nature Trail (0.2 mile), one of the most wheelchair-accessible places to see an unspoiled pine-rockland forest and wetlands. The visitor center has exhibits on Keys biology and ecology. The refuge also provides information on the Key West National Wildlife Refuge and the Great White Heron National Wildlife Refuge. Accessible only by water, both are popular with kayak outfitters. ✉ *Visitor Center–Headquarters, Big Pine Shopping Center, MM 30.5 BS, 28950 Watson Blvd., Big Pine Key* ☎ *305/872–2239* 🌐 *www.fws.gov/nationalkeydeer* 🎟 *Free* 🕒 *Visitor center closed Sun. and Mon.*

WHERE TO EAT

$ 🍴 Good Food Conspiracy. *Vegetarian.* Like good wine, this small natural-foods eatery and market surrenders its pleasures a little at a time. Step inside to the aroma of brewing coffee, and then pick up the scent of fresh strawberries or carrots blending into a smoothie, the green aroma of wheatgrass juice, followed by the earthy odor of hummus. **Known for:** vegetarian and vegan dishes; sandwiches and smoothies; organic items. [$] *Average main: $10* ✉ *MM 30.2 OS, 30150 Overseas Hwy., Big Pine Key* ☎ *305/872–3945* 🌐 *www.goodfoodconspiracy.com* 🕒 *No dinner Sun.*

$$ 🍴 No Name Pub. *American.* This no-frills honky-tonk has been around since 1936, delighting inveterate locals and intrepid vacationers who come for the excellent pizza, cold beer, and *interesting* companionship. The decor, such as it is, amounts to the autographed dollar bills that cover every inch of the place. **Known for:** shrimp pizza and fish sandwich; local and tourist favorite; decor of dollar bills. [$] *Average main: $15* ✉ *MM 30 BS, 30813 Watson Blvd., Big Pine Key* ✣ *From U.S. 1, turn west on Wilder Rd., left on South St., right on Ave. B, right on Watson Blvd.* ☎ *305/872–9115* 🌐 *www.nonamepub.com.*

WHERE TO STAY

$ 🏨 Big Pine Key Fishing Lodge. *Hotel.* There's a congenial atmosphere at this lively, family-owned lodge-campground-marina—a happy mix of tent campers (who have the fabulous waterfront real estate), RVers (who look pretty permanent), and motel dwellers who like to mingle at the rooftop pool and challenge each other to a game of poker. **Pros:** local fishing crowd; nice pool; great price. **Cons:** RV park is too close to motel; deer will eat your food if you're camping; trees and trails recovering from Hurricane Irma. [$] *Rooms from: $134* ✉ *MM 33 OS, 33000 Overseas Hwy., Big Pine Key* ☎ *305/872–2351* 🌐 *www.bpkfl.com* 🛏 *16 rooms* 🍽 *No meals* ☞ *To protect Key deer, no dogs allowed.*

$$$ 🏨 **Deer Run Bed & Breakfast.** *B&B/Inn.* Although Hurricane Irma came ashore here in 2017, the owners of Deer Run have made lemonade from Irma's lemons with a new raised addition that sits adjacent to the main building and houses three guest rooms, all with ocean views, cathedral ceilings, king beds, private baths, small porches, and calming decor. **Pros:** quiet neighborhood; vegan, organic breakfasts; complimentary use of bikes, kayaks, beach towels, and state park passes. **Cons:** major deforestation and loss of mangroves from hurricane; a little hard to find; may be too secluded for some. [$] *Rooms from: $375* ✉ *MM 33 OS, 1997 Long Beach Dr., Big Pine Key* ☎ *305/872–2015* 🌐 *www.deerrunfloridabb.com* 🛏 *4 rooms* 🍴 *Free Breakfast.*

SPORTS AND THE OUTDOORS

BIKING

A good 10 miles of paved roads run from MM 30.3 BS, along Wilder Road, across the bridge to No Name Key, and along Key Deer Boulevard into the National Key Deer Refuge. Along the way you might see some Key deer. Stay off the trails that lead into wetlands, where fat tires can damage the environment.

Big Pine Bicycle Center. Owner Marty Baird is an avid cyclist and enjoys sharing his knowledge of great places to ride. He's also skilled at selecting the right bike for the journey, and he knows his repairs, too. His old-fashioned single-speed, fat-tire cruisers rent by the half or full day. Helmets, baskets, and locks are included. ✉ *MM 30.9 BS, 31 County Rd., Big Pine Key* ☎ *305/872–0130* 🌐 *www.bigpinebikes.com* 🎟 *From $10.*

FISHING

Cast from No Name Key Bridge or hire a charter to take you into backcountry or deep waters for fishing year-round.

Captain Hook's Looe Key Reef Adventures and Strike Zone Charters. Glass-bottom-boat excursions venture into the backcountry and Atlantic Ocean. The five-hour Out Island Excursion and Picnic emphasizes nature and Keys history; besides close encounters with birds, sea life, and vegetation, there's a fish cookout on an island. Snorkel and fishing equipment, food, and drinks are included. This is one of the few nature outings in the Keys with wheelchair access. Deep-sea charter rates for up to six people can be arranged for a half or full day. It also offers flats fishing in the Gulf of Mexico. Dive excursions head to the wreck of the 110-foot *Adolphus Busch,* and scuba and snorkel trips to Looe Key Reef, prime scuba and snorkeling territory, aboard glass-bottom boats. ⊠ *MM 29.6 BS, 29675 Overseas Hwy., Big Pine Key* ☎ *305/872–9863, 800/654–9560* ⊕ *www.captainhooks.com* ⊠ *From $38.*

KAYAKING

There's nothing like the vast expanse of pristine waters and mangrove islands preserved by national refuges from here to Key West. The mazelike terrain can be confusing, so it's wise to hire a guide at least the first time out.

Big Pine Kayak Adventures. There's no excuse to skip a water adventure with this convenient kayak rental service, which delivers them to your lodging or anywhere between Seven Mile Bridge and Stock Island. The company, headed by *The Florida Keys Paddling Guide* author Bill Keogh, will rent you a kayak and then ferry you—called taxi-yakking—to remote islands with clear instructions on how to paddle back on your own. Rentals are by the half day or full day. Three-hour group kayak tours are the cheapest option and explore the mangrove forests of Great White Heron and Key Deer National Wildlife Refuges. More expensive four-hour custom tours transport you to exquisite backcountry areas teeming with wildlife. Kayak fishing charters are also popular. Paddleboard ecotours, rentals, and yoga are available. ⊠ *Old Wooden Bridge Fishing Camp, 1791 Bogie Dr., Big Pine Key* ✦ *From MM 30, turn right at traffic light, continue on Wilder Rd. toward No Name Key; the fishing camp is just before the bridge with a big yellow kayak on the sign out front* ☎ *305/872–7474* ⊕ *www.keyskayaktours. com* ⊠ *From $50.*

SCUBA DIVING AND SNORKELING

Close to Looe Key Reef, this is prime scuba diving and snorkeling territory. Some resorts cater to divers with dive boats that depart from their own dock. Others can make arrangements for you.

LITTLE TORCH KEY

MM 29–10.

Little Torch Key and its neighbor islands, Ramrod Key and Summerland Key, are good jumping-off points for divers headed for Looe Key Reef. The islands also serve as a refuge for those who want to make forays into Key West but not stay in the thick of things.

The undeveloped backcountry at your door makes Little Torch Key an ideal location for fishing and kayaking. Nearby **Ramrod Key,** which also caters to divers bound for Looe Key, derives its name from a ship that wrecked on nearby reefs in the early 1800s.

WHERE TO EAT

$ 🍴 **Baby's Coffee.** *American.* The aroma of rich, roasting coffee beans arrests you at the door of "the Southernmost Coffee Roaster in America." Buy beans by the pound or coffee by the cup, along with sandwiches and sweets. **Known for:** best coffee in the Keys; gluten-free, vegan, and vegetarian specialty foods; excellent service. [$] *Average main: $8* ✉ *MM 15 OS, 3180 Overseas Hwy., Little Torch Key* ☎ *305/744–9866, 800/523–2326* 🌐 *www.babyscoffee.com.*

$$ 🍴 **Geiger Key Smokehouse Bar & Grill.** *American.* There's a strong hint of the Old Keys at this ocean-side marina restaurant, where local fisherman stop for breakfast before heading out to catch the big one, and everyone shows up on Sunday for the barbecue from 4 to 9. "On the backside of paradise," as the sign says, its tiki structures overlook quiet mangroves at an RV park marina. **Known for:** Sunday barbecue; casual atmosphere on the water; conch fritters loaded with conch. [$] *Average main: $16* ✉ *MM 10, 5 Geiger Key Rd., off Boca Chica Rd., Bay Point* ☎ *305/296–3553, 305/294–1230* 🌐 *www.geigerkeymarina.com.*

$$ 🍴 **Mangrove Mama's Restaurant.** *Seafood.* This could be the prototype for a Keys restaurant, given its shanty appearance, lattice trim, and roving sort of indoor-outdoor floor plan. Then there's the seafood, from the ubiquitous fish sandwich (fried, grilled, broiled, or blackened) to lobster Reubens, crab cakes, and coconut shrimp. **Known for:** pizza; award-winning conch chowder; slow service. [$] *Average main: $20* ✉ *MM 20 BS, Sugarloaf Key* ☎ *305/745–3030* 🌐 *www.mangrovemamasrestaurant.com.*

★ Fodor's Choice 🍴 **My New Joint.** *American.* Atop the famed

$ Square Grouper restaurant is a secret spot that locals love and smart travelers seek out for its tapas and well-stocked bar. Sit at a high-top table or on a sofa, and savor made-from-scratch small plates you won't soon forget, like salted carmel puffs or chicken lollipops. **Known for:** craft cocktails and 170 types of beer; cheese or chocolate fondue; raw bar. [$] *Average main: $13* ✉ *22658 Overseas Hwy., 2nd fl. of Square Grouper restaurant, Sugarloaf Key* ☎ *305/745–8880* 🌐 *www.mynewjoint420lounge.com* 🕒 *Closed Sun. and Mon.*

★ **Fodor's Choice** 🍴 **Square Grouper.** *Seafood.* In an unassuming warehouse-looking building on U.S. 1, chef-owner Lynn Bell is creating seafood magic. For starters, try the flash-fried conch with wasabi drizzle or homemade smoked-fish dip. **Known for:** everything made fresh, in-house; long lines in season; outstanding seafood. [$] *Average main: $25* ✉ *MM 22.5 OS, Little Torch Key* ☎ *305/745–8880* 🌐 *www.squaregrouperbarandgrill.com* ⏲ *Closed Sun.; Mon. May–Dec.; and Sept.*

$$$

WHERE TO STAY

★ **Fodor's Choice** 🏨 **Little Palm Island Resort & Spa.** *Resort.* This ultra-luxurious tropical retreat set on a private island was devastated by Hurricane Irma but is scheduled to reopen in late 2019—check the website for updates. **Pros:** secluded setting; heavenly spa; easy wildlife viewing. **Cons:** expensive; might be too quiet for some; only accessible by boat or seaplane. [$] *Rooms from: $1,590* ✉ *MM 28.5 OS, 28500 Overseas Hwy., Little Torch Key* ☎ *305/872–2524, 800/343–8567* 🌐 *www.littlepalmisland.com* ➪ *30 suites* 🍽 *Some meals* ☞ *No one under age 16 allowed on island.*

$$$$

$ 🏨 **Looe Key Reef Resort & Center.** *Hotel.* If your Keys vacation is all about diving, you won't mind the no-frills, basic motel rooms with dated furniture at this scuba-obsessed operation because it's the closest place to stay to the stellar reef. **Pros:** guests get discounts on dive and snorkel trips; inexpensive rates; casual Keys atmosphere. **Cons:** some reports of uncleanliness; unheated pool; close to the road. [$] *Rooms from: $115* ✉ *MM 27.5 OS, 27340 Overseas Hwy., Ramrod Key* ☎ *305/872–2215, 877/816–3483* 🌐 *www.diveflakeys.com* ➪ *24 rooms* 🍽 *No meals.*

$ 🏨 **Parmer's Resort.** *Hotel.* Almost every room at this budget-friendly option has a view of South Pine Channel, with the lovely curl of Big Pine Key in the foreground. **Pros:** bright rooms; pretty setting; good value. **Cons:** a bit out of the way; housekeeping costs extra; little shade around the pool. [$] *Rooms from: $159* ✉ *MM 28.7 BS, 565 Barry Ave., Little Torch Key* ☎ *305/872–2157* 🌐 *www.parmersresort.com* ➪ *47 units* 🍽 *Free Breakfast.*

SPORTS AND THE OUTDOORS

AIR TOURS

Conch Republic BiPlanes. Since 1987, passengers have gotten a bird's-eye view of the waters around Key West to spot sharks, stingrays, and other reef life, not to mention spectacular sunsets. ✉ *3491 S. Roosevelt Blvd., Key West* ☎ *305/851–8359* ⊕ *www.keywestbiplanes.com* 🖃 *From $199.*

SCUBA DIVING AND SNORKELING

This is the closest you can get on land to Looe Key Reef, and that's where local dive operators love to head.

In 1744 the HMS *Looe,* a British warship, ran aground and sank on one of the most beautiful coral reefs in the Keys. Today the key owes its name to the ill-fated ship. The 5.3-square-nautical-mile reef, part of the **Florida Keys National Marine Sanctuary,** has strands of elkhorn coral on its eastern margin, purple sea fans, and abundant sponges and sea urchins. On its seaward side, it drops almost vertically 50 to 90 feet. In its midst, **Shipwreck Trail** plots the location of nine historic wreck sites in 14 to 120 feet of water. Buoys mark the sites, and underwater signs tell the history of each site and what marine life to expect. Snorkelers and divers will find the sanctuary a quiet place to observe reef life—except in July, when the annual Underwater Music Festival pays homage to Looe Key's beauty and promotes reef awareness with six hours of music broadcast via underwater speakers. Dive shops, charters, and private boats transport about 500 divers and snorkelers to hear the spectacle, which includes classical, jazz, New Age, and Caribbean music, as well as a little Jimmy Buffett. There are even underwater Elvis impersonators.

Looe Key Reef Resort & Dive Center. This center, the closest dive shop to Looe Key Reef, offers two affordable trips daily, at 8 am and 12:45 pm (for divers, snorkelers, or bubble watchers). The maximum depth is 30 feet, so snorkelers and divers go on the same boat. Call to check for availability for wreck and night dives. The dive boat, a 45-foot catamaran, is docked at the full-service Looe Key Reef Resort. ✉ *Looe Key Reef Resort, MM 27.5 OS, 27340 Overseas Hwy., Ramrod Key* ☎ *305/872–2215, 877/816–3483* ⊕ *www.diveflakeys.com* 🖃 *From $40.*

WATER SPORTS

★ Fodor'sChoice **Reelax Charters.** For a guided tour, join Captain Andrea Paulson of Reelax Charters, who takes you to remote locations by boat, then hops in a kayak for a tour like no other. Charters carry up to six people at $85 per person and can include snorkeling and beaching on a secluded island in the Keys backcountry. ✉ *Sugarloaf Marina, MM 17 BS, 17015 Overseas Hwy., Sugarloaf Key* ☎ *305/304–1392* ⊕ *www.keyskayaking.com* ✉ *From $255 per boat.*

Sugarloaf Marina. Rates for one-person kayaks are based on an hourly or daily rental. Two-person kayaks are also available. Delivery is free for rentals of three days or more. The folks at the marina can also hook you up with an outfitter for a day of offshore or backcountry fishing. There's also a well-stocked ship store. ✉ *MM 17 BS, 17015 Overseas Hwy., Sugarloaf Key* ☎ *305/745–3135* ⊕ *www.sugarloafkey-marina.com* ✉ *From $15 per hr.*

KEY WEST

Updated
by Jill
Martin

SITUATED 150 MILES FROM MIAMI, 90 miles from Havana, and an immeasurable distance from sanity, this end-of-the-line community has never been like anywhere else. Even after it was connected to the rest of the country—by the railroad in 1912 and by the highway in 1938—it maintained a strong sense of detachment. The United States acquired Key West from Spain in 1821, along with the rest of Florida. The Spanish had named the island Cayo Hueso, or Bone Key, after the Native American skeletons they found on its shores. In 1823, President James Monroe sent Commodore David S. Porter to chase pirates away. For three decades, the primary industry in Key West was wrecking—rescuing people and salvaging cargo from ships that foundered on the nearby reefs. According to some reports, when pickings were lean the wreckers hung out lights to lure ships aground. Their business declined after 1849, when the federal government began building lighthouses.

In 1845, the army began construction on Fort Taylor, which kept Key West on the Union side during the Civil War. After the fighting ended, an influx of Cubans unhappy with Spain's rule brought the cigar industry here. Fishing, shrimping, and sponge gathering became important industries, as did pineapple canning. Throughout much of the 19th century and into the 20th, Key West was Florida's wealthiest city per capita. But in 1929, the local economy began to unravel. Cigar making moved to Tampa, Hawaii dominated the pineapple industry, and the sponges succumbed to blight. Then the Depression hit, and within a few years half the population was on relief.

Tourism began to revive Key West, but that came to a halt when a hurricane knocked out the railroad bridge in 1935. To help the tourism industry recover from that crushing blow, the government offered incentives for islanders to turn their charming homes—many of them built by shipwrights—into guesthouses and inns. That wise foresight has left the town with more than 100 such lodgings, a hallmark of Key West vacationing today. In the 1950s, the discovery of "pink gold" in the Dry Tortugas boosted the economy of the entire region. Catching Key West shrimp required a fleet of up to 500 boats and flooded local restaurants with some of the sweetest shrimp alive. The town's artistic community found inspiration in the colorful fishing boats.

Key West reflects a diverse population: Conchs (natives, many of whom trace their ancestry to the Bahamas), freshwater Conchs (longtime residents who migrated from somewhere else years ago), Hispanics (primarily Cuban immigrants), recent refugees from the urban sprawl of mainland Florida, military personnel, and an assortment of vagabonds, drifters, and dropouts in search of refuge. The island was once a gay vacation hot spot, and it remains a decidedly gay-friendly destination. Some of the once-renowned gay guesthouses, however, no longer cater to an exclusively gay clientele. Key Westers pride themselves on their tolerance of all peoples, all sexual orientations, and even all animals. Most restaurants allow pets, and it's not surprising to see stray cats, dogs, and even chickens roaming freely through the dining rooms. The chicken issue is one that government officials periodically try to bring to an end, but the colorful fowl continue to strut and crow, particularly in the vicinity of Old Town's Bahamian Village.

As a tourist destination, Key West has a lot to sell—an average temperature of 79°F, 19th-century architecture, and a laid-back lifestyle. Yet much has been lost to those eager for a buck. Duval Street is starting to resemble a shopping mall with name-brand storefronts, garish T-shirt shops, and tattoo shops with sidewalk views of the inked action. Cruise ships dwarf the town's skyline and fill the streets with day-trippers gawking at the hippies with dogs in their bike baskets, gay couples walking down the street holding hands, and the oddball lot of locals, some of whom bark louder than the dogs.

PLANNING

WHEN TO GO

Key West has a growing calendar of festivals and artistic and cultural events—including the Conch Republic Celebration in April and the Halloween Fantasy Fest in October. December brings festivity in the form of a lighted boat parade at the Historic Seaport and New Year's Eve revelry that rivals any in the nation. Few cities of its size—a mere 2 miles by 4 miles—celebrate with the joie de vivre of this one.

GETTING HERE AND AROUND

AIR TRAVEL

You can fly directly to Key West on a limited number of flights, most of which connect at other Florida airports. But a lot of folks fly into Miami or Fort Lauderdale and drive down or take the bus.

BOAT TRAVEL

Key West Express operates air-conditioned ferries between the Key West Terminal (Caroline and Grinnell Streets) and Marco Island, and Fort Myers Beach. The trip from Fort Myers Beach takes at least four hours each way and costs $95 one-way, $155 round-trip. Ferries depart from Fort Myers Beach at 8:30 am and from Key West at 6 pm. The Miami and Marco Island ferry costs $95 one-way and $155 round-trip, and departs at 8:30 am. A photo ID is required for each passenger. Advance reservations are recommended and can save money.

BUS AND SHUTTLE TRAVEL TO KEY WEST

Greyhound Lines runs a special Keys Shuttle up to twice a day (depending on the day of the week) from Miami International Airport (departing from Concourse E, lower level) that stops throughout the Keys. Fares run about $45 (web fare) to $57 for Key West. Keys Shuttle runs scheduled service three times a day in 15-passenger vans between Miami Airport and Key West with stops throughout the Keys for $70 to $90 per person. SuperShuttle charges $102 per passenger for trips from Miami International Airport to the Upper Keys. To go farther into the Keys, you must book an entire 11-person van, which costs about $350 to Key West. You need to place your request for transportation back to the airport 24 hours in advance. Uber is also available throughout the Keys and from the airport. *For detailed information on these services, see Air Travel in Travel Smart.*

BUS TRAVEL AROUND KEY WEST

Between mile markers 4 and 0, Key West is the one place in the Keys where you could conceivably do without a car, especially if you plan on staying around Old Town. If you've driven the 106 miles down the chain, you're probably ready to abandon your car in the hotel parking lot anyway. Trolleys, buses, bikes, scooters, and feet are more suitable alternatives. When your feet tire, catch a rickshaw-style pedicab ride, which will run you about $1.50 a minute. But to explore the beaches, New Town, and Stock Island, you'll need a car or taxi.

The City of Key West Department of Transportation has six color-coded bus routes traversing the island from 5:30 am to 11:30 pm. Stops have signs with the international bus symbol. Schedules are available on buses and at hotels, visitor centers, shops, and online. The fare is $2 one-way.

TOP REASONS TO GO

- **Watching the sunset.** Revel in both the beautiful sunset and the gutsy performers at Mallory Square's nightly celebration.

- **The Conch Tour Train.** Hop aboard for a narrated tour of the town's tawdry past and rare architectural treasures.

- **Barhopping.** Nightlife rules in Key West. Do the "Duval Crawl," the local version of club hopping. But first fortify yourself at one of the town's exceptional restaurants.

- **The Hemingway connection.** Visit Ernest Hemingway's historic home for a page out of Key West's literary past.

- **The Dry Tortugas.** Do a day trip to Dry Tortugas National Park for snorkeling and hiking away from the crowds.

5

Its Lower Keys Shuttle bus runs between Marathon to Key West ($4 one-way), with scheduled stops along the way.

VISITOR INFORMATION

Contacts Greater Key West Chamber of Commerce. ✉ 510 Greene St., 1st fl., Key West ☎ 305/294–2587, 800/527–8539 ⊕ www. keywestchamber.org.

HOTELS

Key West's lodgings include historic cottages, restored Conch houses, and large resorts. Quaint guesthouses, the town's trademark, offer a true island experience in residential neighborhoods near Old Town's restaurants, shops, and clubs. A few rooms cost as little as $65 a night in the off-season, but most range from $100 to $300. Please note that certain guesthouses and inns do not welcome children under 16, and most do not permit smoking.

RESTAURANTS

Keys restaurants get most exotic once you reach Key West, and you can pretty much find anything you want, though bargains are hard to come by. Pricier restaurants serve tantalizing fusion cuisine that reflects the influence of Cuba and other Caribbean islands. Tropical fruits and citrus figure prominently on the menus, and mango, papaya, and passion fruit are often featured in beverages. Of course, there are plenty of places that serve local seafood. Key West stays true to island character with a selection of hole-in-the-wall places that couldn't be any more colorful.

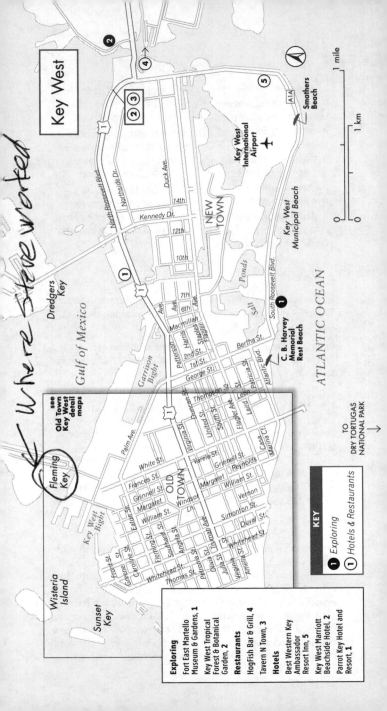

Where Steve worked

Key West

Gulf of Mexico

ATLANTIC OCEAN

Wisteria Island

Sunset Key

Fleming Key

Dredgers Key

Garrison Bight

Key West Bight

see Old Town Key West detail maps

OLD TOWN

NEW TOWN

Key West International Airport

Key West Municipal Beach

Smothers Beach

C. B. Harvey Memorial Rest Beach

Salt Ponds

TO DRY TORTUGAS NATIONAL PARK →

North Roosevelt Blvd.
Northside Dr.
Duck Ave.
South Roosevelt Blvd.
A1A

Kennedy Dr.
14th
12th
10th
7th
6th
Ave.

Palm Ave.
White St.
Frances St.
Grinnell St.
Margaret
William St.
Eaton St.
Southard St.
Angela St.
Fleming St.
Caroline St.
Greene St.
Front St.
Petronia St.
Olivia St.
Truman Ave.
Julia St.
Virginia St.
Amelia St.
Whitehead St.
Thomas St.
Windsor Ln.
Simonton St.
Duval St.
Whitehead St.
Virginia
Macmillan
Patterson
Harris
2nd St.
1st St.
George St.
Bertha St.
Atlantic Blvd.
Patricia St.
Leon
Laird
Flagler Ave.
Flagler
Reynolds
William St.
Vernon
Casa St.
Marina Ct.
Grinnell St.
Varela St.
United St.
South St.
Thompson St.
Duncan St.
Staples
Flagler
Ave.

KEY

- Exploring
- Hotels & Restaurants

Exploring
Fort East Martello Museum & Gardens, **1**
Key West Tropical Forest & Botanical Garden, **2**

Restaurants
HogFish Bar & Grill, **4**
Tavern N Town, **3**

Hotels
Best Western Key Ambassador Resort Inn, **5**
Key West Marriott Beachside Hotel, **2**
Parrot Key Hotel and Resort, **1**

0   1 km
0   1 mile

Restaurant and hotel reviews have been shortened. For full information, visit Fodors.com.

WHAT IT COSTS				
	$	$$	$$$	$$$$
Restaurants	under $15	$15–$20	$21–$30	over $30
Hotels	under $200	$200–$300	$301–$400	over $400

Prices in the restaurant reviews are the average cost of a main course at dinner or, if dinner isn't served, at lunch. Prices in the hotel reviews are the lowest cost of a standard double room in high season.

TOURS

BIKE TOURS

Lloyd's Original Tropical Bike Tour. Explore the natural, non-commercial side of Key West at a leisurely pace, stopping on backstreets and in backyards of private homes to sample native fruits and view indigenous plants and trees with a 45-year Key West veteran. The behind-the-scenes tours run two hours and include a bike rental. ⊠ *Moped Hospital, Truman Ave. and Simonton St., Key West* ☎ *305/304–4700* ⊕ *www.lloydstropicalbiketour.com* ☞ *$49.*

BUS TOURS

Conch Tour Train. The Conch Tour Train is a 90-minute narrated tour of Key West, traveling 14 miles through Old Town and around the island. Board at Mallory Square or Angela Street and Duval Street depot every half hour from 9 to 4:30. Discount tickets are available online. ⊠ *Key West* ☎ *305/294–5161, 888/916–8687* ⊕ *www.conchtourtrain. com* ☞ *$31.45.*

FAMILY **Old Town Trolley.** Old Town Trolley operates trolley-style buses, departing from Mallory Square every 30 minutes from 9 to 4:30, for 90-minute narrated tours of Key West. The smaller trolleys go places the larger Conch Tour Train won't fit and you can ride a second consecutive day for only $15. You may disembark at any of 13 stops and reboard a later trolley. You can save nearly $4 by booking online. It also offers package deals with Old Town attractions. ⊠ *1 Whitehead St., Key West* ☎ *305/296–6688, 855/623–8289* ⊕ *www.trolleytours.com* ☞ *$38.80.*

WALKING TOURS

Historic Florida Keys Foundation. In addition to publishing several good guides on Key West, the foundation conducts tours of the City Cemetery on Tuesday and Thursday at 9:30 am. ✉ *Old City Hall, 510 Greene St., Key West* ☎ *305/292–6718* ⊕ *www.historicfloridakeys.org* ✍ *$15.*

Key West Promotions. If you're not entirely a do-it-yourselfer, Key West Promotions offers a variety of pub tours, from the famous Duval Crawl to a chilling, haunted, and "spirited" adventure. ✉ *424 Greene St., Key West* ☎ *305/294–7170* ⊕ *www.keywestwalkingtours.com.*

EXPLORING

Although the rest of the Keys are known for outdoor activities, Key West has something of a city feel and has a fair number of historic sights. Few open spaces remain, as promoters continue to churn out restaurants, galleries, shops, and museums to interpret the city's intriguing past.

OLD TOWN

The heart of Key West, the historic Old Town area runs from White Street to the waterfront. Beginning in 1822, wharves, warehouses, chandleries, ship-repair facilities, and eventually, in 1891, the U.S. Custom House, sprang up around the deep harbor to accommodate the navy's large ships and other sailing vessels. Wreckers, merchants, and sea captains built lavish houses near the bustling waterfront. A remarkable number of these fine Victorian and pre-Victorian structures have been restored to their original grandeur and now serve as homes, guesthouses, shops, restaurants, and museums. These, along with the dwellings of famous writers, artists, and politicians who've come to Key West over the past 175 years, are among the area's approximately 3,000 historic structures. Old Town also has the city's finest restaurants and hotels, lively street life, and popular nightspots.

TIMING

Allow two full days to see all the Old Town museums and homes, especially if you plan to peruse the shops. For a narrated trip on the tour train or trolley, budget an hour to ride the loop without getting off and an entire day if you plan to get off and on at some of the sights and restaurants.

A GOOD TOUR

You can do this tour via the Old Town Trolley or the Conch Tour Train, but Old Town is also manageable on foot, bicycle, moped, or electric car. However, the area is expansive, so pick and choose from the stops on this tour, or break it into two or more days. Start on Whitehead Street at the **Ernest Hemingway Home and Museum,** then cross the street and climb to the top of the **Key West Lighthouse Museum and Keeper's Quarters** for a spectacular view. Return to Whitehead Street and follow it north to Angela Street, where you'll turn right. At Margaret Street, the **City Cemetery** is worth a look for its aboveground vaults and unusual headstone inscriptions. Head north on Margaret Street, turn left onto Southard Street and follow it through Truman Annex to **Fort Zachary Taylor Historic State Park.** Right before you get to Truman Annex, stop in for a drink at the **Green Parrot Bar,** where they've been serving locals since 1890, at the corner of Southard Street and Whitehead.

Walk west into Truman Annex to see the **Harry S Truman Little White House Museum,** President Truman's vacation residence. Return east on Caroline and turn left on Whitehead to visit the **Audu-bon House and Tropical Gardens,** honoring the famed artist and naturalist. Follow Whitehead north to Greene Street and turn left to see the salvaged sea treasures of the **Mel Fisher Maritime Museum.** At Whitehead's northern end are the **Key West Aquarium** and the **Key West Museum of Art and History,** the former historic U.S. Custom House. By late afternoon you should be ready to cool off with a dip or catch a few rays at the beach. From the aquarium, head east on Whitehead Street about 1½ miles to the Southernmost Point for a famed photo op before continuing on South Street. Turn right on Duval and you'll run into **South Beach.** Like all Key West beaches, it is man-made, with white sand imported from the Bahamas and north Florida. If you've brought your pet, stroll a few blocks east to **Dog Beach,** at the corner of Vernon and Waddell Streets. A little farther east is **Higgs Beach–Astro City,** on Atlantic Boulevard between White and Reynolds Streets. As the sun starts to sink, return to the north end of Old Town and follow the crowds to Mallory Square to watch Key West's nightly sunset spectacle. For dinner, head east on Caroline Street to the **Historic Seaport at Key West Bight.**

5

TOP ATTRACTIONS

Audubon House and Tropical Gardens. If you've ever seen an engraving by ornithologist John James Audubon, you'll understand why his name is synonymous with birds. See his works in this three-story house, which was built in the 1840s for Captain John Geiger and filled with period furniture. It now commemorates Audubon's 1832 stop in Key West while he was traveling through Florida to study birds. After an introduction by a docent, you can do a self-guided tour of the house and gardens. An art gallery sells lithographs of the artist's famed portraits. ⊠ *205 Whitehead St., Key West* ☎ *305/294–2116, 877/294–2470* ⊕ *www. audubonhouse.com* ⊠ *$14.*

★ **Fodor's**Choice **Custom House.** When Key West was designated a U.S. port of entry in the early 1820s, a customhouse was established. Salvaged cargoes from ships wrecked on the reefs were brought here, setting the stage for Key West to become—for a time—the richest city in Florida. The imposing redbrick-and-terra-cotta Richardsonian Romanesque–style building reopened as a museum and art gallery in 1999. Smaller galleries have long-term and changing exhibits about the history of Key West, including a Hemingway room and a permanent Henry Flagler exhibit that commemorates the arrival of Flagler's railroad to Key West in 1912. ⊠ *281 Front St., Key West* ☎ *305/295–6616* ⊕ *www.kwahs.com* ⊠ *$10.*

FAMILY **Dry Tortugas National Park and Historic Key West Bight Museum.** If you can't see Ft. Jefferson in the Dry Tortugas in person, this is the next best thing. Opened in 2013 by the national park's official ferry commissioner, this free attraction located in Key West's historic seaport has an impressive (1:87) scale model of the fort; life-size figures including the fort's most famous prisoner, Dr. Samuel Mudd; and even a junior ranger station for the little ones with hands-on educational fun. The exhibits are housed in a historic site as well, the old Thompson Fish House, where local fisherman would bring their daily catch for processing. History lingers on within these walls, but to get a whiff of the sea and days gone past, you'll have to walk the docks out front. ⊠ *240 Margaret St., Key West* ☎ *305/294–7009* ⊕ *www. drytortugas.com* ⊠ *Free.*

★ **Fodor's**Choice **The Ernest Hemingway Home and Museum.** Amusing anecdotes spice up the guided tours of Ernest Hemingway's home, built in 1801 by the town's most successful wrecker.

While living here between 1931 and 1942, Hemingway wrote about 70% of his life's work, including classics like *For Whom the Bell Tolls*. Few of his belongings remain aside from some books, and there's little about his actual work, but photographs help you visualize his day-to-day life. The famous six-toed descendants of Hemingway's cats—many named for actors, artists, authors, and even a hurricane—have free rein of the property. Tours begin every 10 minutes and take 30 minutes; then you're free to explore on your own. Be sure to find out why there is a urinal in the garden! ⊠ *907 Whitehead St., Key West* ☎ *305/294–1136* ⊕ *www.hemingwayhome.com* 🖾 *$14.*

Fort Zachary Taylor Historic State Park. Construction of the fort began in 1845 but was halted during the Civil War. Even though Florida seceded from the Union, Yankee forces used the fort as a base to block Confederate shipping. More than 1,500 Confederate vessels were detained in Key West's harbor. The fort, finally completed in 1866, was also used in the Spanish-American War. Take a 30-minute guided walking tour of the redbrick fort, a National Historic Landmark, at noon and 2, or self-guided tour anytime between 8 and 5. In February a celebration called Civil War Heritage Days includes costumed reenactments and demonstrations. From mid-January to mid-April the park serves as an open-air gallery for pieces created for Sculpture Key West. One of its most popular features is its man-made beach, a rest stop for migrating birds in the spring and fall; there are also picnic areas, hiking and biking trails, and a kayak launch. ⊠ *Southard St., at end of street, through Truman Annex, Key West* ☎ *305/292–6713* ⊕ *www.floridastateparks.org/park/ Fort-Taylor* 🖾 *$4 for single-occupant vehicles, $6 for 2–8 people in a vehicle, plus a 50¢ per person county surcharge.*

Harry S Truman Little White House Museum. Renovations to this circa-1890 landmark have restored the home and gardens to the Truman era, down to the wallpaper pattern. A free photographic review of visiting dignitaries and presidents—John F. Kennedy, Jimmy Carter, and Bill Clinton are among the chief executives who passed through here—is on display in the back of the gift shop. Engaging 45-minute tours begin every 20 minutes until 4:30. They start with an excellent 10-minute video on the history of the property and Truman's visits. On the grounds of **Truman Annex,** a 103-acre former military parade grounds and barracks, the home served as a "winter White House" for presidents Truman, Eisenhower, and Kennedy. Entry is cheaper when

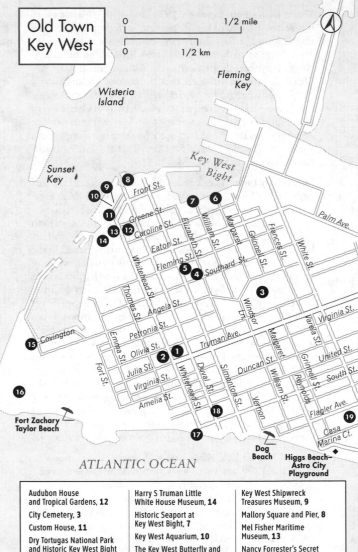

Old Town Key West

0   1/2 mile

0   1/2 km

Fleming Key

Wisteria Island

Sunset Key

Key West Bight

Front St.
Greene St.
Caroline St.
Eaton St.
Fleming St.
Southard St.
Angela St.
Petronia St.
Olivia St.
Julia St.
Virginia St.
Amelia St.

Whitehead St.
Thomas St.
Emma St.
Fort St.
William St.
Elizabeth St.
Margaret St.
Grinnell St.
Frances St.
White St.
Windsor Ln.
Truman Ave.
Duncan St.
Simonton St.
Divall St.
Vernon
Covington
Palm Ave.
Virginia St.
Varela St.
Grinnel St.
United St.
Reynolds
South St.
Flagler Ave.
Casa Marina Ct.

Fort Zachary Taylor Beach

ATLANTIC OCEAN

Dog Beach

Higgs Beach–Astro City Playground

Audubon House and Tropical Gardens, **12**	Harry S Truman Little White House Museum, **14**	Key West Shipwreck Treasures Museum, **9**
City Cemetery, **3**	Historic Seaport at Key West Bight, **7**	Mallory Square and Pier, **8**
Custom House, **11**	Key West Aquarium, **10**	Mel Fisher Maritime Museum, **13**
Dry Tortugas National Park and Historic Key West Bight Museum, **6**	The Key West Butterfly and Nature Conservatory, **18**	Nancy Forrester's Secret Garden, **4**
Eco-Discovery Center, **15**	Key West Garden Club at West Martello Tower, **19**	The Southernmost Point, **17**
The Ernest Hemingway Home and Museum, **1**	Key West Library, **5**	
Fort Zachary Taylor Historic State Park, **16**	Key West Lighthouse Museum and Keeper's Quarters, **2**	

purchased in advance online; tickets bought on-site add sales tax. ■TIP➔ **The house tour does require climbing steps. Visitors can do a free self-guided botanical tour of the grounds with a brochure from the museum store.** ✉ *111 Front St., Key West* ☎ *305/294–9911* ⊕ *www.trumanlittlewhitehouse.com* 💲 *$21.45*.

Historic Seaport at Key West Bight. What was once a funky—in some places even seedy—part of town is a 20-acre historic restoration of businesses, including waterfront restaurants, open-air bars, museums, clothing stores, and water-sports concessions. It's all linked by the 2-mile waterfront **Harborwalk,** which runs between Front and Grinnell Streets, passing big ships, schooners, sunset cruises, fishing charters, and glass-bottom boats. This is where the locals go for great music and good drinks. ✉ *100 Grinnell St., Key West* ⊕ *www.keywesthistoricseaport.com*.

5

NEED A BREAK? Coffee Plantation. Bakery. Get your morning (or afternoon) buzz, and hook up to the Internet in the comfort of a homelike setting in a circa-1890 Conch house. Sit inside or out and munch on sandwiches, wraps, and pastries, and sip a hot or cold espresso beverage. Known for: tropical macchiatos; Almond Joy lattes; homemade quiche of the day. ✉ 713 Caroline St., Key West ☎ 305/295–9808 ⊕ www.coffeeplantationkeywest. com ⊙ Closed Sun.

FAMILY **The Key West Butterfly and Nature Conservatory.** This air-conditioned refuge for butterflies, birds, and the human spirit gladdens the soul with hundreds of colorful wings—more than 45 species of butterflies alone—in a lovely glass-encased bubble. Waterfalls, artistic benches, paved pathways, birds, and lush, flowering vegetation elevate this above most butterfly attractions. The gift shop and gallery are worth a visit on their own. ✉ *1316 Duval St., Key West* ☎ *305/296–2988, 800/839–4647* ⊕ *www.keywestbutterfly. com* 💲 *$12*.

Key West Library. Check out the pretty palm garden next to the Key West Library at 700 Fleming Street, just off Duval. This leafy, outdoor reading area, with shaded benches, is the perfect place to escape the frenzy and crowds of downtown Key West. There's free Internet access in the library, too. ✉ *700 Fleming St., Key West* ☎ *305/292–3595* ⊕ *www. keyslibraries.org* ⊙ *Closed Sun*.

Key West Lighthouse Museum and Keeper's Quarters. For the best view in town, climb the 88 steps to the top of this 1847 lighthouse. The 92-foot structure has a Fresnel lens, which was installed in the 1860s at a cost of $1 million. The keeper lived in the adjacent 1887 clapboard house, which now exhibits vintage photographs, ship models, nautical charts, and artifacts from all along Key West's reefs. A kids' room is stocked with books and toys. ✉ *938 Whitehead St., Key West* ☎ *305/294–0012* ⊕ *www.kwahs.com* 🎟 *$10.*

Mallory Square and Pier. For cruise-ship passengers, this is the disembarkation point for an attack on Key West. For practically every visitor, it's the requisite venue for a nightly sunset celebration that includes street performers—human statues, sword swallowers, tightrope walkers, musicians, and more—plus craft vendors, conch-fritter fryers, and other regulars who defy classification. With all the activity, don't forget to watch the main show: a dazzling tropical sunset. ✉ *Mallory Sq., Key West.*

The Southernmost Point. Possibly the most photographed site in Key West (even though the actual geographic southern-most point in the continental United States lies across the bay on a naval base, where you see a satellite dish), this is a must-see. Have your picture taken next to the big striped buoy that's been marking the southernmost point in the continental United States since 1983. A plaque next to it honors Cubans who lost their lives trying to escape to America, and other signs tell Key West history. ✉ *Whitehead and South sts., Key West.*

WORTH NOTING

City Cemetery. You can learn almost as much about a town's history through its cemetery as through its historic houses. Key West's celebrated 20-acre burial place may leave you wanting more, with headstone epitaphs such as "I told you I was sick," and, for a wayward husband, "Now I know where he's sleeping at night." Among the interesting plots are a memorial to the sailors killed in the sinking of the battleship USS *Maine,* carved angels and lambs marking graves of children, and grand abo-veground crypts that put to shame many of the town's dwellings for the living. There are separate plots for Catholics, Jews, and refugees from Cuba. You're free to walk around the cemetery on your own, but the best way to see it is on a 90-minute tour given by the staff and volunteers of the Historic Florida Keys Foundation. Tours

Hemingway Was Here

In a town where Pulitzer Prize–winning writers are almost as common as coconuts, Ernest Hemingway stands out. Many bars and restaurants around the island claim that he ate or drank there.

Hemingway came to Key West in 1928 at the urging of writer John Dos Passos and rented a house with his second wife, Pauline Pfeiffer. They spent winters in the Keys and summers in Europe and Wyoming, occasionally taking African safaris. Along the way, they had two sons, Patrick and Gregory. In 1931, Pauline's wealthy uncle Gus gave the couple the house at 907 Whitehead Street. Now known as the Ernest Hemingway Home & Museum, it's Key West's number one tourist attraction. Renovations included the addition of a pool and a tropical garden.

In 1935, when the visitor bureau included the house in a tourist brochure, Hemingway promptly built the brick wall that surrounds it today. He wrote of the visitor bureau's offense in a 1935 essay for *Esquire*, saying, "The house at present occupied by your correspondent is listed as number eighteen in a compilation of the forty-eight things for a tourist to see in Key West. So there will be no difficulty in a tourist finding it or any other of the sights of the city, a map has been prepared by the local F.E.R.A. authorities to be presented to each arriving visitor. This is all very flattering to the easily bloated ego of your correspondent but very hard on production."

During his time in Key West, Hemingway penned some of his most important works, including *A Farewell to Arms, To Have and Have Not, Green Hills of Africa,* and *Death in the Afternoon.* His rigorous schedule consisted of writing almost every morning in his second-story studio above the pool, then promptly descending the stairs at midday. By afternoon and evening he was ready for drinking, fishing, swimming, boxing, and hanging around with the boys.

One close friend was Joe Russell, a craggy fisherman and owner of the rugged bar Sloppy Joe's, originally at 428 Greene Street but now at 201 Duval Street. Russell was the only one in town who would cash Hemingway's $1,000 royalty check. Russell and Charles Thompson introduced Hemingway to deep-sea fishing, which became fodder for his writing.

Hemingway stayed in Key West for 11 years before leaving Pauline for his third wife. Pauline and the boys stayed on in the house, which sold in 1951 for $80,000, 10 times its original cost.

5

leave from the main gate, and reservations are required. ✉ *Margaret and Angela sts., Key West* ☎ *305/292–6718* ⊕ *www.historicfloridakeys.org* 🎫 *Tours $15.*

FAMILY **Eco-Discovery Center.** While visiting Fort Zachary Taylor Historic State Park, stop in at this colorful 6,400-square-foot interactive attraction, which encourages visitors to venture through a variety of Florida Keys habitats from pinelands, beach dunes, and mangroves to the deep sea. Walk through a model of NOAA's (National Oceanic and Atmospheric Administration) Aquarius, a unique underwater ocean laboratory 9 miles off Key Largo, to virtually discover what lurks beneath the sea. Touch-screen computer displays, a dramatic movie, a 2,500-gallon aquarium, and live underwater web cameras show off North America's only contiguous barrier coral reef. You'll leave with a new understanding of the native animals and unique plants of the Florida Keys. ✉ *35 E. Quay Rd., at end of Southard St. in Truman Annex, Key West* ☎ *305/809–4750* ⊕ *eco-discovery.com* 🎫 *Free (donations accepted)* ◷ *Closed Sun. and Mon.*

FAMILY **Key West Aquarium.** Pet a nurse shark and explore the fascinating underwater realm of the Keys without getting wet at this historic aquarium. Hundreds of tropical fish and enormous sea creatures live here—all locals. A touch tank enables you to handle starfish, sea cucumbers, horseshoe and hermit crabs, even horse and queen conchs—living totems of the Conch Republic. Built in 1934 by the Works Progress Administration as the world's first open-air aquarium, most of the building has been enclosed for all-weather viewing. Guided tours, included in the admission price, feature shark feedings. Tickets are cheaper when booked online. ✉ *1 Whitehead St., Key West* ☎ *305/296–2051* ⊕ *www.keywestaquarium.com* 🎫 *$17.19.*

Key West Garden Club at West Martello Tower. For over 65 years, the Key West Garden Club has maintained lush gardens among the arches and ruins of this redbrick Civil War–era fort. In addition to the impressive collection of native and tropical plants, you can meander past fountains, sculptures, and a picture-perfect gazebo on your self-guided tour. These volunteers hold art, orchid, and flower shows February through April and lead private garden tours one weekend in March. ✉ *1100 Atlantic Blvd., where White St. and the Atlantic Ocean meet, Key West* ☎ *305/294–3210* ⊕ *www.keywestgardenclub.com* 🎫 *Donation welcome.*

FAMILY **Key West Shipwreck Treasures Museum.** Much of Key West's history, early prosperity, and interesting architecture come from ships that ran aground on its coral reef. Artifacts from the circa-1856 *Isaac Allerton,* which yielded $150,000 worth of wreckage, comprise the museum portion of this multifaceted attraction. Actors and films add a bit of Disneyesque drama. The final highlight is climbing to the top of the 65-foot lookout tower, a reproduction of the 20 or so towers used by Key West wreckers during the town's salvaging heyday. ⊠ *1 Whitehead St., Key West* ☎ *305/292–8990* ⊕ *www.keywestshipwreck.com* ⚏ *$16.11.*

FAMILY **Mel Fisher Maritime Museum.** In 1622, a flotilla of Spanish galleons laden with riches left Havana en route to Spain, but foundered in a hurricane 40 miles west of the Keys. In 1985 diver Mel Fisher recovered the treasures from two of the lost ships, including the *Nuestra Señora de Atocha,* said to carry the mother lode of treasures, and the *Santa Margarita.* Fisher's incredible adventures tracking these fabled hoards and battling the state of Florida for rights is as amazing as the loot you'll see, touch, and learn about in this museum. Artifacts include a 77.76-carat natural emerald crystal worth almost $250,000. Exhibits on the second floor rotate and might cover slave ships, including the excavated 17th-century *Henrietta Marie,* or the evolution of Florida maritime history. ⊠ *200 Greene St., Key West* ☎ *305/294–2633* ⊕ *www.melfisher.org* ⚏ *$15.*

FAMILY **Nancy Forrester's Secret Garden.** A few blocks away from the parties of Duval Street lies a purely selfless labor of love in the form of a backyard garden whose paths lead to colorful (and happily squawking) rescued parrots and macaws. Step inside the nondescript side gate and you'll meet Nancy, an environmental artist, and her flock of feathered children (which you can hold and feed). At 10 am she personally gives a tour, or come between 11 am and 3 pm and do the self-guided version. Bring a lunch and have a picnic in the shade, or just meander and learn. It's Parroting 101, and it might just be the most memorable day of your Key West vacation. ⊠ *518 Elizabeth St., Key West* ✛ *Between Southard and Fleming St.* ☎ *305/294–0015* ⊕ *nancyforrester.com* ⚏ *$10* ☞ *Leashed dogs are welcome.*

THE CONCH REPUBLIC

Beginning in the 1970s, pot smuggling became a source of income for islanders who knew how to dodge detection in the maze of waterways in the Keys. In 1982, the U.S. Border Patrol threw a roadblock across the Overseas Highway just south of Florida City to catch drug runners and undocumented aliens. Traffic backed up for miles as Border Patrol agents searched vehicles and demanded that the occupants prove U.S. citizenship. Officials in Key West, outraged at being treated like foreigners by the federal government, staged a protest and formed their own "nation," the so-called Conch Republic. They hoisted a flag and distributed mock border passes, visas, and Conch currency. The embarrassed Border Patrol dismantled its roadblock, and now an annual festival recalls the city's victory.

NEW TOWN

The Overseas Highway splits as it enters Key West, the two forks rejoining to encircle New Town, the area east of White Street to Cow Key Channel. The southern fork runs along the shore as South Roosevelt Boulevard (Route A1A) and skirts Key West International Airport, while the northern fork runs along the north shore as North Roosevelt Boulevard and turns into Truman Avenue once it hits Old Town. Part of New Town was created with dredged fill. The island would have continued growing this way had the Army Corps of Engineers not determined in the early 1970s that it was detrimental to the nearby reef.

TIMING

Allow one to two hours to include brief stops at each attraction. If your interests lie in art, gardens, or Civil War history, you'll need three or four hours. Throw in time at the beach and make it a half-day affair.

Fort East Martello Museum & Gardens. This redbrick Civil War fort never saw a lick of action during the war. Today it serves as a museum, with historical exhibits about the 19th and 20th centuries. Among the latter are relics of the USS *Maine*, cigar factory and shipwrecking exhibits, and the citadel tower you can climb to the top. The museum, operated by the Key West Art and Historical Society, also has a collection of Stanley Papio's "junk art" sculptures inside and out, and a gallery of Cuban folk artist Mario

Sanchez's chiseled and painted wooden carvings of historic Key West street scenes. ⊠ *3501 S. Roosevelt Blvd., Key West* ☎ *305/296–3913* ⊕ *www.kwahs.com* ⊠ *$10.*

Key West Tropical Forest & Botanical Garden. Established in 1935, this unique habitat is the only frost-free botanical garden in the continental United States. You won't see fancy topiaries and exotic plants, but you'll see a unique ecosystem that naturally occurs in this area and the Caribbean. There are paved walkways that take you past butterfly gardens, mangroves, Cuban palms, lots of birds like herons and ibis, and ponds where you can spy turtles and fish. It's a nice respite from the sidewalks and shops, and offers a natural slice of Keys paradise. ⊠ *5210 College Rd., Key West* ☎ *305/296–1504* ⊕ *www.kwbgs.org* ⊠ *$7.*

BEACHES

OLD TOWN

Dog Beach. Next to Louie's Backyard restaurant, this tiny beach—the only one in Key West where dogs are allowed unleashed—has a shore that's a mix of sand and rocks. **Amenities:** none. **Best for:** walking. ⊠ *Vernon and Waddell sts., Key West* ⊠ *Free.*

FAMILY **Fort Zachary Taylor Beach.** The park's beach is the best and safest place to swim in Key West. There's an adjoining picnic area with barbecue grills and shade trees, a snack bar, and rental equipment, including snorkeling gear. A café serves sandwiches and other munchies. Water shoes are recommended since the bottom is rocky here. **Amenities:** food and drink; showers; toilets; water sports. **Best for:** swimming; snorkeling. ⊠ *End of Southard St., through Truman Annex, Key West* ☎ *305/292–6713* ⊕ *www.fortzacharytaylor.com* ⊠ *$4 for single-occupant vehicles, $6 for 2–8 people, plus $0.50 per person county surcharge.*

FAMILY **Higgs Beach–Astro City Playground.** This Monroe County park with its groomed pebbly sand is a popular sunbathing spot. A nearby grove of Australian pines provides shade, and the West Martello Tower provides shelter should a storm suddenly sweep in. Kayak and beach-chair rentals are available, as is a volleyball net. The beach also has the largest AIDS memorial in the country and a cultural exhibit commemorating the grave site of 295 enslaved Africans who died after being rescued from three South America–bound slave ships in 1860. An athletic trail with 10 fitness stations is also available. Hungry? Grab a bite to eat at the on-site restaurant, Salute. Across the street, **Astro City Playground** is popular with young children. **Amenities:** parking; toilets; water sports. **Best for:** swimming; snorkeling. ⊠ *Atlantic Blvd. between White and Reynolds sts., Key West* ▣ *Free*.

NEW TOWN

C. B. Harvey Memorial Rest Beach. This beach and park were named after Cornelius Bradford Harvey, former Key West mayor and commissioner. Adjacent to Higgs Beach, it has half a dozen picnic areas across the street, dunes, a pier, and a wheelchair and bike path. **Amenities:** none. **Best for:** walking. ⊠ *Atlantic Blvd., east side of White St. Pier, Key West* ▣ *Free*.

Smathers Beach. This wide beach has nearly 1 mile of nice white sand, plus beautiful coconut palms, picnic areas, and volleyball courts, all of which make it popular with the spring-break crowd. Trucks along the road rent rafts, Windsurfers, and other beach "toys." **Amenities:** food and drink; parking; toilets; water sports. **Best for:** partiers. ⊠ *S. Roosevelt Blvd., Key West* ▣ *Free*.

WHERE TO EAT

Bring your appetite, a sense of daring, and a lack of preconceived notions about propriety. A meal in Key West can mean overlooking the crazies along Duval Street, watching roosters and pigeons battle for a scrap of food that may have escaped your fork, relishing the finest in what used to be the dining room of a 19th-century Victorian home, or gazing out at boats jockeying for position in the marina. And that's just the diversity of the setting. Seafood dominates local menus, but the treatment afforded that fish or crustacean can range from Cuban and New World to Asian and Continental.

OLD TOWN

$$ ✕**Ambrosia.** *Japanese.* Ask any savvy local where to get the best sushi on the island and you'll undoubtedly be pointed to this bright and airy dining room with a modern indoor waterfall literally steps from the Atlantic. Grab a seat at the sushi bar and watch owner and head sushi chef Masa (albeit not the famous chef from New York and Las Vegas)

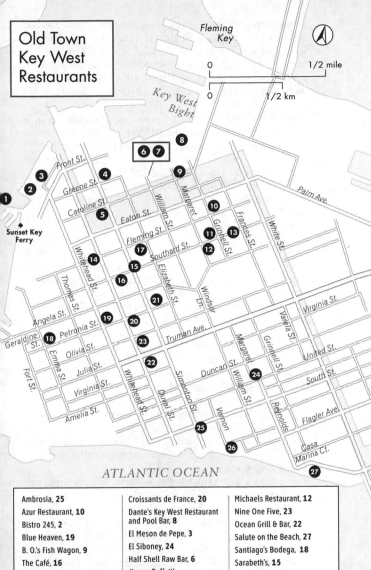

Old Town Key West Restaurants

Fleming Key

Key West Bight

Front St.

Greene St.

Caroline St.

Eaton St.

Fleming St.

Southard St.

Palm Ave.

Sunset Key Ferry

Whitehead St.

Thomas St.

Angela St.

Geraldine St.

Petronia St.

Olivia St.

Julia St.

Virginia St.

Amelia St.

Emma St.

Fort St.

Duval St.

William St.

Margaret

Grinnell St.

Frances St.

White St.

Elizabeth St.

Windsor Ln.

Truman Ave.

Simonton St.

Duncan St.

Vernon

Margaret

William St.

Grinnell St.

Varela St.

Virginia St.

United St.

South St.

Reynolds

Flagler Ave.

Casa Marina Ct.

ATLANTIC OCEAN

Ambrosia, **25**	Croissants de France, **20**	Michaels Restaurant, **12**
Azur Restaurant, **10**	Dante's Key West Restaurant and Pool Bar, **8**	Nine One Five, **23**
Bistro 245, **2**	El Meson de Pepe, **3**	Ocean Grill & Bar, **22**
Blue Heaven, **19**	El Siboney, **24**	Salute on the Beach, **27**
B. O.'s Fish Wagon, **9**	Half Shell Raw Bar, **6**	Santiago's Bodega, **18**
The Café, **16**	Jimmy Buffett's Margaritaville Cafe, **14**	Sarabeth's, **15**
Café Marquesa, **17**	Latitudes, **1**	Seven Fish, **21**
Café Solé, **13**	Louie's Backyard, **26**	Turtle Kraals, **7**
Camille's Restaurant, **5**	Mangia Mangia, **11**	
Conch Republic Seafood Company, **4**		

0   1/2 mile

0   1/2 km

prepare an impressive array of sashimi delicacies. **Known for:** consistently good fish; great tempura and teriyaki bento lunch specials; the Ambrosia special, with a mix of sashimi, sushi, and rolls. $ *Average main: $20* ⊠ *Santa Maria Resort, 1401 Simonton St., Key West* ☎ *305/293–0304* ⊕ *www. ambrosiasushi.com* ⊘ *Closed 2 wks after Labor Day. No lunch weekends.*

$$$ ✕ **Azur Restaurant.** *Eclectic.* In a contemporary setting with indoor and outdoor seating, welcoming staff serve original, eclectic dishes that stand out from those at the hordes of Key West restaurants. Key lime–stuffed French toast and yellowtail snapper Benedict make breakfast a pleasant wake-up call. **Known for:** homemade gnocchi; a nice variety of fish specials; daily brunch. $ *Average main: $26* ⊠ *425 Grinnell St., Key West* ☎ *305/292–2987* ⊕ *www. azurkeywest.com.*

$$$$ ✕ **Bistro 245.** *Seafood.* The sunset views alone are worth a visit, but the food here is stellar as well. Enjoy a key lime martini at the bar or a seafood dinner in the air-conditioned dining room or the open-air patio. **Known for:** upstairs bar overlooking Mallory Square; "Key West Pink" shrimp; popular weekend brunch. $ *Average main: $35* ⊠ *Margaritaville Resort & Marina, 245 Front St., Key West* ☎ *305/294–4000* ⊕ *www.margaritavillekeywestresort.com/bistro-245.*

$$$ ✕ **Blue Heaven.** *Caribbean.* The outdoor dining area here is often referred to as "the quintessential Keys experience," and it's hard to argue. There's much to like about this historic Caribbean-style restaurant where Hemingway refereed boxing matches and customers cheered for cockfights. **Known for:** shrimp and grits; lobster Benedict with key lime hollandaise; the wait for a table and lack of parking. $ *Average main: $24* ⊠ *729 Thomas St., Key West* ☎ *305/296–8666* ⊕ *www.blueheavenkw.com* ⊘ *Closed after Labor Day for 6 wks.*

★   Fodor'sChoice ✕ **B.O.'s Fish Wagon.** *Seafood.* What started out
$$ as a fish house on wheels appears to have broken down on the corner of Caroline and William streets and is today the cornerstone for one of Key West's junkyard-chic dining institutions. Step up to the window and order a grouper sandwich fried or grilled and topped with key lime sauce. **Known for:** lots of Key West charm; Friday-night jam sessions; all seating on picnic tables in the yard. $ *Average main: $18* ⊠ *801 Caroline St., Key West* ☎ *305/294–9272* ⊕ *bosfishwagon.com.*

$ 🍴 **The Café.** *Vegetarian.* You don't have to be a vegetarian to love this new-age café decorated with bright artwork and a corrugated-tin-fronted counter. Local favorites include homemade soup, veggie sandwiches and burgers (order them with a side of sweet-potato fries), grilled portobello mushroom salad, seafood, vegan specialties, stir-fry dinners, and grilled veggie pizzas. **Known for:** vegan options; homemade sangria; weekend brunch. [$] *Average main: $11* ✉ *509 Southard St., Key West* ☎ *305/296–5515* 🌐 *www.thecafekw.com.*

★ $$$ **Fodor's Choice** 🍴 **Café Marquesa.** *European.* You'll find seven or more inspired entrées on a changing menu each night, including anything from yellowtail snapper to seared duck breast. End your meal on a sweet note with chocolate pot de crème and homemade ice cream—there's also a fine selection of wines and custom martinis. **Known for:** relaxed but elegant setting; good wine and martini lists; desserts worth ordering. [$] *Average main: $30* ✉ *600 Fleming St., Key West* ☎ *305/292–1244* 🌐 *www.marquesa.com* 🕒 *No lunch.*

$$$ 🍴 **Café Solé.** *French.* This little corner of France hides behind a high wall in a residential neighborhood. Inside, French training intertwines with local ingredients, creating delicious takes on classics, including a must-try conch carpaccio and some of the best bouillabaisse that you'll find outside Marseilles. **Known for:** hogfish in several different preparations; intimate, romantic atmosphere; award-winning key lime pie. [$] *Average main: $28* ✉ *1029 Southard St., Key West* ☎ *305/294–0230* 🌐 *www.cafesole.com.*

$$$ FAMILY 🍴 **Camille's Restaurant.** *Modern American.* Break out the stretchy pants because everything on the menu at this affordable hot spot not only sounds scrumptious, it is. Start your day with a shrimp, lobster, or crab-cake Benedict—the latter was voted best in the Florida Keys. **Known for:** popularity with both locals and tourists; fresh seafood daily; BOGO menu from 3 pm to closing daily. [$] *Average main: $21* ✉ *1202 Simonton St., at Catherine St., Key West* ☎ *305/296–4811.*

$$$ FAMILY 🍴 **Conch Republic Seafood Company.** *Seafood.* Because of its location where the fast ferry docks, Conch Republic does a brisk business. It's huge, open-air, on the water, and the menu is ambitious, offering more than just standard seafood fare. **Known for:** "Royal Reds" peel-and-eat shrimp; no reservations; live music most nights. [$] *Average main: $25* ✉ *631 Greene St., at Elizabeth St., Key West* ☎ *305/294–4403* 🌐 *www.conchrepublicseafood.com.*

$ 🍴 **Croissants de France.** *French.* Pop into the bakery for something sinfully sweet or spend some time people-watching at the sidewalk café next door. You can get breakfast or lunch at the café, and the bakery is open late. **Known for:** gluten-free buckwheat crepes; popularity with both locals and visitors; great coffee and croissants. [$] *Average main: $14* ✉ *816 Duval St., Key West* ☎ *305/294–2624* 🌐 *www.croissantsdefrance.com.*

$$ 🍴 **Dante's Key West Restaurant and Pool Bar.** *Seafood.* With the motto "Come be an aquaholic," Dante's is as unique as Key West itself. Sun loungers, tiki bars, and tables with umbrellas and chairs surround a large free-form swimming pool. **Known for:** food and drink minimum at some key tables; popular happy hour; "Hook and Cook" (bring your fresh catch and they cook it for you). [$] *Average main: $18* ✉ *Conch Harbor Marina, 951 Caroline St., Key West* ☎ *305/423–2001* 🌐 *www.danteskeywest.com.*

$$ 🍴 **El Meson de Pepe.** *Cuban.* If you want a taste of the island's Cuban heritage, this is the place to dine alfresco or in the dining room on refined Cuban classics. Begin with a megasize mojito while you browse the expansive menu offering *tostones rellenos* (green plantains with different traditional fillings), ceviche, and more. **Known for:** authentic plantain chips; Latin band during the nightly sunset celebration; touristy atmosphere. [$] *Average main: $19* ✉ *Mallory Sq., 410 Wall St., Key West* ☎ *305/295–2620* 🌐 *www.elmesondepepe.com.*

$ 🍴 **El Siboney.** *Cuban.* Dining at this family-style restaurant is like going to Mom's for Sunday dinner—if your mother is Cuban. The dining room is noisy, and the food is traditional *cubano*. To make a good thing even better, the prices are very reasonable and the homemade sangria is *muy bueno*. **Known for:** memorable paella and traditional dishes; wine and beer only; cheaper than more touristy options close to Duval. [$] *Average main: $11* ✉ *900 Catherine St., Key West* ☎ *305/296–4184* 🌐 *www.elsiboneyrestaurant.com.*

$$ 🍴 **Half Shell Raw Bar.** *Seafood.* Smack-dab on the docks, this
FAMILY legendary institution gets its name from the oysters, clams, and peel-and-eat shrimp that are a departure point for its seafood-based diet. It's not clever recipes or fine dining (or even air-conditioning) that packs 'em in; it's fried fish, po'boy sandwiches, and seafood combos. **Known for:** daily happy hour with food and drink deals; few non-seafood options; good people-watching spot. [$] *Average main: $16* ✉ *Lands End Village at Historic Seaport, 231 Margaret St., Key West* ☎ *305/294–7496* 🌐 *www.halfshellrawbar.com.*

$$ 🍴 **Jimmy Buffett's Margaritaville Cafe.** *American.* If you must have your cheeseburger in paradise, it may as well be here. The first of Buffett's line of chain eateries, it belongs here more than anywhere else, but quite frankly it's more about the name, music, and attitude (and margaritas) than the food. The menu has a Cajun-Caribbean flair, and live bands pack the place come dinner and into the wee hours. **Known for:** pricey Caribbean bar food; good and spicy conch chowder; raucous party atmosphere almost all the time. [$] *Average main: $18* ✉ *500 Duval St., Key West* ☎ *305/292–1435* 🌐 *www.margaritaville.com.*

$$$ 🍴 **Latitudes.** *Eclectic.* For a special treat, take the short boat ride to lovely Sunset Key for lunch or dinner on the beach. Creativity and quality ingredients combine for dishes that are bound to impress as much as the setting, like the fish tacos with chipotle aioli. **Known for:** amazing sunset views; sophisticated atmosphere and expensive food; lobster bisque. [$] *Average main: $28* ✉ *Sunset Key Guest Cottages, 245 Front St., Key West* ☎ *305/292–5300, 888/477–7786* 🌐 *www.sunsetkeycottages.com/latitudes-key-west* ☞ *Reservations are required to catch the ferry: no reservation, no ride.*

$$$$ 🍴 **Louie's Backyard.** *Eclectic.* Feast your eyes on a steal-your-breath-away view and beautifully presented dishes prepared by executive chef Doug Shook. Once you get over sticker shock on the seasonally changing menu, settle in on the outside deck and enjoy dishes like cracked conch with mango chutney, lamb chops with sun-dried tomato relish, and tamarind-glazed duck breast. **Known for:** fresh, pricey seafood and steaks; affordable lunch menu; late night drinks at Afterdeck Bar, directly on the water. [$] *Average main: $36* ✉ *700 Waddell Ave., Key West* ☎ *305/294–1061* 🌐 *www.louiesbackyard.com* ⏲ *Closed Labor Day–mid-Sept. Café closed Sun. and Mon.*

$$ 🍴 **Mangia Mangia.** *Italian.* This longtime favorite serves large portions of homemade pastas that can be matched with any of the homemade sauces. Tables are arranged in a brick garden hung with twinkling lights and in a cozy, casual dining room in an old house. **Known for:** extensive wine list with a nice range of prices; gluten-free and organic pastas; outdoor seating in the garden. [$] *Average main: $18* ✉ *900 Southard St., Key West* ☎ *305/294–2469* 🌐 *www.mangia-mangia.com* ⏲ *No lunch.*

$$$$ 🍴 **Michaels Restaurant.** *American.* White tablecloths, subdued lighting, and romantic music give Michaels the feel of an urban eatery, while garden seating reminds you that you are in the Keys. Chef-owner Michael Wilson flies in prime

5

rib, cowboy steaks, and rib eyes from Allen Brothers in Chicago, which has supplied top-ranked steak houses for more than a century. **Known for:** elegant, romantic atmosphere; small plates available until 7:30 Sunday–Thursday; steak and seafood. Ⓢ *Average main: $32* ✉ *532 Margaret St., Key West* ☎ *305/295–1300* ⊕ *www.michaelskeywest. com* ⊗ *No lunch.*

$$$$ ✕ **Nine One Five.** *Eclectic.* Twinkling lights draped along the lower- and upper-level outdoor porches of a 100-year-old Victorian home set an unstuffy and comfortable stage here. If you like to sample and sip, you'll appreciate the variety of smaller-plate selections and wines by the glass. **Known for:** fun place to people-watch; intimate and inviting atmosphere; light jazz during dinner. Ⓢ *Average main: $32* ✉ *915 Duval St., Key West* ☎ *305/296–0669* ⊕ *www.915duval. com* ⊗ *No lunch Mon. and Tues.*

$$$ ✕ **Ocean Grill & Bar.** *Seafood.* Whether it's breakfast, lunch, or dinner, Ocean Grill serves up fresh Key West seafood in good portions at fair prices. The "Scalouper" is just of one the unique offerings: jumbo diver scallops sliced on the diagonal and served atop pan-seared, local black grouper with a mint puree—sounds odd, but it tastes delightfully fresh. **Known for:** shrimp and grits; bottomless Bloody Marys and mimosas every day 9–3:30; creamy lobster bisque. Ⓢ *Average main: $30* ✉ *1075 Duval St., Key West* ⊹ *Between Duval and Simonton in the Duval Square Mall* ☎ *305/296–4300* ⊕ *www.oceangrillandbar.com.*

$$$ ✕ **Salute on the Beach.** *Italian.* Sister restaurant to Blue Heaven, this colorful establishment sits on Higgs Beach, giving it one of the island's best lunch views—and a bit of sand and salt spray on a windy day. The intriguing menu is Italian with a Caribbean flair and will not disappoint. **Known for:** amazing water views; casual, inviting atmosphere; pricey slice of key lime pie. Ⓢ *Average main: $22* ✉ *Higgs Beach, 1000 Atlantic Blvd., Key West* ☎ *305/292– 1117* ⊕ *www.saluteonthebeach.com.*

★ **Fodor'sChoice** ✕ **Santiago's Bodega.** *Tapas.* Picky palates will be
$ satisfied at this funky, dark, and sensuous tapas restaurant, which is well off the main drag—it's a secret spot for local foodies in the know. Small plates include yellowfin tuna ceviche with hunks of avocado and mango, and filet mignon with creamy Gorgonzola butter. **Known for:** legendary bread pudding; homemade white or red sangria; a favorite with local chefs. Ⓢ *Average main: $14* ✉ *Bahama Village, 207 Petronia St., Key West* ☎ *305/296–7691* ⊕ *www.santiagosbodega.com.*

$$ 🍴 **Sarabeth's.** *American.* Named for the award-winning jam-maker and pastry chef Sarabeth Levine, who runs the kitchen, this restaurant serves all-day breakfast, best enjoyed in the picket-fenced front yard of this circa-1870 synagogue. Lemon ricotta pancakes, pumpkin waffles, and homemade jams make the meal. **Known for:** homemade granola and old-fashioned porridge; daily specials including meat loaf and mac and cheese; orange apricot bread pudding. [$] *Average main: $20* ✉ *530 Simonton St., at Souhard St., Key West* ☎ *305/293–8181* 🌐 *www.sarabethskeywest.com* 🕒 *Closed Mon. and Tues.*

$$$ 🍴 **Seven Fish.** *Seafood.* This local hot spot exudes a casual Key West vibe with an eclectic mix of dishes. The specialty is the local fish of the day (like snapper with creamy Thai curry). **Known for:** fresh seafood; busy spot requiring reservations; amazing foccacia bread. [$] *Average main: $26* ✉ *921 Truman Ave., Key West* ☎ *305/296–2777* 🌐 *www.7fish.com* 🕒 *Closed Tues. No lunch.*

5

$$ 🍴 **Turtle Kraals.** *Seafood.* Named for the kraals, or corrals,
FAMILY where sea turtles were once kept until they went to the cannery, this place calls to mind the island's history. The menu offers an assortment of marine cuisine that includes seafood enchiladas, mesquite-grilled fish of the day, and mango crab cakes. **Known for:** mesquite-grilled oysters with Parmesan and cilantro; Peruvian-style ceviche; great views of the harbor. [$] *Average main: $16* ✉ *231 Margaret St., Key West* ☎ *305/294–2640* 🌐 *www.turtlekraals.com.*

NEW TOWN

$$ 🍴 **Hogfish Bar & Grill.** *Seafood.* It's worth a drive to Stock Island, one of Florida's last surviving working waterfronts, just outside Key West, to indulge in the freshness you'll witness at this down-to-earth spot. Hogfish is the specialty, of course. **Known for:** pricey fish sandwiches; a taste of local life; fried grouper cheeks. [$] *Average main: $17* ✉ *6810 Front St., Stock Island, Key West* ☎ *305/293–4041* 🌐 *www.hogfishbar.com.*

$$$$ 🍴 **Tavern N Town.** *Eclectic.* This handsome and warm restaurant has an open kitchen that adds lovely aromas from the wood-fired oven. The dinner menu offers a variety of options, including small plates and full entrées. **Known for:** upscale atmosphere (and prices); popular happy hour; noisy when busy. [$] *Average main: $33* ✉ *Key West Marriott Beachside Resort, 3841 N. Roosevelt Blvd., Key West* ☎ *305/296–8100, 800/546–0885* 🌐 *www.taverntown.com* 🕒 *No lunch.*

WHERE TO STAY

Historic cottages, restored century-old Conch houses, and large resorts are among the offerings in Key West, the majority charging between $100 and $300 a night. In high season, Christmas through Easter, you'll be hard-pressed to find a decent room for less than $200, and most places raise prices considerably during holidays and festivals. Many guesthouses and inns do not welcome children under 16, and most do not permit smoking indoors. Most tariffs include an expanded Continental breakfast and, often, an afternoon glass of wine or snack.

LODGING ALTERNATIVES

The Lodging Association of Key West and the Florida Keys is an umbrella organization for dozens of local properties. Key West Vacations lists historic cottages, homes, and condominiums for rent. Rent Key West Vacations specializes in renting vacation homes and condos for a week or longer. Vacation Key West lists all kinds of properties throughout Key West. In addition to these local agencies, 🌐 *airbnb.com* and 🌐 *vrbo.com* have many offerings in Key West.

Lodging Association of Key West and the Florida Keys. ☎ *800/492–1911* 🌐 *www.keywestinns.com.*

Key West Vacations. ☎ *888/775–3993* 🌐 *www.keywestvacations.com.*

Rent Key West Vacations. ✉ *1075 Duval St., Suite C11, Key West* ☎ *305/294–0990, 800/833–7368* 🌐 *www.rentkeywest.com.*

Vacation Key West. ✉ *100 Grinnell St., Key West Ferry Terminal, Key West* ☎ *305/295–9500, 800/595–5397* 🌐 *www.vacationkw.com.*

OLD TOWN

$$$ 🏨 **Ambrosia Key West.** *B&B/Inn.* If you desire personal attention, a casual atmosphere, and a dollop of style, stay at these twin inns spread out on nearly 2 acres. **Pros:** spacious rooms; breakfast served poolside; great location. **Cons:** on-street parking can be tough to come by; a little too spread out; high windows in some rooms let in the early morning light. [$] *Rooms from: $385* ✉ *615, 618, 622 Fleming St., Key West* ☎ *305/296–9838, 800/535–9838* 🌐 *www.ambrosiakeywest.com* ⇨ *20 rooms* 🍴 *Free Breakfast.*

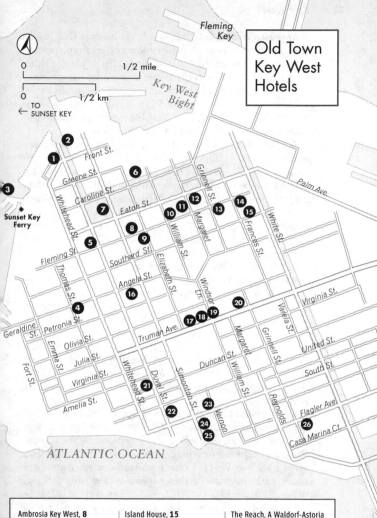

Old Town Key West Hotels

Fleming Key

Key West Bight

TO ← SUNSET KEY

Sunset Key Ferry

0 — 1/2 mile

0 — 1/2 km

ATLANTIC OCEAN

Front St.
Greene St.
Caroline St.
Eaton St.
Fleming St.
Southard St.
Angela St.
Petronia St.
Olivia St.
Julia St.
Virginia St.
Amelia St.
Truman Ave.
Duncan St.
Whitehead St.
Thomas St.
Emma St.
Fort St.
Geraldine St.
Elizabeth St.
William St.
Margaret
Windsor Ltr.
Grinnell St.
Francis St.
White St.
Palm Ave.
Virginia St.
United St.
South St.
Varela St.
Reynolds
Duval St.
Simonton St.
Vernon
Flagler Ave.
Casa Marina Ct.

Ambrosia Key West, **8**

Angelina Guest House, **4**

Azul Key West, **20**

Casa Marina, A Waldorf-Astoria Resort, **26**

Crowne Plaza La Concha Hotel and Spa, **5**

Eden House, **13**

The Gardens Hotel, **16**

Heron House, **14**

Island City House, **10**

Island House, **15**

Key Lime Inn, **17**

La Pensione, **19**

The Marker, **6**

Marquesa Hotel, **9**

Mermaid & the Alligator, **18**

NYAH: Not Your Average Hotel, **11**

Ocean Key Resort & Spa, **1**

Pier House Resort and Spa, **2**

The Reach, A Waldorf-Astoria Resort, **25**

Santa Maria Suites , **24**

Simonton Court, **7**

Southernmost Beach Resort, **22**

Southwinds, **23**

Speakeasy Inn, **21**

Sunset Key , **3**

Westwinds Inn, **12**

$ 🏨 **Angelina Guest House.** *B&B/Inn.* In the heart of Old Town, this adults-only home away from home offers simple, clean, attractively priced accommodations. **Pros:** good value; nice garden; friendly staff. **Cons:** thin walls; basic rooms with no TVs; shared balcony and four of the rooms share a bathroom. [$] *Rooms from: $159* ✉ *302 Angela St., Key West* ☎ *305/294–4480, 888/303–4480* 🌐 *www.angelinaguesthouse.com* 🛏 *13 rooms* 🍴 *Free Breakfast.*

$$ 🏨 **Azul Key West.** *B&B/Inn.* The ultramodern—nearly minimalistic—redo of this classic circa-1903 Queen Anne mansion is a break from the sensory overload of Key West's other abundant Victorian guesthouses. **Pros:** lovely building; marble-floored baths; luxurious linens. **Cons:** on a busy street; modern isn't for everyone; two-night minimum stay, five nights in season. [$] *Rooms from: $289* ✉ *907 Truman Ave., Key West* ☎ *305/296–5152, 888/253–2985* 🌐 *www.azulhotels.us* 🛏 *11 rooms* 🍴 *Free Breakfast.*

$$$ FAMILY 🏨 **Casa Marina, A Waldorf-Astoria Resort.** *Resort.* This luxurious property is on the largest private beach in Key West, and it has the same richly appointed lobby with beamed ceilings, polished pine floor, and original art as it did when it opened on New Year's Eve 1920. **Pros:** hugh beach; on-site dining, bars, and water sports; away from the crowds. **Cons:** long walk to central Old Town; expensive resort fee; spa is across the street in a separate building. [$] *Rooms from: $399* ✉ *1500 Reynolds St., Key West* ☎ *305/296–3535, 866/203–6392* 🌐 *www.casamarinaresort.com* 🛏 *311 rooms* 🍴 *No meals.*

$$$ 🏨 **Crowne Plaza La Concha Hotel and Spa.** *Hotel.* History and franchises can mix, as this 1920s-vintage hotel proves with its handsome atrium lobby and sleep-conducive rooms. **Pros:** location is everything; good on-site restaurant and wine bar; free Wi-Fi. **Cons:** high-traffic area; rooms are small, bathrooms are smaller; expensive valet-only parking. [$] *Rooms from: $350* ✉ *430 Duval St., Key West* ☎ *305/296–2991* 🌐 *www.laconchakeywest.com* 🛏 *178 rooms* 🍴 *No meals.*

$$ 🏨 **Eden House.** *Hotel.* From the vintage metal rockers on the streetside porch to the old neon hotel sign in the lobby, this 1920s rambling Key West mainstay hotel is high on character, low on gloss. **Pros:** free parking; hot tub is actually hot; daily happy hour around the pool. **Cons:** pricey for older rooms; brown towels take getting used to; parking is first-come, first-served. [$] *Rooms from: $225* ✉ *1015 Fleming St., Key West* ☎ *305/296–6868, 800/533–5397* 🌐 *www.edenhouse.com* 🛏 *44 rooms* 🍴 *No meals.*

★ **Fodor'sChoice** 🏨 **The Gardens Hotel.** *Hotel.* Built in 1875, this
$$$$ gloriously shaded, well-loved property was a labor of love from the get-go, and it covers a third of a city block in Old Town. **Pros:** luxurious bathrooms; secluded garden seating; free Wi-Fi. **Cons:** hard to get reservations; expensive; nightly secure parking fee. [$] *Rooms from: $415* ✉ *526 Angela St., Key West* ☎ *305/294–2661, 800/526–2664* 🌐 *www.gardenshotel.com* 🛏 *23 rooms* 🍴 *Free Breakfast.*

$$ 🏨 **Heron House.** *B&B/Inn.* Built in the 1850s, rooms at this hotel just off Duval (not to be confused with Heron House Court, although they are sister properties) are outfitted in rattan and tropical watercolors, and bathrooms are updated with a touch of granite. **Pros:** vintage charm; close enough to the action but quiet; friendly staff. **Cons:** early bird gets the hot food at breakfast; furnishings need updating; no designated parking lot. [$] *Rooms from: $229* ✉ *512 Simonton St., Key West* ☎ *305/294–8477, 800/294–1644* 🌐 *www.heronhousehotels.com* 🛏 *23 rooms* 🍴 *Free Breakfast.*

$$$ 🏨 **Island City House Hotel.** *B&B/Inn.* A private garden with brick walkways, tropical plants, and a canopy of palms sets this convivial guesthouse apart from the pack. **Pros:** lush gardens; knowledgeable staff; bike rentals on-site. **Cons:** spotty Wi-Fi service; front desk is only staffed 8 am–8 pm; no parking. [$] *Rooms from: $320* ✉ *411 William St., Key West* ☎ *305/294–5702, 800/634–8230* 🌐 *www.islandcityhouse.com* 🛏 *24 suites* 🍴 *No meals.*

$$$$ 🏨 **Island House.** *Hotel.* Geared specifically toward gay men, this hotel features a health club, a video lounge, a café and bar, and rooms in historic digs. **Pros:** lots of privacy; just the place to get that all-over tan; free happy hour for guests. **Cons:** no women allowed; three rooms share a bath; day passes bring visitors of every age, which is a pro or con depending on your mood. [$] *Rooms from: $459* ✉ *1129 Fleming St., Key West* ☎ *305/294–6284, 800/890–6284* 🌐 *www.islandhousekeywest.com* 🛏 *34 rooms* 🍴 *No meals.*

$$ 🏨 **Key Lime Inn.** *B&B/Inn.* This 1854 Grand Bahama–style house on the National Register of Historic Places succeeds by offering amiable service, a great location, and simple rooms with natural-wood furnishings. **Pros:** walking distance to clubs and bars; some rooms have private outdoor spaces; free Wi-Fi. **Cons:** over a mile to the sunset end of Duval Street; pool faces a busy street; $20 daily parking fee. [$] *Rooms from: $259* ✉ *725 Truman Ave., Key West* ☎ *305/294–5229, 800/549–4430* 🌐 *www.keylimeinn.com* 🛏 *37 rooms* 🍴 *Free Breakfast.*

$$ [H] **La Pensione.** *B&B/Inn.* Hospitality and period furnishings make this 1891 home, once owned by a cigar executive, a wonderful glimpse into Key West life in the late 19th century. **Pros:** pine-paneled walls; first-come, first-served parking included; some rooms have wraparound porches. **Cons:** street-facing rooms are noisy; rooms do not have TVs; rooms only accommodate two people. [$] *Rooms from: $258* ✉ *809 Truman Ave., Key West* ☎ *305/292–9923, 800/893–1193* 🌐 *www.lapensione.com* 🛏 *9 rooms* 🍴 *Free Breakfast.*

$$$ [H] **The Marker.** *Resort.* The Marker is one of Key West's newest hotels, and a welcome and luxurious addition to the waterfront in Old Town, with Conch-style architecture and an authentic Keys aesthetic. **Pros:** convenient Old Town location; on-site restaurant Cero Bodega; three saltwater pools, including one for adults only. **Cons:** hefty resort and parking fees nightly; "locals welcome" policy means pool loungers can be hard to come by; lots of walking if your room isn't near the amenities. [$] *Rooms from: $400* ✉ *200 William St., Key West* ☎ *305/501–5193* 🌐 *www.themarkerkeywest.com* 🛏 *96 rooms* 🍴 *No meals.*

★ $$$ **Fodor's Choice** [H] **Marquesa Hotel.** *Hotel.* In a town that prides itself on its laid-back luxury, this complex of four restored 1884 houses stands out. **Pros:** room service; romantic atmosphere; turndown service. **Cons:** street-facing rooms can be noisy; expensive rates; no elevator. [$] *Rooms from: $395* ✉ *600 Fleming St., Key West* ☎ *305/292–1919, 800/869–4631* 🌐 *www.marquesa.com* 🛏 *27 rooms* 🍴 *No meals.*

$$ [H] **Mermaid & the Alligator.** *B&B/Inn.* An enchanting combination of flora and fauna makes this 1904 Victorian house a welcoming retreat. **Pros:** hot plunge pool; massage pavilion; island-getaway feel. **Cons:** minimum stay required (length depends on season); dark public areas; plastic lawn chairs. [$] *Rooms from: $278* ✉ *729 Truman Ave., Key West* ☎ *305/294–1894, 800/773–1894* 🌐 *www.kwmermaid.com* 🛏 *9 rooms* 🍴 *Free Breakfast.*

$$$ [H] **NYAH: Not Your Average Hotel.** *B&B/Inn.* From its charming white picket fence, it may look similar to other Victorian-style Key West B&Bs, but that's where the similarities end. **Pros:** central location; perfect for traveling with a group of friends; free daily happy hour. **Cons:** small rooms, even smaller closets; street parking only; no toiletries provided. [$] *Rooms from: $349* ✉ *420 Margaret St., Key West* ☎ *305/296–2131* 🌐 *www.nyahotels.com* 🛏 *36 rooms* 🍴 *Free Breakfast* ☞ *Age 18 and over only.*

★ **Fodor's Choice** 🏨 **Ocean Key Resort & Spa.** *Resort.* This full
$$$$ resort—relatively rare in Key West—has large, tropical-look rooms with private balconies and excellent amenities, including a pool and bar overlooking Sunset Pier and a Thai-inspired spa. **Pros:** well-trained staff; lively pool scene; fantastic location at the busy end of Duval. **Cons:** daily valet parking and resort fee; too bustling for some; rooms are starting to show their age. [$] *Rooms from: $495* ✉ *Zero Duval St., Key West* ☎ *305/296–7701, 800/328–9815* 🌐 *www.oceankey.com* 🛏 *100 rooms* 🍴 *No meals.*

$$$$ 🏨 **Pier House Resort and Spa.** *Resort.* This upscale resort, near Mallory Square in the heart of Old Town, offers a wide range of amenities, including a beach and comfortable, traditionally furnished rooms. **Pros:** beautiful beach; free Wi-Fi; nice spa and restaurant. **Cons:** lots of conventions; poolside rooms are small; not really suitable for children under 16. [$] *Rooms from: $470* ✉ *1 Duval St., Key West* ☎ *305/296–4600, 800/327–8340* 🌐 *www.pierhouse.com* 🛏 *145 rooms* 🍴 *No meals.*

$$$ 🏨 **The Reach, A Waldorf Astoria Resort.** *Resort.* Embracing Key West's only natural beach, this full-service, luxury resort offers sleek rooms, all with balconies and modern amenities as well as reciprocal privileges to its sister Casa Marina resort nearby. **Pros:** removed from Duval hubbub; great sunrise views; pullout sofas in most rooms. **Cons:** expensive resort fee; high rates; some say it lacks the grandeur you'd expect of a Waldorf property. [$] *Rooms from: $399* ✉ *1435 Simonton St., Key West* ☎ *305/296–5000, 888/318–4316* 🌐 *www.reachresort.com* 🛏 *150 rooms* 🍴 *No meals.*

★ **Fodor's Choice** 🏨 **Santa Maria Suites.** *Resort.* It's odd to call this
$$$$ a hidden gem when it sits on a prominent corner just one block off Duval, but you'd never know what luxury awaits behind its concrete facade, which creates total seclusion from the outside world. **Pros:** amenities galore; front desk concierge services; private parking lot. **Cons:** daily resort fee; poolside units must close curtains for privacy; only two-bedroom units available. [$] *Rooms from: $549* ✉ *1401 Simonton St., Key West* ☎ *866/726–8259, 305/296–5678* 🌐 *www.santamariasuites.com* 🛏 *35 suites* 🍴 *No meals.*

$$$ 🏨 **Simonton Court.** *B&B/Inn.* A small world all its own, this adults-only maze of accommodations and four swimming pools makes you feel deliciously sequestered from Key West's crasser side but keeps you close enough to get there on foot. **Pros:** lots of privacy; well-appointed accommodations; friendly staff. **Cons:** minimum stay required in high season; off-street parking $25 nightly; some street noise

in basic rooms. Ⓢ *Rooms from: $310* ⊠ *320 Simonton St., Key West* ☎ *305/294–6386, 800/944–2687* ⊕ *www.simontoncourt.com* ⮑ *29 rooms* ⓞ *Free Breakfast.*

$$$ 🖼 **Southernmost Beach Resort.** *Hotel.* Rooms at this hotel on the quiet end of Duval—a 20-minute walk from downtown—are modern and sophisticated, and it's far enough from the hubub that you can relax but close enough that you can participate if you wish. **Pros:** pool attracts a lively crowd; access to nearby properties and beach; free parking and Wi-Fi. **Cons:** can get crowded around the pool and public areas; expensive nightly resort fee; beach is across the street. Ⓢ *Rooms from: $359* ⊠ *1319 Duval St., Key West* ☎ *305/296–6577, 800/354–4455* ⊕ *www.southernmostbeachresort.com* ⮑ *118 rooms* ⓞ *No meals.*

$$ 🖼 **Southwinds.** *B&B/Inn.* Operated by the same company as the ultra-high-end Santa Maria Suites, this motel-style property, though still pretty basic, has been modestly upgraded and is a good value-oriented option in pricey Key West. **Pros:** early (2 pm) check-in may be available; clean and spacious rooms; free parking and Wi-Fi. **Cons:** bland decor; small pools; thin walls. Ⓢ *Rooms from: $200* ⊠ *1321 Simonton St., Key West* ☎ *305/296–2829, 877/879–2362* ⊕ *www.keywestsouthwinds.com* ⮑ *58 rooms* ⓞ *Free Breakfast.*

$ 🖼 **Speakeasy Inn.** *B&B/Inn.* During Prohibition, Raul Vasquez made this place popular by smuggling in rum from Cuba; today its reputation is for having reasonably priced rooms within walking distance of the beach. **Pros:** good location; all rooms have kitchenettes; first-come, first-served free parking. **Cons:** no pool; on busy Duval; rooms are fairly basic. Ⓢ *Rooms from: $189* ⊠ *1117 Duval St., Key West* ☎ *305/296–2680* ⊕ *www.speakeasyinn.com* ⮑ *7 suites* ⓞ *Free Breakfast.*

★ **Fodor's**Choice 🖼 **Sunset Key.** *Resort.* This luxurious private
$$$$ island retreat with its own sandy beach feels completely cut off from the world, yet you're just minutes away from the action: a 10-minute ride from Mallory Square on the 24-hour free ferry. **Pros:** all units have kitchens; roomy verandas; free Wi-Fi. **Cons:** luxury doesn't come cheap; beach shore is rocky; launch runs only every 30 minutes. Ⓢ *Rooms from: $780* ⊠ *245 Front St., Key West* ☎ *305/292–5300, 888/477–7786* ⊕ *www.sunsetkeycottages.com* ⮑ *40 cottages* ⓞ *Free Breakfast.*

$$ 🖼 **Westwinds Inn.** *B&B/Inn.* This cluster of historic gingerbread-trimmed houses has updated, individually decorated rooms that make you feel right at home with their muted tropical colors and simple furnishings. **Pros:** away from

THE HOLIDAYS KEY WEST STYLE

On New Year's Eve, Key West celebrates the turning of the calendar page with three separate ceremonies that parody New York's dropping-of-the-ball drama. Here they let fall a 6-foot conch shell from Sloppy Joe's Bar, a pirate wench from the towering mast of a tall ship at the Historic Seaport, and a drag queen (elegantly decked out in a ball gown and riding an oversize red high-heel shoe) at Bourbon Street Pub. You wouldn't expect any less from America's most outrageous city.

Key West is one of the nation's biggest party towns, so the celebrations here take on a colorful hue. In keeping with Key West's rich maritime heritage, its monthlong Bight Before Christmas begins Thanksgiving Eve at Key West Bight. The Lighted Boat Parade creates a quintessential Florida spectacle with live music and decorated vessels of all shapes and sizes.

Some years, the Tennessee Williams Theatre hosts a Key West version of *The Nutcracker*. In this unorthodox retelling, the heroine sails to a coral reef and is submerged in a diving bell. (What? No sugarplum fairies?) Between Christmas and New Year's Day, the Holiday House and Garden Tour is another yuletide tradition.

Old Town's bustle; lots of character; affordable rates. **Cons:** small lobby; confusing layout; a long walk from Duval Street. Ⓢ *Rooms from: $210* ✉ *914 Eaton St., Key West* ☎ *305/296–4440, 800/788–4150* ⊕ *www.westwindskeywest.com* ➺ *21 rooms, 4 suites* ⦿ *Free Breakfast.*

NEW TOWN

$$ 🏨 **Best Western Key Ambassador Resort Inn.** *Hotel.* You know what to expect from this chain hotel: well-maintained rooms, predictable service, and competitive prices. **Pros:** big pool area; popular tiki bar serves liquor and food; most rooms have screened-in balconies. **Cons:** roar of airplanes from nearby airport; lacks personality; far from Duval Street. Ⓢ *Rooms from: $300* ✉ *3755 S. Roosevelt Blvd., New Town* ☎ *305/296–3500, 800/432–4315* ⊕ *www.keyambassador.com* ➺ *100 rooms* ⦿ *Free Breakfast.*

$$$$ 🏨 **Key West Marriott Beachside Hotel.** *Hotel.* This hotel vies
FAMILY for convention business with the biggest ballroom in Key West, but it also appeals to families with its spacious condo units decorated with impeccable good taste. **Pros:** private

tanning beach; poolside cabanas; complimentary shuttle to Old Town and airport. **Cons:** no swimming at its beach; lots of conventions and conferences; cookie-cutter facade. [$] *Rooms from: $409* ✉ *3841 N. Roosevelt Blvd., New Town* ☎ *305/296–8100, 800/546–0885* 🌐 *www.keywest-marriottbeachside.com* 🛏 *93 rooms, 93 1-bedroom suites, 10 2-bedroom suites, 26 3-bedroom suites* 🍴 *No meals.*

$$$ ⊡ **Parrot Key Hotel and Resort.** *Hotel.* This revamped destination resort feels like an old-fashioned beach community with picket fences and rocking-chair porches. **Pros:** four pools; finely appointed units; access to marina and other facilities at three sister properties in Marathon. **Cons:** not in walking distance to Old Town; no transportation provided; hefty resort fee. [$] *Rooms from: $355* ✉ *2801 N. Roosevelt Blvd., New Town* ☎ *305/809–2200* 🌐 *www.parrotkeyresort.com* 🛏 *222 units* 🍴 *No meals.*

NIGHTLIFE AND PERFORMING ARTS

NIGHTLIFE

Rest up: much of what happens in Key West occurs after dark. Open your mind and take a stroll. Scruffy street performers strum next to dogs in sunglasses. Characters wearing parrots or iguanas try to sell you your photo with their pet. Brawls tumble out the doors of Sloppy Joe's. Drag queens strut across stages in Joan Rivers garb. Tattooed men lick whipped cream off women's body parts. And margaritas flow like a Jimmy Buffett tune.

NIGHTLIFE TOURS

Best of the Bars. Southernmost Scavenger Hunt's "Best of the Bars" challenge has teams of two to five touring the bars of Key West for clues, libations, and prizes. It hosts the event at 7 pm most Fridays, Saturdays, and Sundays, starting at Sloppy Joe's. ☎ *305/292–9994* 🌐 *www.keywest-hunt.com* 🎟 *$20.*

BARS AND LOUNGES

Capt. Tony's Saloon. When it was the original Sloppy Joe's in the mid-1930s, Hemingway was a regular. Later, a young Jimmy Buffett sang here and made this watering hole famous in his song "Last Mango in Paris." Captain Tony was even voted mayor of Key West. Yes, this place is a beloved landmark. Stop in and take a look at the "hanging tree" that grows through the roof, listen to live music seven nights a week, and play some pool. ✉ *428 Greene St., Key West* ☎ *305/294–1838* ⊕ *www.capttonyssaloon.com.*

Cowboy Bill's Honky Tonk Saloon. Ride the mechanical bucking bull, listen to live bands croon cry-in-your-beer tunes, and grab some pretty decent chow at the indoor-outdoor spread known as Cowboy Bill's Honky Tonk Saloon. There's live music from Tuesday through Saturday. Wednesday brings—we kid you not—sexy bull riding. ✉ *610½ Duval St., Key West* ☎ *305/295–8219* ⊕ *www.cowboybillskw.com.*

Durty Harry's. This megasize entertainment complex is home to eight different bars and clubs, both indoor and outdoor. Their motto is "Eight Famous Bars, One Awesome Night," and they're right. You'll find pizza, dancing, live music, Rick's Key West, and the infamous Red Garter strip club. ✉ *208 Duval St., Key West* ☎ *305/296–5513* ⊕ *www. ricksbarkeywest.com.*

The Garden of Eden. Perhaps one of Duval's more unusual and intriguing watering holes, The Garden of Eden sits atop the Bull & Whistle saloon and has a clothing-optional policy. Most drinkers are lookie-loos, but some actually bare it all, including the barmaids. ✉ *Bull & Whistle Bar, 224 Duval St., Key West* ☎ *305/396–4565.*

Green Parrot Bar. Pause for a libation in the open air and breathe in the spirit of Key West. Built in 1890 as a grocery store, this property has been many things to many people over the years. It's touted as the oldest bar in Key West and the sometimes-rowdy saloon has locals outnumbering out-of-towners, especially on nights when bands play. ✉ *601 Whitehead St., at Southard St., Key West* ☎ *305/294–6133* ⊕ *www.greenparrot.com.*

Hog's Breath Saloon. Belly up to the bar for a cold mug of the signature Hog's Breath Lager at this infamous joint, a must-stop on the Key West bar crawl. Live bands play daily 1 pm–2 am (except when the game's on TV). You never know who'll stop by and perhaps even jump on stage for an impromptu concert (can you say Kenny Chesney?). ✉ *400 Front St., Key West* ☎ *305/296–4222* ⊕ *www.hogs-breath.com.*

Mangoes. On a busy corner right on bustling Duval Street, it's the perfect spot for people-watching and being part of the action. Find a seat at the bar, especially at happy hour, for half-price appetizers and drink deals. ✉ *700 Duval St.,* *corner of Angela St., Key West* ☎ *305/294–8002* ⊕ *www. mangoeskeywest.com.*

Margaritaville Café. A youngish, touristy crowd mixes with aging Parrot Heads. It's owned by former Key West resident and recording star Jimmy Buffett, who has been known to perform here. The drink of choice is, of course, a margarita, made with Jimmy's own brand of Margaritaville tequila. There's live music nightly, as well as lunch and dinner. ⊠ *500 Duval St., Key West* ☎ *305/292–1435* ⊕ *www.margaritavillekeywest.com.*

Pier House. The party here begins at the Beach Bar with live entertainment daily to celebrate the sunset on the beach, then moves to the funky Chart Room. It's small and odd, but there are free hot dogs and peanuts, and its history is worth learning. ⊠ *1 Duval St., Key West* ☎ *305/296–4600, 800/327–8340* ⊕ *www.pierhouse.com.*

Schooner Wharf Bar. This open-air waterfront bar and grill in the historic seaport district retains its funky Key West charm and hosts live entertainment daily. Its margaritas rank among Key West's best, as does the bar itself, voted Best Local's Bar six years in a row. For great views, head up to the second floor and be sure to order up some fresh seafood and fritters and Dark and Stormy cocktails. ⊠ *202 William St., Key West* ☎ *305/292–3302* ⊕ *www.schoonerwharf.com.*

Sloppy Joe's. There's history and good times at the successor to a famous 1937 speakeasy named for its founder, Captain Joe Russell. Decorated with Hemingway memorabilia and marine flags, the bar is popular with travelers and is full and noisy all the time. A Sloppy Joe's T-shirt is a de rigueur Key West souvenir, and the gift shop sells them like crazy. Grab a seat (if you can) and be entertained by the bands and by the parade of people in constant motion. ⊠ *201 Duval St., Key West* ☎ *305/294–5717* ⊕ *www.sloppyjoes.com.*

Two Friends Patio Lounge. Love karaoke? Get it out of your system at Two Friends Patio Lounge, where your performance gets a live Internet feed via the bar's Karaoke Cam. The singing starts at 8:30 pm most nights. The Bloody Marys are famous. ⊠ *512 Front St., Key West* ☎ *305/296–3124* ⊕ *www.twofriendskeywest.com.*

GAY AND LESBIAN BARS

Aqua. Key West's largest gay bar, Aqua hosts karaoke contests, dancing, and live entertainment at three bars, including one outside on the patio. For an evening like no other, come see the Aquanettes at their "Reality is a Drag" show. ✉ *711 Duval St., Key West* ☎ *305/294–0555* ⊕ *www. aquakeywest.com.*

Bourbon Street Complex. Pick your entertainment at the Bourbon Street Complex, a club within an all-male guesthouse. There are 10 video screens along with dancers grooving to the latest music spun by DJs at the Bourbon Street Pub. ✉ *724 Duval St., Key West* ☎ *305/293–9800* ⊕ *www.bourbonstpub.com.*

Island House Café + Bar. Part of a men's resort, Island House Café + Bar serves frozen and other cocktails along with creative cuisine in tropical gardens with a pool where clothing is optional. It is open 24 hours. ✉ *Island House, 1129 Fleming St., Key West* ☎ *305/294–6284, 800/890–6284* ⊕ *www.islandhousekeywest.com.*

La Te Da Hotel and Bar. This venue hosts female impersonators (catch Christopher Peterson when he's on stage) and riotously funny cabaret shows nightly in the Crystal Room Cabaret Lounge ($). There is also live entertainment nightly, featuring a variety of local stars including the ever-popular Debra in the ultracool piano bar. ✉ *1125 Duval St., Key West* ☎ *305/296–6706* ⊕ *www.lateda.com.*

PERFORMING ARTS

Red Barn Theatre. Since the 1980s, the Red Barn Theatre, a small professional theater company, has performed dramas, comedies, and musicals, including works by new playwrights. Big things happen in this little theater, and it's well worth a visit while you're here. ✉ *319 Duval St. (rear), Key West* ☎ *305/296–9911, 866/870–9911* ⊕ *www. redbarntheatre.com.*

South Florida Symphony. Key West native and nationally recognized conductor Sebrina Maria Alfonso directs the South Florida Symphony (formerly the Key West Symphony). This traveling group of symphonic musicians is based in Fort Lauderdale, and performs at the Glynn Archer Performing Arts Center while in Key West. ☎ *954/522–8445* ⊕ *www. southfloridasymphony.org.*

Tennessee Williams Fine Arts Center. On Stock Island, the Tennessee Williams Fine Arts Center presents chamber music, dance, jazz concerts, and dramatic and musical plays with major stars, as well as other performing arts events. ✉ *Florida Keys Community College, 5901 College Rd., Key West* ☎ *305/296–1520 administration, 305/295–7676 box office* ⊕ *twstages.com.*

Tropic Cinema. Catch the classics and the latest art, independent, and foreign films shown daily in this four-screen theater. A full-concession café with beer and wine is available. This is thee place to catch a show in Key West. ✉ *416 Eaton St., Key West* ☎ *305/294–5857, 877/761–3456* ⊕ *www. tropiccinema.com.*

Waterfront Playhouse. Home to the Key West Players, the community-run Waterfront Playhouse is an 1880s ice warehouse that was converted into a 180-seat regional theater presenting comedy and drama from December to May. The troupe first banded together in 1940, counting Tennessee Williams among its members. ✉ *Mallory Sq., Key West* ☎ *305/294–5015* ⊕ *www.waterfrontplayhouse.org.*

SHOPPING

On these streets, you'll find colorful local art of widely varying quality, key limes made into everything imaginable, and the raunchiest T-shirts in the civilized world. Browsing the boutiques—with frequent pub stops along the way—makes for an entertaining stroll down Duval Street. Cocktails certainly help the appreciation of some goods, such as the figurine of a naked man blowing bubbles out his backside or the swashbuckling pirate costumes that are no longer just for Halloween.

Sculpture Key West. Key West bursts with art, especially every year between January and April, when artists unveil their latest works at two exhibitions in Fort Zachary Taylor State Park and West Martello Tower. More than 30 artists from around the country are selected to bring their contemporary sculpture for outdoor exhibitions. In years past, sculptures have ranged from a dinosaur surfacing in a pond and a giant Key West chicken to heads floating in the water and abstract formations suggesting sea and seaside vegetation.

ARTS AND CRAFTS

Key West is filled with art galleries, and the variety is truly amazing. Most of them congregate around the south end of Duval Street. The town's large artist community locally produces much of the art, but many galleries carry international artists from as close as Haiti and as far away as France. Local artists do a great job of preserving the island's architecture and spirit.

Alan S. Maltz Gallery. The owner, declared the state's official wildlife photographer by the Wildlife Foundation of Florida, captures the state's nature and character in stunning portraits. Spend four figures for large-format images on canvas or save on small prints and closeouts. ⊠ *1210 Duval St., Key West* ☎ *305/294–0005* ⊕ *www.alanmaltz.com.*

Art@830. This inviting gallery carries a little bit of everything, from pottery to paintings and jewelry to sculptures. Most outstanding is its selection of glass art, particularly the jellyfish lamps. Take time to admire all that is here. ⊠ *830 Caroline St., Historic Seaport* ☎ *305/295–9595* ⊕ *www. art830.com.*

Frangipani Gallery. Fran Decker, an artist herself, is dedicated to promoting local talent, so this gallery is her longtime dream come true. You'll see Fran's colorful acrylic works that capture the colors of the Keys along with a bevy of tropical paintings, sculptures, ceramics, jewelry, stained glass, and photography. Everyone is invited to Art Stroll, from 6 to 9 pm every first Friday. ⊠ *Upper Duval Art District, 1102 Duval St., Key West* ☎ *305/296–0440* ⊕ *www. frangipanigallery.com.*

Gallery on Greene. This is the largest gallery–exhibition space in Key West and it showcases 37 museum-quality artists. It prides itself on being the leader in the field of representational fine art, painting, sculptures, and reproductions from the Florida Keys and Key West. You can see the love immediately from gallery curator Nancy Frank, who aims to please everyone, from the casual buyer to the established collector. ⊠ *606 Greene St., Key West* ☎ *305/294–1669* ⊕ *www.galleryongreene.com.*

Gingerbread Square Gallery. The oldest private art gallery in Key West represents local and internationally acclaimed artists on an annually changing basis, in media ranging from paintings to art glass. ⊠ *1207 Duval St., Key West* ☎ *305/296–8900* ⊕ *www.gingerbreadsquaregallery.com.*

Key West Pottery. You won't find any painted coconuts here, but you will find a collection of contemporary tropical ceramics. Wife-and-husband owners Kelly Lever and Adam Russell take real pride in this working studio that, in addition to their own creations, features artists from around the country. This is one of the island's few specialty galleries. ⊠ *1203 Duval St., Key West* ☎ *305/900–8303* ⊕ *www. keywestpottery.com.*

Lucky Street Gallery. High-end contemporary paintings are the focus at this gallery that has been in business for over 30 years. There are also a few pieces of jewelry by internationally recognized Key West–based artists. Changing exhibits, artist receptions, and special events make this a lively venue. Although the location has changed, the passionate staff remain the same. ⊠ *1204 White St., Key West* ☎ *305/294–3973* ⊕ *www.luckystreetgallery.com.*

Wyland Gallery. A painter, sculptor, and photographer, Robert Wyland is world renowned for his marine-life art pieces and conservation efforts. You'll get your first glimpse of his work as you enter the Keys; he chose the Bimini Blue paint for the concrete safety walls that stretch from the mainland to Key Largo. At mile marker 99.2, you can't miss *Keys to the Seas,* one of his famed "whaling wall" murals; *Florida's Radiant Reef* is in Marathon, at mile marker 55.5; *Florida's Living Reef* is in Key West at the foot of William Street (Guy Harvey even helped on this one). Get to this gallery to see many incredible works by Wyland and other marine-life artists. You might not be able to afford anything, but it's the equivalent of exploring underwater without getting your hair wet, and a place to experience truly jaw-dropping talent. ⊠ *623 Duval St., Key West* ☎ *305/292–4998* ⊕ *www.wylandkw.com.*

BOOKS

Key West Island Bookstore. This home away from home for the large Key West writers' community carries new, used, and rare titles. It specializes in Hemingway, Tennessee Williams, and South Florida mystery writers. ⊠ *513 Fleming St., Key West* ☎ *305/294–2904* ⊕ *www.keywestislandbooks.com.*

CLOTHING AND FABRICS

Fairvilla Megastore. Don't leave town without a browse through the legendary shop. Although it's not really a clothing store, you'll find an astonishing array of fantasy wear, outlandish costumes (check out the pirate section), as well as other "adult" toys. (Some of the products may make you blush.) ✉ *520 Front St., Key West* ☎ *305/292–0448* ⊕ *www.fairvilla.com.*

Kino Sandals. A pair of Kino sandals was once a public declaration that you'd been to Key West. The attraction? You can watch these inexpensive items being made. The factory has been churning out several styles since 1966. Walk up to the counter, grab a pair, try them on, and lay down some cash. It's that simple. ✉ *107 Fitzpatrick St., Key West* ☎ *305/294–5044* ⊕ *www.kinosandalfactory.com.*

Seam Shoppe. Take home a shopping bag full of scarlet hibiscus, fuchsia heliconias, blue parrotfish, and even pink flamingo fabric, selected from the city's widest selection of tropical-print fabrics. ✉ *1113 Truman Ave., Key West* ☎ *305/296–9830* ⊕ *www.tropicalfabricsonline.com.*

FOOD AND DRINK

Fausto's Food Palace. Since 1926 Fausto's has been the spot to catch up on the week's gossip and to chill out in summer—it has groceries, organic foods, marvelous wines, a sushi chef on duty 8 am–3 pm, and box lunches and dinners-by-the-pound to go. There are two locations you can shop at in Key West (the other is at 1105 White Street) plus a recently opened online store. ✉ *522 Fleming St., Key West* ☎ *305/296–5663* ⊕ *www.faustos.com.*

★ Fodor'sChoice **Kermit's Key West Lime Shoppe.** You'll see Kermit himself standing on the corner every time a trolley passes, pie in hand. Besides pie, his shop carries a multitude of key lime products from barbecue sauce to jelly beans. His prefrozen pies, topped with a special long-lasting whipped cream instead of meringue, travels well. This is a must-stop shop while in Key West. The key lime pie is the best on the island; once you try it frozen on a stick, dipped in chocolate, you may consider quitting your job and moving here. Savor every bite on the outdoor patio-garden area, or come for breakfast or lunch at the on-site café. A smaller second location is on the corner of Duval and Front streets.

✉ *200 Elizabeth St., Historic Seaport* ☎ *305/296–0806, 800/376–0806* ⊕ *www.keylimeshop.com.*

Peppers of Key West. If you like it hot, you'll love this collection of hundreds of sauces, salsas, and sweets guaranteed to heat you up. Take a seat at the tasting bar and see which products light your fire. ✉ *602 Greene St., Key West* ☎ *305/295–9333, 800/597–2823* ⊕ *www.peppersofkey-west.com.*

GIFTS AND SOUVENIRS

Cayo Hueso y Habana. Part museum, part shopping center, this circa-1879 warehouse includes a hand-rolled-cigar shop, one-of-a-kind souvenirs, a Cuban restaurant, and exhibits that tell of the island's Cuban heritage. Outside, a memorial garden pays homage to the island's Cuban ancestors. ✉ *410 Wall St., Mallory Sq., Key West* ☎ *305/293–7260.*

Papa's Pilar Rum Distillery. A beautiful 1879 brick building (formerly a tobacco warehouse) is where you'll find the flagship store and tour for Papa Hemingway's rum distillery. Broaden your rum knowledge and let the distiller be your guide, or just quench your thirst for adventure with a tasting. Either way, you'll see lots of Hemingway memorabilia on display and for sale. The Hemingway Foundation gives a portion of the proceeds to causes that Papa was passionate about, like ocean conservation. ✉ *201 Simonton St., Historic Seaport* ☎ *305/414–8754* ⊕ *www. papaspilar.com* ⌦ *Tour $10.*

HEALTH AND BEAUTY

Key West Aloe. This shop produces hundreds of soap, candle, sunscreen, and skin-care products for men and women. A second location is at 1075 Duval. Soothe your skin from head to toe and slather on natural, tropical products that boast an added boost from science. ✉ *416 Greene St., at Simonton St., Key West* ☎ *305/735–4927, 800/445–2563* ⊕ *www.keywestaloe.com.*

SHOPPING CENTERS

Not sure where to start? There are no malls in Key West, but there is a convenient collection of shops, bars, and restaurants in Old Town.

Bahama Village. Where to start your shopping adventure? This cluster of spruced-up shops, restaurants, and vendors is responsible for the restoration of the colorful historic district where Bahamians settled in the 19th century. The village lies roughly between Whitehead and Fort streets and Angela and Catherine streets. Hemingway frequented the bars, restaurants, and boxing rings in this part of town. ⊠ *Between Whitehead and Fort sts. and Angela and Catherine sts., Key West.*

SPORTS AND THE OUTDOORS

Unlike the rest of the region, Key West isn't known primarily for outdoor pursuits. But everyone should devote at least half a day to relaxing on a boat tour, heading out on a fishing expedition, or pursuing some other adventure at sea. The ultimate excursion is a boat or seaplane trip to Dry Tortugas National Park for snorkeling and exploring Ft. Jefferson. Other excursions cater to nature lovers, scuba divers, and snorkelers, and folks who just want to get out in the water and enjoy the scenery and sunset. For those who prefer land-based recreation, biking is the way to go. Hiking is limited, but walking the streets of Old Town provides plenty of exercise.

AIR TOURS

Conch Republic Air Force. Up to two passengers can fly in a 1942 Waco; tours range from a 15- to 18-minute Best of Key West to a 30- to 35-minute Island and Reef excursion. ⊠ *Key West Airport, 3469 S. Roosevelt Blvd., Key West* ☎ *305/851–8359* ⊕ *www.keywestbiplanes.com* 🖃 *From $200.*

BIKING

Key West was practically made for bicycles, but don't let that lull you into a false sense of security. Narrow and one-way streets along with car traffic result in several bike accidents a year. Some hotels rent or lend bikes to guests; others will refer you to a nearby shop and reserve a bike for you. Rentals usually start at about $12 a day, but some places also rent by the half day. ■ TIP➔ **Lock up; bikes—and porch chairs!—are favorite targets for local thieves.**

A&M Rentals. Rent beach cruisers with large baskets, scooters, and electric mini-cars. Look for the huge American flag on the roof, or call for free airport, ferry, or cruise-ship pickup. A second location is on South Street. ⌂ *523 Truman Ave., Key West* ☎ *305/294–0399* ⊕ *www.amscoot-erskeywest.com* 🚲 *Bicycles from $15, scooters from $35, electric cars from $139.*

Eaton Bikes. Tandem, three-wheel, and children's bikes are available in addition to the standard beach cruisers and hybrid bikes. Delivery is free for all Key West rentals. ⌂ *830 Eaton St., Key West* ☎ *305/294–8188* ⊕ *www.eatonbikes. com* 🚲 *From $18 per day.*

Moped Hospital. This outfit supplies balloon-tire bikes with yellow safety baskets for adults and kids, as well as scooters and even double-seater scooters. ⌂ *601 Truman Ave., Key West* ☎ *305/296–3344, 866/296–1625* ⊕ *www.mopedhos-pital.com* 🚲 *Bicycles from $12 per day, scooters from $35 per day.*

BOATING

Key West is surrounded by marinas, so it's easy to find what you're looking for, whether it's sailing with dolphins or paddling in the mangroves. In addition to its popular kayaking trips, Key West Eco-Tours offers sunset sails and private charters. (*See also Kayaking.*)

★ **Fodor's Choice Classic Harbor Line.** The *Schooner America 2.0* is refined and elegant, and her comfortable seating makes her a favorite when she sails Key West each November–April. Two-hour sunset champagne cruises are an island highlight. Make reservations well in advance. These sailings are popular with locals and visitors. ⌂ *202-R Williams St., Key West* ☎ *305/293–7245* ⊕ *www.sail-keywest.com* 🚲 *Day sails from $55, sunset sails from $85.*

FAMILY **Dancing Dolphin Spirit Charters.** Victoria Impallomeni-Spencer, a wilderness guide and environmental marine science walking encyclopedia, invites up to six nature lovers—especially children—aboard the *Imp II*, a 25-foot Aquasport, for four- and seven-hour ecotours that frequently include encounters with wild dolphins. While island-hopping, you visit underwater gardens and reefs, natural shoreline, and mangrove habitats. For the "Dolphin Day for Humans" tour, you'll be pulled through the water, equipped with mask and snorkel, on a specially designed "dolphin water massage board" that simulates dolphin swimming motions. All equipment is supplied. Captain Victoria is known around these parts as the dolphin whisperer as she's been guiding for over 40 years. ⊠ *MM 5 OS, Murray's Marina, 5710 Overseas Hwy., Key West* ☎ *305/304–7562, 305/745–9901* ⊕ *www. dancingdolphinspirits.com* ⊠ *From $600.*

Wind and Wine Sunset Sail. Of the hundreds of things to do in Key West, this sailing trip is justifiably one of the most popular. Set sail on a historic 65-foot schooner and catch the famous sunset as you drink wines from around the world (eight are presented each sailing, three whites, four reds, and a champagne). Nosh on nibbles like Gouda and crackers, Brie and apples, and sausage rounds, which will hold you over until you grab dinner afterwards. Beer is also available. ⊠ *Margaritaville Marina, 245 Front St., Key West* ☎ *305/304–7999* ⊕ *www.dangercharters.com* ⊠ *$85.*

FISHING

Any number of local fishing guides can take you to where the big ones are biting, either in the backcountry for snapper and snook or to the deep water for the marlins and shark that lured Hemingway here.

Key West Bait & Tackle. Prepare to catch a big one with the live bait, frozen bait, and fishing equipment provided here. They even offer rod and reel rentals (starting at $15 for one day, $5 each additional day). Stop by their on-site Live Bait Lounge where you can sip $3.25 ice-cold beer while telling fish tales. ⊠ *241 Margaret St., Key West* ☎ *305/292–1961* ⊕ *www.keywestbaitandtackle.com.*

Key West Pro Guides. This outfitter offers private charters, and you can choose four-, five-, six-, or eight-hour trips. Choose from flats, backcountry, reef, offshore fishing, and even specialty trips to the Dry Tortugas. Whatever your fishing (even spearfishing) pleasure, their captains will hook you up. ⊠ *G–31 Miriam St., Key West* ☎ *866/259–4205* ⊕ *www.keywestproguides.com* ⊠ *From $450.*

GOLF

Not in the least a golfing destination, Key West does have one course on Stock Island.

Key West Golf Club. Key West isn't a major golf destination, but there is one course on Stock Island designed by Rees Jones that will downright surprise you with its water challenges and tropical beauty. It's also the only "Caribbean" golf course in the United States, boasting 200 acres of unique Florida foliage and wildlife. Hole 8 is the famous "Mangrove Hole," which will give you stories to tell. It's a 143-yard par 3 that is played completely over a mass of mangroves with their gnarly roots and branches completely intertwined. Bring extra balls and book your tee time early in season. Nike rental clubs are available. ⊠ *6450 E. College Rd., Key West* ☎ *305/294–5232* ⊕ *www.keywestgolf.com* 🖙 *$55–$99* 🏌 *18 holes, 6500 yards, par 70.*

KAYAKING

Key West Eco-Tours. Key West is surrounded by marinas, so it's easy to find a water-based activity or tour, whether it's sailing with dolphins or paddling in the mangroves. These sail-kayak-snorkel excursions take you into backcountry flats and mangrove forests without the crowds. The 4½-hour trip includes a light lunch, equipment, and even dry camera bags. Private sunset sails, backcountry boating adventures, kayak, and paddleboard tours are available, too. ⊠ *Historic Seaport behind Turtle Kraals, 231 Margaret St., Key West* ☎ *305/294–7245* ⊕ *www.keywestecotours. com* 🖙 *From $115.*

Lazy Dog. Take a two-hour backcountry mangrove ecotour or a four-hour guided sea kayak–snorkel tour around the mangrove islands just east of Key West. Costs include transportation, bottled water, a snack, and supplies, including snorkeling gear. Paddleboard tours, PaddleYoga, and PaddleFit classes are also available, as are maps and rentals for self-touring. ⊠ *5114 Overseas Hwy., Key West* ☎ *305/295– 9898* ⊕ *www.lazydog.com* 🖙 *From $50.*

SCUBA DIVING AND SNORKELING

The Florida Keys National Marine Sanctuary extends along Key West and beyond to the Dry Tortugas. Key West National Wildlife Refuge further protects the pristine waters. Most divers don't make it this far out in the Keys, but if you're looking for a day of diving as a break from the nonstop party in Old Town, expect to pay about $65 and upward for a two-tank dive. Serious divers can book dive trips to the Dry Tortugas. The USS *Vandenberg* is another popular dive spot, known for its world's-first underwater transformative art exhibit on an artificial reef.

Captain's Corner. This PADI-certified dive shop has classes in several languages and twice-daily snorkel and dive trips to reefs and wrecks aboard a 60-foot dive boat, the *Sea Eagle*.

Use of weights, belts, masks, and fins is included. ✉ *125 Ann St., Key West* ☎ *305/296–8865* ⊕ *www.captainscorner. com* 🔁 *From $45.*

Dive Key West. Operating over 40 years, Dive Key West is a full-service dive center that has charters, instruction, gear rental, sales, and repair. You can take either snorkel excursions or scuba trips with this outfit that is dedicated to coral reef education and preservation. ✉ *3128 N. Roosevelt Blvd., Key West* ☎ *305/296–3823* ⊕ *www.divekeywest.com* 🔁 *Snorkeling from $69, scuba from $95.*

FAMILY **Snuba of Key West.** If you've always wanted to dive but never found the time to get certified, Snuba is for you. You can dive safely using a regulator tethered to a floating air tank with a simple orientation. Ride out to the reef on a catamaran, then follow your guide underwater for a one-hour tour of the coral reefs. It's easy and fun. No prior diving or snorkeling experience is necessary, but you must know how to swim and be at least eight years old. The price includes beverages. ✉ *Garrison Bight Marina, Palm Ave. between Eaton St. and N. Roosevelt Blvd., Key West* ☎ *305/292–4616* ⊕ *www.snubakeywest.com* 🔁 *From $109.*

STAND-UP PADDLEBOARDING

SUP Key West. This ancient sport from Hawaii involves a surfboard and a paddle and has quickly become a favorite Florida water sport known as SUP (stand-up paddleboarding). SUP Key West gives lessons and morning, afternoon, or sunset tours of the estuaries. What's more, your tour guides are experts (one's even a PhD) in marine biology and ecology. Call ahead to make arrangements. ✉ *110 Grinnell St., Key West* ☎ *305/240–1426* ⊕ *www.supkeywest.com* 🔁 *From $45.*

EXCURSION TO DRY TORTUGAS NATIONAL PARK

70 miles southwest of Key West.

The Dry Tortugas lie in the central time zone. Key West Seaplane pilots like to tell their passengers that they land 15 minutes before they take off. If you can't do the time-consuming and (by air, at least, expensive) trip, the national park operates an interpretive center in the Historic Seaport at Old Key West Bight.

GETTING HERE AND AROUND

For now, the *Yankee Freedom III* ferryboat departs from a marina in Old Town and does day trips to Garden Key. Key West Seaplane Adventures has half- and full-day trips to the Dry Tortugas, where you can explore Ft. Jefferson, built in 1846, and snorkel on the beautiful protected reef. Departing from the Key West airport, the flights include soft drinks and snorkel equipment for $265 half-day, $465 full-day, plus there's a $15 park fee (cash only). If you want to explore the park's other keys, look into renting a boat or hiring a private charter. The Dry Tortugas National Park and Historic Key West Bight Museum at 240 Margaret Street is a way to experience it for free. *See Exploring in Key West.*

Key West Seaplane Adventures. The 35- to 40-minute trip to the Dry Tortugas skims above the trademark window-pane-clear waters of the Florida Keys. The seaplane perspective provides an awesome experience that could result in a stiff neck from craning to look out the window and down from 500 feet above. In the flats that edge Key West, you can spot stingrays, sea turtles, and sharks in the shallow water. In the area dubbed The Quicksands, water plunges to 30-foot depths and sand undulates in dunelike formations. Shipwrecks also festoon these waters; here's where Mel Fisher harvested treasure from the *Atocha* and *Margarita*. His 70-foot work ship, the *Arbutus,* deteriorated and eventually sank at the northern edge of the treasure sites. With its mast poking out above water, it's easy to spot and fun to photograph. From there, the water deepens from emerald hues to shades of deep blue as depths reach 70 feet. Seaplanes of Key West's most popular trip is the half-day option, where you spend about 2½ hours on Garden Key. The seaplanes leave during your stay, so be prepared to carry all of your possessions with you. The morning trip beats the ferries to the island, so you'll have it to yourself until the others arrive. Snorkeling equipment, soft drinks, and birding lists are supplied. ✉ *3471 S. Roosevelt Blvd., Key West* ☎ *305/615–7429* ⊕ *www.keywestseaplanecharters.com* 🖃 *From $342.*

Yankee Freedom III. The fast, sleek, 110-foot catamaran *Yankee Freedom III* travels to the Dry Tortugas in 2¼ hours. The time passes quickly on the roomy vessel equipped with four restrooms, three warm freshwater showers, and two bars. Stretch out on two decks that are both air-conditioned, with cushioned seating. There is also an open sundeck with sunny and shaded seating. Continental breakfast and lunch are included. On arrival, a naturalist leads a 45-minute guided tour, which is followed by lunch and a free afternoon for swimming, snorkeling (gear included), and exploring. The vessel is ADA-certified for visitors using wheelchairs. The Dry Tortugas lies in the central time zone. ⊠ *Ticket booth, 240 Margaret St., Key West* ☎ *305/294–7009, 800/634–0939* ⊕ *www.drytortugas.com* ⊠ *$180; parking $19 in city garage* ⚲ *Vessel departs from the Ferry Terminal at 100 Grinnell St. in the Historic Seaport.*

EXPLORING

Dry Tortugas National Park. This park, 70 miles off the shores of Key West, consists of seven small islands. Tour the fort; then lay out your blanket on the sunny beach for a picnic before you head out to snorkel on the protected reef. Many people like to camp here ($15 per site for one of eight sites, plus a group site and overflow area; first-come, first-served), but note that there's no freshwater supply and you must carry off whatever you bring onto the island.

The typical visitor from Key West, however, makes it no farther than the waters of Garden Key. Home to 19th-century Ft. Jefferson, it is the destination for seaplane and fast ferry tours out of Key West. With 2½ to 6½ hours to spend on the island, visitors have time to tour the mammoth fort-prison and then cool off with mask and snorkel along the fort's moat wall.

History buffs might remember long-deactivated Ft. Jefferson, the largest brick building in the western hemisphere, as the prison that held Dr. Samuel Mudd, who unwittingly set John Wilkes Booth's leg after the assassination of Abraham Lincoln. Three other men were also held there for complicity in the assassination. Original construction on the fort began in 1846 and continued for 30 years, but was never completed because the invention of the rifled cannon made it obsolete. That's when it became a Civil War prison and later a wildlife refuge. In 1935 President Franklin Roosevelt declared it a national monument for its historic and natural value.

The brick fort acts as a gigantic, almost 16-acre reef. Around its moat walls, coral grows and schools of snapper, grouper, and wrasses hang out. To reach the offshore coral heads requires about 15 minutes of swimming over sea-grass beds. The reef formations blaze with the color and majesty of brain coral, swaying sea fans, and flitting tropical fish. It takes a bit of energy to swim the distance, but the water depth pretty much measures under 7 feet all the way, allowing for sandy spots to stop and rest. (Standing in sea-grass meadows and on coral is detrimental to marine life.)

Serious snorkelers and divers head out farther offshore to epic formations, including Palmata Patch, one of the few surviving concentrations of elkhorn coral in the Keys. Day-trippers congregate on the sandy beach to relax in the sun and enjoy picnics. Overnight tent campers have use of restroom facilities and achieve a total getaway from noise, lights, and civilization in general. Remember that no matter how you get here, the park's $15 admission fee must be paid in cash.

The park has signposted a self-guided tour that takes about 45 minutes. You should budget more time if you're into photography, because the scenic shots are hard to pass up. Ranger-guided tours are also available at certain times. Check in at the visitor center for a schedule. The small office also shows an orientation video, sells books and other educational materials, and, most importantly, provides a blast of air-conditioning on hot days.

Birders in the know bring binoculars to watch some 100,000 nesting sooty terns at their only U.S. nesting site, Bush Key, adjacent to Garden Key. Noddy terns also nest in the spring. During winter migrations, birds fill the airspace so thickly they literally fall from the sky to make their pit stops, birders say. Nearly 300 species have been spotted in the park's seven islands, including frigate birds, boobies, cormorants, and broad-winged hawks. Bush Key is closed to foot traffic during nesting season, January through September. ✉ *Key West* ⊕ *www.nps.gov/drto* 🕮 *$15.*

6

GATEWAYS TO
THE KEYS

ALTHOUGH IT'S POSSIBLE TO FLY into Key West, many people don't, because of the expense and limited number of flights. Furthermore, if you are visiting the Upper or Middle Keys, there is a drive, regardless of which airport you fly into. This means that many visitors flying into Florida to visit the Keys will pass through Miami. In some cases, people choose to stay a while to absorb some of the new luxe hotels, hot nightlife, and stylish restaurants—not to mention the expansive beaches, of which the Keys do not have in abundance. Travelers on more of a budget may want to look a bit farther afield to either Homestead or Florida City, both south of Miami, the two major gateways to both the Keys and the Everglades.

PLANNING

See Travel Smart for information on flights and car rentals in Miami.

HOTELS

If you are looking for the hot spots, then you need look no farther than Miami's South Beach, which is awash with both new high-rises and restored art deco gems. The choices in Homestead and Florida City are more pedestrian, but also friendlier to the wallet and closer to the Keys. Given the driving distance, if you arrive late in Miami, you may just want to sleep before getting an early start to drive down to the Keys; in that case, a basic room may be just what the travel agent ordered.

RESTAURANTS

Miami has a vibrant dining scene, with prices to match, but you can still find reasonably priced local restaurants and chains, mostly outside the trendy South Beach area. Most restaurants south of Miami are small, mom-and-pop establishments serving homey food or local specialties such as alligator, fish, stone crab, frogs' legs, and fresh Florida lobster from the Keys. There are plenty of chain restaurants and fast-food establishments, especially in the Homestead and Florida City areas.

Restaurant and hotel reviews have been shortened. For full information, visit Fodors.com.

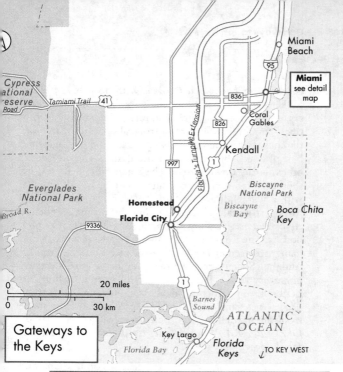

Gateways to the Keys

MIAMI

Updated by Paul Rubio

In the 1950s, Miami was best known for alligator wrestlers and "U-pick" strawberry fields and citrus groves. Well, things have changed. Mainland Miami is now South Florida's commercial hub, while its sultry sister, Miami Beach (America's Riviera), encompasses 17 islands in Biscayne Bay. Seducing winter refugees with its sunshine, beaches, palms, and nightlife, Miami Beach is what most people envision when they think of Miami. Exploring the city will require a car if you intend to go beyond South Beach.

EXPLORING

TOP ATTRACTIONS

FAMILY **Fairchild Tropical Botanic Garden.** With 83 acres of lakes, sunken gardens, a 560-foot vine pergola, orchids, bellflowers, coral trees, bougainvillea, rare palms, and flowering trees, Fairchild is the largest tropical botanical garden in the continental United States. The tram tour highlights the best of South Florida and exotic flora; then you can set off exploring on your own. The 2-acre Simons Rainforest showcases tropical plants from around the world complete with a waterfall and stream. The conservatory is home to rare tropical plants, including the Burmese endemic *Amherstia nobilis,* flowering annually with orchidlike pink flowers. The Keys Coastal Habitat, created in a marsh and mangrove area in 1995 with assistance from the Tropical Audubon Society, provides food and shelter to resident and migratory birds. The excellent bookstore–gift shop carries books on gardening and horticulture, and the Garden Café serves sandwiches and, seasonally, smoothies made from the garden's own crop of tropical fruits. ⊠ *10901 Old Cutler Rd., Coral Gables* ☎ *305/667–1651* ⊕ *www.fairchildgarden.org* ⊠ *$25.*

FAMILY **Jungle Island.** Originally located deep in south Miami and known as Parrot Jungle, South Florida's original tourist attraction opened in 1936 and moved closer to Miami Beach in 2003. Now on Watson Island, a small stretch of land between downtown Miami and South Beach, Jungle Island is far more than a place where cockatoos ride tricycles; this interactive zoological park is home to just about every unusual and endangered species you would want to see (if you are into seeing them in zoo-like settings, that is), including a rare albino alligator, a liger (lion and tiger mix), and myriad exotic birds. With an emphasis on the experiential versus mere observation, the park now offers several new attractions and activities, including private beaches, treetop ziplining, aquatic activities, adventure trails, cultural activities, and enhanced VIP packages where you mingle with an array of furry and feathered friends. Jungle Island offers complimentary shuttle service to most downtown Miami and South Beach hotels. ⊠ *Watson Island, 1111 Parrot Jungle Trail, off MacArthur Causeway (I–395), Downtown* ☎ *305/400–7000* ⊕ *www.jungleisland.com* ⊠ *$39.95, plus $10 parking.*

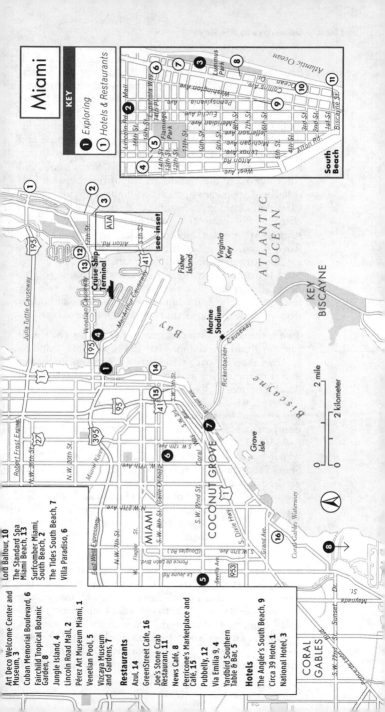

Miami

KEY

1 Exploring

① Hotels & Restaurants

Art Deco Welcome Center and
Museum, **3**
Cuban Memorial Boulevard, **6**
Fairchild Tropical Botanic
Garden, **8**
Jungle Island, **4**
Lincoln Road Mall, **2**
Pérez Art Museum Miami, **1**
Venetian Pool, **5**
Vizcaya Museum
and Gardens, **7**

Lord Balfour, **10**
The Standard Spa
Miami Beach, **13**
Surfcomber Miami,
South Beach, **2**
The Tides South Beach, **7**
Villa Paradiso, **6**

Restaurants

Azul, **14**
GreenStreet Cafe, **16**
Joe's Stone Crab
Restaurant, **11**
News Café, **8**
Perricone's Marketplace and
Café, **15**
Pubbelly, **12**
Via Emilia 9, **4**
Yardbird Southern
Table & Bar, **5**

Hotels

The Angler's South Beach, **9**
Circa 39 Hotel, **1**
National Hotel, **3**

South Beach

Atlantic Ocean

Lummus Park

Ocean Dr.
Collins Ave.
Washington Ave.
Española Way
Lincoln Rd. Mall
Pennsylvania Ave.
Euclid Ave
Meridian Ave.
Jefferson Ave.
Michigan Ave
Lenox Ave.
West Ave.
Alton Rd.

16th St.
15th St.
14th St.
14th Pl.
13th St.
11th St.
9th St.
7th St.
5th St.
4th St.
3rd St.
2nd St.
1st St.

Biscayne St.

Flamingo Park

ATLANTIC OCEAN

Julia Tuttle Causeway

Robert Frost Expwy.

195

Venetian Causeway

MacArthur Causeway

Cruise Ship Terminal

see inset

Alton Rd.

A1A

41

Fisher Island

BISCAYNE

BAY

Marine Stadium

Rickenbacker Causeway

Virginia Key

KEY BISCAYNE

ATLANTIC OCEAN

N.W. 36th St.
N.W. 20th St.

East-West Expressway

N.W. 7th St.

Miami River

395

W. Flagler St.

MIAMI

S.W. 8th St.

S.W. 2nd St.

Ponce de León Blvd

Le Jeune Rd.
(Douglas Rd.)

Coral Way

S.W. 22nd Ave.
N.W. 17th Ave.
N.W. 12th Ave.

S.W. 17th Ave.

S.W. 27th Ave.
S.W. 32nd Ave.
S.W. 37th Ave.

Sevilla Ave.

Grand Ave.

COCONUT GROVE

Grove Isle

Coral Gables Waterway

CORAL GABLES

S.W. 72nd St.

Sunset Dr.

Maynada St.

Calle de la Luna

0   2 mile
0   2 kilometer

★ Fodor'sChoice **Lincoln Road Mall.** This open-air pedestrian mall
FAMILY flaunts some of Miami's best people-watching. The eclectic
interiors of myriad fabulous restaurants, colorful boutiques,
art galleries, lounges, and cafés are often upstaged by the
bustling outdoor scene. It's here among the prolific alfresco
dining enclaves that you can pass the hours easily behold-
ing the beautiful people. Indeed, outdoor restaurant and
café seating take center stage along this wide pedestrian
road adorned with towering date palms, linear pools, and
colorful broken-tile mosaics. A few of the shops on Lincoln Road are owner-operated boutiques carrying a smart
variety of clothing, furnishings, jewelry, and decorative
elements. But more often you'll find typical upscale chain
stores—Apple Store, Nespresso, Gap, and so on. Lincoln
Road is fun, lively, and friendly for people—old, young,
gay, and straight—and their dogs. Lincoln Road is a great
place to cool down with an icy treat while touring South
Beach. If you visit on a Sunday, stop at one of the many
juice vendors, who'll whip up made-to-order smoothies
from mangoes, oranges, and other fresh local fruits.

Two landmarks worth checking out at the eastern end of
Lincoln Road are the massive 1940s keystone building
at 420 Lincoln Road, which has a 1945 Leo Birchanky
mural in the lobby, and the 1921 Mission-style Miami
Beach Community Church, at Drexel Avenue. The Lincoln
Theatre (541–545 Lincoln Rd.), at Pennsylvania Avenue,
is a classical four-story art deco gem with friezes, which
now houses H&M. At Euclid Avenue there's a monument
to Morris Lapidus, the brains behind Lincoln Road Mall,
who in his nineties watched the renaissance of his whimsical
South Beach creation. At Lenox Avenue, a black-and-white
art deco movie house with a Mediterranean barrel-tile roof
is now the Colony Theater (1040 Lincoln Rd.), where live
theater and experimental films are presented. ⊠ *Lincoln
Rd., between Washington Ave. and Alton Rd., South Beach*
⊕ *www.lincolnroadmall.com.*

★ Fodor'sChoice **Pérez Art Museum Miami**(*PAMM*). Opened in
FAMILY December 2013, the Pérez Art Museum Miami, known
locally as PAMM, shines as the city's first true world-class
museum. This über-high-design architectural masterpiece
on Biscayne Bay is a sight to behold. Double-story, cylin-
drical hanging gardens sway from high atop the museum,
anchored to stylish wood trusses that help create this gotta-
see-it-to-believe-it indoor-outdoor museum. Large sculptures, Asian-inspired gardens, sexy white benches, and steel

frames envelop the property. Inside, the 120,000-square-foot space houses multicultural art from the 20th and 21st centuries, some of which were previously on display at the Miami Art Museum. (Note: downtown's Miami Art Museum no longer exists, and the collection has now been incorporated into PAMM.) Most of the interior space is devoted to temporary exhibitions, which have included the likes of *Ai Weiwei: According to What?* and *Edouard Duval-Carrié: Imagined Landscapes.* Even if you aren't a "museum type," come check out this magnum opus over lunch at Verde at PAMM, the museum's sensational waterfront restaurant and bar. ■TIP→ **Admission is free every first Thursday of the month and every second Saturday of the month.** ⊠ *1103 Biscayne Blvd., Downtown* ☎ *305/375–3000* ⊕ *www.pamm.org* 🖾 *$16* ⊘ *Closed Wed.*

FAMILY **Venetian Pool.** Sculpted from a rock quarry in 1923 and fed by artesian wells, this 820,000-gallon municipal pool had a major face-lift in 2010 and again in 2015. It remains quite popular because of its themed architecture—a fantasy version of a waterfront Italian village—created by Denman Fink. The pool has earned a place on the National Register of Historic Places and showcases a nice collection of vintage photos depicting 1920s beauty pageants and swank soirees held long ago. Paul Whiteman played here, Johnny Weissmuller and Esther Williams swam here, and you should, too (but no kids under age three—no exceptions). A snack bar, lockers, and showers make this must-see user-friendly as well, and there's free parking across De Soto Boulevard. ⊠ *2701 De Soto Blvd., at Toledo St., Coral Gables* ☎ *305/460–5306* ⊕ *www.coralgables.com* 🖾 *$13.*

★ **Fodor's Choice Vizcaya Museum and Gardens.** Of the 10,000 people living in Miami between 1912 and 1916, about 1,000 of them were gainfully employed by Chicago industrialist James Deering to build this European-inspired residence. Once comprising 180 acres, this National Historic Landmark now occupies a 30-acre tract that includes a rockland hammock (native forest) and more than 10 acres of formal gardens with fountains overlooking Biscayne Bay. The house, open to the public, contains 70 rooms, 34 of which are filled with paintings, sculpture, antique furniture, and other fine and decorative arts. The collection spans 2,000 years and represents the Renaissance, baroque, rococo, and neoclassical periods. The 90-minute self-guided Discover Vizcaya Audio Tour is available in multiple languages for an additional $5. Moonlight tours, offered on evenings that are nearest the full moon, provide a magical look at the gardens; call for reservations. ✉ *3251 S. Miami Ave., Coconut Grove* ☎ *305/250–9133* ⊕ *www.vizcaya.org* 💲 *$18* ☉ *Closed Tues.*

WORTH NOTING

Art Deco Welcome Center and Museum. Run by the Miami Design Preservation League, the center provides information about the buildings in the district. An official art deco Museum opened within the center in October 2014, and an improved gift shop sells 1930s–50s art deco memorabilia, posters, and books on Miami's history. Several tours—covering Lincoln Road, Española Way, North Beach, and the entire Art Deco District, among others—start here. You can choose from a self-guided iPod audio tour or join one of the regular morning walking tours at 10:30 every day. On Thursday a second tour takes place at 6:30 pm. Pre-purchase tickets online and arrive at the center 15 minutes beforehand; all tours leave from the gift shop. All of the options provide detailed histories of the art deco hotels as well as an introduction to the art deco, Mediterranean revival, and Miami Modern (MiMo) styles found within the Miami Beach Architectural Historic District. Don't miss the special boat tours during Art Deco Weekend, in early January. ✉ *1001 Ocean Dr., South Beach* ☎ *305/672–2014, 305/531–3484 for tours* ⊕ *www.mdpl.org* 💲 *Tours $25.*

Cuban Memorial Boulevard. Four blocks in the heart of Little Havana are filled with monuments to Cuba's freedom fighters. South of Calle Ocho (8th Street), Southwest 13th Avenue becomes a ceiba tree–lined parkway known as Cuban Memorial Boulevard, divided at the center by a narrow grassy mall with a walking path through the various memorials. Among them is the *Eternal Torch of the Brigade 2506*, blazing with an endless flame and commemorating those who were killed in the failed Bay of Pigs invasion of 1961. Another is a bas-relief map of Cuba depicting each of its *municipios*. There's also a bronze statue in honor of Nestory (Tony) Izquierdo, who participated in the Bay of Pigs invasion and served in Nicaragua's Somozan forces. ✉ *S.W. 13th Ave., between S.W. 8th and S.W. 12th sts., Little Havana.*

BEACHES

Almost every east–west side street in Miami Beach dead-ends at the ocean. Sandy shores also stretch along the southern side of the Rickenbacker Causeway to Key Biscayne, where you'll find more popular beaches. Greater Miami is best known for its ocean beaches, but there's freshwater swimming here, too, in pools and lakes. Below are the highlights for the get-wet set.

CORAL GABLES

FAMILY **Matheson Hammock Park and Beach.** Kids love the gentle waves and warm (albeit often murky) waters of this beach in Coral Gables's suburbia, near Fairchild Tropical Botanic Garden. But the beach is only part of the draw—the park includes a boardwalk trail, a playground, and a golf course. Plus, the park is a prime spot for kiteboarding. The man-made lagoon, or "atoll pool," is perfect for inexperienced swimmers, and it's one of the best places in mainland Miami for a picnic. Most tourists don't make the trek here; this park caters more to locals who don't want to travel all the way to Miami Beach. The park also offers a full-service marina. ■TIP→ **With an emphasis on family fun, it's not the best place for singles. Amenities:** parking (fee); toilets. **Best for:** swimming. ⊠ *9610 Old Cutler Rd., Coral Gables* ☎ *305/665–5475* ⊕ *www.miamidade.gov/parks/matheson-hammock. asp* ☜ *$5 per vehicle weekdays, $7 weekends.*

KEY BISCAYNE

★ **Fodor's** Choice **Bill Baggs Cape Florida State Park.** Thanks to inviting beaches, sunsets, and a tranquil lighthouse, this park at Key Biscayne's southern tip is worth the drive. In fact, the 1-mile stretch of pure beachfront has been named several times in Dr. Beach's revered America's Top 10 Beaches list. It has 18 picnic pavilions available as daily rentals, two cafés that serve light lunches that include several Cuban specialties, and plenty of space to enjoy the umbrella and chair rentals. A stroll or ride along walking and bicycle paths provides wonderful views of Miami's dramatic skyline. From the southern end of the park you can see a handful of houses rising over the bay on wooden stilts, the remnants of Stiltsville, built in the 1940s and now protected by the Stiltsville Trust. The nonprofit group was established in 2003 to preserve the structures, because they showcase the park's rich history. Bill Baggs has bicycle rentals, a playground, fishing piers, and guided tours of the **Cape Florida Lighthouse,** South Florida's oldest structure. The lighthouse was erected in 1845 to replace an earlier one damaged in an 1836 Seminole attack, in which the keeper's helper was killed. Free tours are offered at the restored cottage and lighthouse at 10 am and 1 pm, Thursday to Monday. Be there a half hour beforehand. **Amenities:** food and drink; lifeguards; parking (no fee); showers; toilets. **Best for:** solitude; sunset; walking. ⊠ *1200 S. Crandon Blvd., Key Biscayne* ☎ *305/361–5811* ⊕ *www.floridastateparks.org/ park/Cape-Florida* ⛱ *$8 per vehicle; $2 per pedestrian.*

SOUTH BEACH

★ **Fodor's Choice South Beach.** A 10-block stretch of white sandy beach hugging the turquoise waters along Ocean Drive from 5th to 15th Street is one of the most popular in America, known for drawing unabashedly model-like sunbathers and posers. With the influx of new luxe hotels and hot spots from 1st to 5th and 16th to 25th Street, the South Beach stand-and-pose scene is now bigger than ever and stretches yet another dozen-plus blocks. The beaches crowd quickly on the weekends with a blend of European tourists, young hipsters, and sun-drenched locals. Separating the sand from the traffic of Ocean Drive is palm-fringed **Lummus Park,** with its volleyball nets and chickee huts (huts made of palmetto thatch over a cypress frame) for shade. The beach at **12th Street** is popular with gays, in a section often marked with rainbow flags. Locals hang out on 3rd Street beach, in an area called **SoFi** (South of Fifth) where they watch fit Brazilians play foot volley, a variation of volleyball that uses everything but the hands. Because much of South Beach leans toward skimpy sunning—women are often in G-strings and casually topless—many families prefer the tamer sections of Mid- and North Beach (save Haulover nude beach). Metered parking spots next to the ocean are a rare find. Instead, opt for a public garage a few blocks away and enjoy the people-watching as you walk to find your perfect spot on the sand. **Amenities:** food and drink; lifeguards; parking (fee); showers; toilets. **Best for:** partiers; sunrise; swimming; walking. ⊠ *Ocean Dr. from 5th to 15th St., then Collins Ave. to 25th St., South Beach.*

WHERE TO EAT

Because Miami dining is a part of the trendy nightlife scene, most dinners don't start until 8 or 9 pm and may go well into the night. To avoid a long wait among the late-night partiers at hot spots, arrive before 7 or make reservations. Attire is usually casual chic, but patrons like to dress to impress. When you get your bill, check whether a gratuity is already included; most restaurants add between 15% and 20% (ostensibly for the convenience of, and protection from, the many Latin American and European tourists who are used to this practice in their homelands), but supplement it depending on your opinion of the service.

$$$$ ✕ **Azul.** *Eclectic.* A restaurant known for producing celebrity chefs and delivering dining fantasies of Food Network proportions, Azul is a Miami foodie institution. With its *Forbes* five-star, award-winning team, Azul offers a haute-cuisine experience on par with a two– or three–Michelin star restaurant. **Known for:** special-occasion dining; gastronomic excellence; sublime bayside views. [$] *Average main: $48* ✉ *Mandarin Oriental, Miami, 500 Brickell Key Dr., Downtown* ☎ *305/913–8358* 🌐 *www.mandarinoriental.com/miami* ⏲ *Closed Sun. and Mon. No lunch.*

$$ ✕ **GreenStreet Cafe.** *Mediterranean.* A tried-and-true locals' hangout since it was founded in the early 1990s—with regulars including athletes, politicians, entrepreneurs, artists, and other prominent area names—this cozy café serves up simple French-Mediterranean delights. Despite the restaurant's see-and-be-seen reputation, diners are encouraged to sit back and simply enjoy the experience with relaxed decor, good food, and friendly service. **Known for:** fruity cocktails; great breakfast; late-night lounging and noshing. [$] *Average main: $17* ✉ *3468 Main Hwy., Coconut Grove* ☎ *305/444–0244* 🌐 *www.greenstreetcafe.net.*

★ **Fodor'sChoice** ✕ **Joe's Stone Crab Restaurant.** *Seafood.* In South
$$$$ Beach's decidedly new-money scene, the stately Joe's Stone Crab is an old-school testament to good food and good service. Stone crabs, served with legendary mustard sauce, crispy hash brown potatoes, and creamed spinach, remain the staple. **Known for:** the best of the best stone crab claws; long waits (up to three hours on weekends); decadent side dishes. [$] *Average main: $49* ✉ *11 Washington Ave., South Beach* ☎ *305/673–0365, 305/673–4611 for takeout* 🌐 *www.joesstonecrab.com* ⏲ *No lunch Sun. and Mon. and mid-May–mid-Oct.*

$$ ✕ **News Café.** *American.* No first-time trip to Miami is complete without a stop at this Ocean Drive landmark, though the food is nothing special. The 24-hour café attracts a crowd with snacks, light meals, drinks, periodicals, and the people parade on the sidewalk out front. **Known for:** late-night and early-morning dining; people-watching;

newspaper selection. $ *Average main: $18* ✉ *800 Ocean Dr., South Beach* ☎ *305/538–6397* 🌐 *www.newscafe.com.*

$$$ ✕ **Perricone's Marketplace and Café.** *Italian.* Brickell Avenue south of the Miami River is a haven for Italian restaurants, and this lunch place for local bigwigs is arguably the best and most popular. It's housed partially outdoors and partially indoors in an 1880s barn that was brought down from Vermont. **Known for:** rustic setting; tree-lined garden seating area; excellent Italian food. $ *Average main: $22* ✉ *Mary Brickell Village, 15 S.E. 10th St., Downtown* ☎ *305/374–9449* 🌐 *www.perricones.com.*

★ $$$ **Fodor's Choice** ✕ **Pubbelly.** *Eclectic.* This petite eatery, on a residential street in SoBe's western reaches, still attracts the "who's who" of beach socialites, hipsters, and the occasional tourist coming to chow down on inventive Asian-Latin small plates, dumplings, charcuterie, and seasonal large plates by executive chef–owner Jose Mendin. From bay scallops "à la escargot" to short-rib tartare, Pubbelly constantly pushes the envelope on inventive cuisine, and locals simply can't get enough. **Known for:** chef's tasting menu; hypercreative "pb culture" small plates; modern dim sum. $ *Average main: $28* ✉ *1418 20th St., South Beach* ☎ *305/532–7555* 🌐 *www.pubbellyboys.com/miami/pubbelly.*

★ $$ **Fodor's Choice** ✕ **Via Emilia 9.** *Italian.* If you're longing for a *true* taste of Italy and a respite from the overpriced SoBe dining scene, head to this adorable hole-in-the-wall restaurant off Alton Road. It is owned and operated by Italian chef Wendy Cacciatori and his lovely wife. **Known for:** authentic Italian fare; homemade flatbreads; variety of stuffed pastas. $ *Average main: $17* ✉ *1120 15th St., South Beach* ☎ *786/216–7150* 🌐 *www.viaemilia9.com.*

$$$ ✕ **Yardbird Southern Table & Bar.** *Southern.* There's a helluva lot of Southern lovin' from the Lowcountry at this lively and funky South Beach spot. Miami's A-list puts calorie-counting aside for decadent nights filled with comfort foods and innovative drinks. **Known for:** high-calorie delights; Mama's chicken biscuits; 27-hour marinated fried chicken. $ *Average main: $30* ✉ *1600 Lenox Ave., South Beach* ☎ *305/538–5220* 🌐 *www.runchickenrun.com.*

WHERE TO STAY

South Beach is the center of the action in Miami Beach, but it's also expensive. If you are looking for a budget-conscious hotel, you'll almost certainly have to choose one that's a few blocks from the beach rather than one located right across the street.

$$$ 🏨 **The Angler's South Beach.** *Hotel.* This boutique hotel, one of several in Miami under the Kimpton brand, has an air of serenity and privacy that pervades this discreet little oasis of personality-driven villas (built in 1930 by architect Henry Maloney) and modern tower units, together capturing the feel of a sophisticated private Mediterranean villa community. **Pros:** gardened private retreat; excellent service; daily complimentary wine hour. **Cons:** on busy Washington Avenue; not directly on beach. [$] *Rooms from: $379* ✉ *660 Washington Ave., South Beach* ☎ *305/534–9600* 🌐 *www.anglershotelmiami.com* 🛏 *44 rooms* 🍴 *No meals.*

$ 🏨 **Circa 39 Hotel.** *Hotel.* Located in the heart of Mid-Beach, this stylish yet affordable boutique hotel pays attention to every detail and gets them all right, with amenities that include a swimming pool and sundeck complete with cabanas and umbrella-shaded chaises that invite all-day lounging. **Pros:** affordable; beach chairs provided; art deco fireplace. **Cons:** not on the beach side of Collins Avenue. [$] *Rooms from: $170* ✉ *3900 Collins Ave., Mid-Beach* ☎ *305/538–4900* 🌐 *www.circa39.com* 🛏 *96 rooms* 🍴 *No meals.*

$$ 🏨 **National Hotel.** *Hotel.* Fully renovated in 2014, the National Hotel maintains its distinct art deco heritage —the chocolate- and ebony-hue pieces in the lobby date back to the 1930s, and the baby grand piano headlines the throwback Blues Bar—while trying to keep up with SoBe's glossy newcomers. **Pros:** stunning pool; perfect location; Blues Bar. **Cons:** street noise on the weekends; smaller rooms in art deco tower; $19/daily resort fee. [$] *Rooms from: $295* ✉ *1677 Collins Ave., South Beach* ☎ *305/532–2311, 800/327–8370 reservations* 🌐 *www.nationalhotel.com* 🛏 *152 rooms* 🍴 *No meals.*

$$ 🏨 **Room Mate Lord Balfour.** *Hotel.* Quickly making a name for itself in South Beach's emerging SoFi (South of Fifth) neighborhood, the luxurious, boutique, and retro-chic Lord Balfour hotel—part of the Spain's RoomMate brand—exudes style, sophistication, and the full-throttle, present-day Miami Beach experience. **Pros:** great European crowd; whimsical interior design; excellent service. **Cons:** rooms on smaller side; occasional street noise from some

rooms; small resort fee. [$] *Rooms from: $219* ✉ *350 Ocean Dr., South Beach* ☎ *855/471–2739, 305/673–0401* 🌐 *www.lordbalfour.room-matehotels.com* 🛏 *64 rooms* 🍴 *No meals.*

$$ 🏨 **The Standard Spa Miami Beach.** *Resort.* An extension of André Balazs's trendy and hip—yet budget-conscious—brand, this shabby-chic boutique spa hotel is a mile from South Beach on an island just over the Venetian Causeway and boasts one of South Florida's most renowned spas, trendiest bars, and hottest pool scenes. **Pros:** free bike and kayak rentals; swank pool scene; great spa. **Cons:** slight trek to South Beach; small rooms with no views. [$] *Rooms from: $263* ✉ *40 Island Ave., Belle Isle* ☎ *305/673–1717* 🌐 *www.standardhotels.com* 🛏 *105 rooms* 🍴 *No meals.*

$$ 🏨 **Surfcomber Miami, South Beach.** *Hotel.* As part of the hip Kimpton Hotel group, South Beach's legendary Surfcomber hotel reflects a vintage luxe aesthetic and an oceanside freshness, as well as a reasonable price point that packs the place with a young, sophisticated, yet unpretentious crowd. **Pros:** stylish but not pretentious; pet-friendly; on the beach. **Cons:** small bathrooms; front desk often busy. [$] *Rooms from: $279* ✉ *1717 Collins Ave., South Beach* ☎ *305/532–7715* 🌐 *www.surfcomber.com* 🛏 *186 rooms* 🍴 *No meals.*

$$$$ 🏨 **The Tides South Beach.** *Hotel.* The Tides South Beach, which celebrated its 80th anniversary in 2016, is an exclusive Ocean Drive art deco hotel of all ocean-facing suites adorned with soft pinks and corals, gilded accents, and marine-inspired decor. **Pros:** superior service; great beach location; ocean views from all suites plus the terrace restaurant (where we recommend cocktails only). **Cons:** tiny elevators; on touristy Ocean Drive; taxidermy in rooms and common areas. [$] *Rooms from: $445* ✉ *1220 Ocean Dr., South Beach* ☎ *305/604–5070* 🌐 *www.tidessouthbeach.com* 🛏 *45 suites* 🍴 *No meals.*

$ 🏨 **Villa Paradiso.** *B&B/Inn.* This hotel is one of South Beach's best deals for budget travelers (and for those who don't plan on lingering in their rooms all day), with huge (but basic) rooms with kitchens and a charming tropical courtyard with benches for hanging out at all hours. **Pros:** great hangout spot in courtyard; good value; great location. **Cons:** no pool; no restaurant; not trendy. [$] *Rooms from: $139* ✉ *1415 Collins Ave., South Beach* ☎ *305/532–0616* 🌐 *www.villaparadisohotel.com* 🛏 *17 rooms* 🍴 *No meals.*

NIGHTLIFE

One of Greater Miami's most popular pursuits is barhopping. Bars range from intimate enclaves to showy see-and-be-seen lounges to loud, raucous frat parties. There's a New York–style flair to some of the newer lounges, which are increasingly catering to the Manhattan party crowd who escape to South Beach for long weekends. Undoubtedly, Miami's pulse pounds with nonstop nightlife that reflects the area's potent cultural mix. On sultry, humid nights with the huge full moon rising out of the ocean and fragrant night-blooming jasmine intoxicating the senses, who can resist Cuban salsa with some disco and hip-hop thrown in for good measure? When this place throws a party, hips shake, fingers snap, and bodies touch. It's no wonder many clubs are still rocking at 5 am. If you're looking for a relatively nonfrenetic evening, your best bet is one of the chic hotel bars on Collins Avenue.

How to get past the velvet ropes at the hottest South Beach nightspots? First, if you're staying at a hotel, use the concierge. Decide which clubs you want to check out (consult *Ocean Drive* magazine's celebrity pages if you want to be among the glitterati), and the concierge will email, fax, or call in your names to the clubs so you'll be on the guest list when you arrive. This means much easier access and usually no cover charge (which can be upward of $20) if you arrive before midnight. Guest list or no guest list, follow these pointers: Make sure there are more women than men in your group. Dress up—casual chic is the dress code. For men this means no sneakers, no shorts, no sleeveless vests, and no shirts unbuttoned past the top button. For women, provocative and seductive is fine; overly revealing is not. Black is always right. At the door: Don't name-drop—no one takes it seriously. Don't be pushy while trying to get the doorman's attention. Wait until you make eye contact, and then be cool and easygoing. If you decide to tip him (which most bouncers don't expect), be discreet and pleasant, not big-bucks obnoxious—a $10 or $20 bill quietly passed will be appreciated, however.

SHOPPING

Beyond its fun-in-the-sun offerings, Miami has evolved into a world-class shopping destination. People fly to Miami from all over the world just to shop. The city teems with sophisticated malls—from multistory, climate-controlled temples of consumerism to sun-kissed, open-air retail enclaves—and bustling avenues and streets, lined at once with affordable chain stores, haute couture boutiques, and one-off "only in Miami"–type shops.

Give your plastic a workout in South Beach shopping at the many high-profile tenants on this densely packed stretch of **Collins Avenue** between 5th and 10th streets, with stores like Steve Madden, Club Monaco, The Webster, MAC Cosmetics, Ralph Lauren, and Intermix. Sprinkled among the upscale vendors are hair salons, spas, cafés, and such familiar stores as The Gap and Sephora. Be sure to head over one street east to Ocean Drive or west to Washington Avenue for a drink or a light bite, or go for more retail therapy on Lincoln Road.

The eight-block-long pedestrianized **Lincoln Road Mall** between Alton Road and Washington Avenue is the trendiest place on Miami Beach. Home to more than 200 shops, art galleries, restaurants and cafés, and the renovated Colony Theatre, Lincoln Road is like the larger, more sophisticated cousin of Ocean Drive. The see-and-be-seen theme is furthered by outdoor seating at every restaurant, where tourists and locals lounge and discuss the people (and pet) parade passing by. An 18-screen movie theater anchors the west end of the street, which is where most of the worthwhile shops are; the far east end is mostly discount and electronics shops. Due to higher rents, you are more likely to see big corporate stores like Armani, H&M, and Victoria's Secret than original boutiques. However, a few emporiums and stores with unique personalities, like Alchemist, Base, and Books & Books, remain.

HOMESTEAD

Updated by Lynne Helm

30 miles southwest of Miami.

Since recovering from Hurricane Andrew in 1992, Homestead has redefined itself as a destination for tropical agro- and ecotourism. At a crossroads between Miami and the Keys as well as Everglades and Biscayne National Parks, the area has the added dimension of shopping centers, residential development, hotel chains, and the Homestead-Miami Speedway—when car races are scheduled, hotels hike rates and require minimum stays. The historic downtown has become a preservation-driven Main Street. Krome Avenue, where it cuts through the city's heart, is lined with restaurants, an arts complex, antiques shops, and low-budget, sometimes undesirable, accommodations. West of north–south Krome Avenue, miles of fields grow fresh fruits and vegetables. Some are harvested commercially, and others beckon with "U-pick" signs. Stands selling farm-fresh produce and nurseries that grow and sell orchids and tropical plants abound. In addition to its agricultural legacy, the town has an eclectic flavor, attributable to its population mix: descendants of pioneer Crackers, Hispanic growers and farm workers, professionals escaping the Miami hubbub, and latter-day northern retirees.

EXPLORING

★ Fodor'sChoice **Dante Fascell Visitor Center.** Go outside on the
FAMILY wide veranda to soak up views across mangroves and Biscayne Bay at this Convoy Point visitor center, which opened in 2002. Inside the museum, artistic vignettes and on-request videos including the 11-minute *Spectrum of Life* explore the park's four ecosystems, while the Touch Table gives both kids and adults a feel for bones, feathers, and coral. Facilities include the park's canoe and tour concession, restrooms with showers, a ranger information area, gift shop with books, and vending machines. Various ranger programs take place daily during busy fall and winter seasons. Rangers give informal tours on Boca Chita Key, but these must be arranged in advance. A short trail and boardwalk lead to a jetty, and there are picnic tables and grills. This is the only area of the park accessible without a boat. You can snorkel from shore, but the water is shallow, with sea grass and a mud bottom. ⊠ *9700 S.W. 328th St., Homestead* ☎ *305/230–7275* ⊕ *www.nps.gov/bisc* ⊠ *Free.*

★ Fodor'sChoice **Fruit & Spice Park.** Because it officially qualifies
FAMILY for tropical status, this 37-acre park in Homestead's Redland historic agricultural district is the only public botanical garden of its type in the United States. More than 500 varieties of fruit, nuts, and spices typically grow here, and there are 75 varieties of bananas alone, plus 160 of mango. Tram tours (included in admission) run three times daily, and you can sample fresh fruit at the gift shop, which also stocks canned and dried fruits plus cookbooks. The Mango Café, open daily from 11:30 to 4:30, serves mango salsa, smoothies, and shakes along with salads, wraps, sandwiches, and a yummy Mango Passion Cheesecake. Picnic in the garden at tables or on your own blankets. Annual park events include January's Redland Heritage Festival and

June's Summer Fruit Festival. Kids age six and under are free. ✉ *24801 S.W. 187th Ave., Homestead* ☎ *305/247–5727* 🌐 *www.fruitandspicepark.com* 🎫 *$8.*

Schnebly Redland's Winery. Homestead's fruity bounty comes in liquid form at this growing enterprise that began producing wines of lychee, mango, guava, and other fruits as a way to avoid waste from family groves each year—bounty not perfect enough for shipping. Over the years, this grape-free winery (now with a beer brewery, too) has expanded with a reception-tasting indoor area serving snacks and a lush plaza picnic area landscaped in coral rock, tropical plants, and waterfalls—topped with a thatched-roof chickee. Tours and tastings are offered on the weekend. The Ultimate Tasting includes five wines and an etched Schnebly glass you can keep. Redlander Restaurant operates daily with an ever-changing menu. On Sunday, and on other occasions, there's yoga on the lawn. Count on a cover charge at the restaurant after 6 pm on Friday and Saturday nights. ✉ *30205 S.W. 217th Ave., Homestead* ☎ *305/242–1224, 888/717–9463 (WINE)* 🌐 *www.schneblywinery.com* 🎫 *Winery tours (weekends only) $8; tastings $12.95.*

WHERE TO EAT

$ 🍴 **Royal Palm Grill.** *American.* You may have a déjà vu moment if you drive down Krome Avenue, where two Royal Palm Grills are just a hop-skip away from each other. This popular "breakfast all day, every day" enterprise has two locations, only a few blocks apart, to accommodate a steady stream of customers for the aforementioned breakfast fare from omelets and pancakes to biscuits and gravy, plus salads, steaks, and seafood. **Known for:** early open, early close; popular for breakfast; nostalgic setup at the original location. [$] *Average main: $10* ✉ *Royal Palm Pharmacy, 806 N. Krome Ave., Homestead* ☎ *305/246–5701* 🌐 *royalpalmgrillfl.com* 🕒 *No dinner.*

$$ 🍴 **Shiver's BBQ.** *Barbecue.* Piggin' out since the 1960s, Shiver's
FAMILY ranks as a lip-smackin' must for lovers of hickory-smoked barbecue pork, beef, and chicken in assorted forms from baby back ribs to briskets. Longtime owners Martha and Perry Curtis are typically on hand attending to traditions with original recipes, although Martha does offer her new, alternative "secret recipe" sauce. **Known for:** corn-bread soufflé; picnic table seating; popular for takeout. [$] *Average main: $15* ✉ *28001 S. Dixie Hwy., Homestead* ☎ *305/248–2272* 🌐 *www.shiversbbq.com.*

WHERE TO STAY

$ [H] **Hotel Redland.** *Hotel.* Of downtown Homestead's smattering of mom-and-pop lodging options, this historic inn is by far the most desirable with its Victorian-style rooms done up in pastels and reproduction antique furniture. **Pros:** historic character; convenient to downtown and near antiques shops; free Wi-Fi. **Cons:** traffic noise; small rooms. [$] *Rooms from: $120* ✉ *5 S. Flagler Ave., Homestead* ☎ *305/246–1904, 800/595–1904* 🌐 *www.hotelredland.com* 🛏 *13 rooms* 🍴 *No meals.*

SPORTS AND THE OUTDOORS

AUTO RACING

Homestead-Miami Speedway. Buzzing more than 280 days each year, the 600-acre speedway hosts racing, manufacturer testing, car-club events, driving schools, and ride-along programs. The facility has 65,000 grandstand seats, club seating eight stories above racing action, and two tracks—a 2.21-mile continuous road course and a 1.5-mile oval. A packed schedule includes GRAND-AM and NASCAR events. Two tunnels on the grounds are below sea level. Parking includes space for 30,000 vehicles. ✉ *1 Speedway Blvd., Homestead* ☎ *866/409–7223* 🌐 *www.homesteadmiamispeedway.com.*

BOATING

Homestead Bayfront Park. Boaters, anglers, and beachgoers give high ratings to facilities at this recreational area adjacent to Biscayne National Park. The 174-slip Herbert Hoover Marina, accommodating up to 50-foot vessels, has a ramp, dock, bait-and-tackle shop, fuel station, ice, and dry storage. The park also has a snack bar, tidal swimming area, a beach with lifeguards, playground, ramps for people with disabilities, and a picnic pavilion with grills, showers, and restrooms. ✉ *9698 S.W. 328th St., Homestead* ☎ *305/230–3033* 🎟 *$7 per passenger vehicle on weekends; $12 per vehicle with boat Mon.–Thurs., $15 Fri.–Sun.; $15 per RV or bus.*

FLORIDA CITY

Updated by Lynne Helm

2 miles southwest of Homestead.

Florida's Turnpike ends in Florida City, the southernmost town on the Miami-Dade County mainland, spilling thousands of vehicles onto U.S. 1 and eventually west to Everglades National Park, east to Biscayne National Park, or south to the Florida Keys. Although Florida City begins immediately south of Homestead, the difference in towns couldn't be more noticeable. As the last outpost before 18 miles of mangroves and water, this stretch of U.S. 1 is lined with fast-food eateries, service stations, hotels, bars, dive shops, and restaurants. Hotel rates increase significantly during NASCAR races at the nearby Homestead-Miami Speedway. Like Homestead, Florida City is rooted in agriculture, with expanses of farmland west of Krome Avenue and a huge farmers' market that ships produce nationwide.

EXPLORING

Tropical Everglades Visitor Center. Run by the nonprofit Tropical Everglades Visitor Association, this pastel-pink center with teal sign posting offers abundant printed material plus tips from volunteer experts on exploring South Florida, especially Homestead, Florida City, and the Florida Keys. ✉ *160 U.S. 1, Florida City* ☎ *305/245–9180, 800/388–9669* 🌐 *www.tropicaleverglades.com.*

WHERE TO EAT

$ ✕ **Farmers' Market Restaurant.** *Seafood.* Although this eatery is within the farmers' market on the edge of town and is big on serving fresh vegetables, seafood figures prominently on the menu. A family of anglers runs the place, so fish and shellfish are only hours from the sea, and there's a fish fry on Friday night. **Known for:** early opening for breakfast; seafood-centric menu; using fresh produce from the market. [$] *Average main: $13* ✉ *300 N. Krome Ave., Florida City* ☎ *305/242–0008.*

$ ✕ **La Panaderia Favorita.** *Bakery.* To pick up treats for picnics in the Everglades, look no further than La Panaderia Favorita, truly a fave among locals for savory café con leche, seductive sweet rolls, whimsical cookies, breads, and other bakery delights. Early birds appreciate the 5:30 am opening hour. **Known for:** the area's best bakery; a few grocery staples also for sale; early opening. [$] *Average main: $10* ✉ *337 W. Palm Dr., Florida City* ☎ *305/245–0436.*

$$ ✕ **Mutineer Restaurant.** *Seafood.* Families and older couples flock to this kitschy roadside outpost that is shaped like a ship. Florida lobster tails, stuffed grouper, shrimp, and snapper top the menu, along with another half dozen daily seafood specials. **Known for:** family-friendly atmosphere; kitschy decor; the Wharf Lounge, with live entertainment

on weekends. $ *Average main: $20* ✉ *11 S.E. 1st Ave. (U.S. 1), at Palm Dr., Florida City* ☎ *305/245–3377* 🌐 *www.mutineerrestaurant.com.*

WHERE TO STAY

$ 🏨 **Best Western Gateway to the Keys.** *Hotel.* For easy access to Everglades and Biscayne National Parks as well as the Keys, you'll be well situated at this sprawling, two-story motel two blocks off Florida's Turnpike. **Pros:** convenient to parks, outlet shopping, and dining; free Wi-Fi and breakfast; attractive pool area. **Cons:** traffic noise; fills up fast in high season. $ *Rooms from: $135* ✉ *411 S. Krome Ave., Florida City* ☎ *305/246–5100, 888/981–5100* 🌐 *www.bestwestern.com/gatewaytothekeys* 🛏 *114 rooms* 🍴 *Breakfast.*

$ 🏨 **Fairway Inn.** *Hotel.* With a waterfall pool, this two-story motel with exterior room entry has some of the area's lowest chain rates, and it's next to the Chamber of Commerce visitor center so you'll have easy access to tourism brochures and other information. **Pros:** affordable; convenient to restaurants, parks, and raceway. **Cons:** plain, small rooms; no-pet policy. $ *Rooms from: $89* ✉ *100 S.E. 1st Ave., Florida City* ☎ *305/248–4202, 888/340–4734* 🛏 *160 rooms* 🍴 *Breakfast.*

6

$ 🏨 **Quality Inn.** *Hotel.* Amid an asphalt complex of hotels, gas stations, and eateries just off U.S. 1, this two-story Quality Inn with exterior corridors has a friendly front desk staff offering tips on Everglades or Keys adventures, or race action at the nearby track. **Pros:** close to restaurants and services. **Cons:** no elevator; noisy location. $ *Rooms from: $90* ✉ *333 S. E. 1st Ave., Florida City* ☎ *305/248–4009, 888/352–2489* 🌐 *www.qualityinn.com* 🛏 *123 rooms* 🍴 *Breakfast.*

$ 🏨 **Ramada Inn.** *Hotel.* If you're seeking an uptick from other chains, this kid-friendly property offers more amenities and comfort, such as 32-inch flat-screen TVs, free Wi-Fi, duvet-covered beds, closed closets, and stylish furnishings. **Pros:** extra room amenities; convenient location; guest laundry facilities. **Cons:** chain anonymity. $ *Rooms from: $99* ✉ *124 E. Palm Dr., Florida City* ☎ *305/247–8833* 🌐 *www.wyndhamhotels.com* 🛏 *118 rooms* 🍴 *Breakfast.*

$ 🏨 **Travelodge.** *Hotel.* This bargain motor lodge is close to Florida's Turnpike, the Everglades and Biscayne national parks, and Homestead-Miami Speedway. **Pros:** convenience to race track and U.S. 1; nice pool; complimentary breakfast. **Cons:** busy location; some small rooms; no pets. $ *Rooms from: $89* ✉ *409 S.E. 1st Ave., Florida City* ☎ *305/248–9777, 800/758–0618* 🌐 *www.tlflcity.com* 🛏 *88 rooms* 🍴 *Breakfast.*

SHOPPING

FAMILY **Robert Is Here.** Want take-home gifts? This historic fruit stand sells more than 100 types of jams, jellies, honeys, and salad dressings, along with its vegetables, juices, fabulous fresh-fruit milk shakes (try the papaya key lime or guanabana, under $6), and some 30 kinds of tropical fruits, including (in season) carambola, lychee, egg fruit, monstera, sapodilla, dragonfruit, genipa, sugar apple, and tamarind. Back in 1960, the stand got started when pint-size Robert sat at this spot hawking his father's bumper cucumber crop. Now with his own book (*Robert Is Here: Looking East for a Lifetime*), Robert can still be found on the scene daily with wife and kids, shipping nationwide, and donating seconds to needy families. An assortment of animals out back—from goats to iguanas and emus—and a splash pool add to the fun. Picnic tables, benches, and a waterfall with a koi pond provide serenity. It's on the way to Everglades National Park, and Robert opens at 8 am, operating until at least 7, shutting down from Labor Day until November. ✉ *19200 S.W. 344th St., Florida City* ☎ *305/246–1592.*

TRAVEL SMART
FLORIDA KEYS

GETTING HERE AND AROUND

Key West International Airport is the only airport in the Keys that accommodates commercial flights; three major airlines and a few small companies serve the airport. Because flights to Key West can be limited and expensive, most visitors fly into Miami International Airport and either drive to their destination in the Keys or take an air shuttle to Key West. The drive is long and slow. It can be done in a half day, but it's better to break up the drive and spend some time exploring the Keys outside of Key West.

■ TIP→ **Ask the local tourist board about hotel and local transportation packages that include tickets to major museum exhibits or other special events.**

❚ AIR TRAVEL

About 760,000 passengers use Key West International Airport (EYW) each year; its most recent renovation includes a beach where travelers can catch their last blast of rays after clearing security. Because direct flights to Key West are few, many prefer flying into Miami International Airport (MIA) or Fort Lauderdale–Hollywood International Airport (FLL) and driving the 110-mile Overseas Highway (aka U.S. 1).

AIRPORTS

The fittingly tiny, laid-back Key West International Airport (EYW) has greeted domestic passengers and overseas private planes since 1957. The McCoy Terminal sits atop a 475-car parking ramp.

The airport is a short drive from Old Town, so should your flight get delayed (it happens often enough), jump in a taxi and enjoy a few more hours of Key West freedom. Note that ⊕ *www.keywestinternationalairport.com* is *not* the official airport site; it is operated by an outside travel agency.

Contacts Fort Lauderdale–Hollywood International Airport(*FLL*) ✉ *100 Terminal Dr., Fort Lauderdale* ☏ *866/435–9355* ⊕ *www.broward. org/airport.* **Key West International Airport**(*EYW*) . ✉ *3491 S. Roosevelt Blvd., Key West* ☏ *305/809–5200* ⊕ *eyw.com.* **Miami International Airport**(*MIA*). ✉ *N.E. 20th St. and LeJeune Rd., Miami* ☏ *305/876–7000* ⊕ *www.miami-airport.com.*

GROUND TRANSPORTATION

Keys Transportation provides private airport transfers to any destination in the Keys from either MIA or FLL. Prices start at $49 per person for transportation to Key Largo and get more expensive as you move south. Call or email for a price quote.

Greyhound Lines runs a special Keys shuttle twice a day (times depend on the day of the week) from Miami International Airport (departing from Concourse E, lower level) and stops throughout the Keys. Fares run from around $25 for Key Largo (MM 99.6) or Islamorada (Burger King, MM 82) to around $45 for Key West (3535 S. Roosevelt, Key West International Airport).

Keys Shuttle runs scheduled service six times a day in 15-passenger vans (nine passengers maximum) between Miami and Fort Lauderdale airports and Key West with stops throughout the Keys for $60 to $90 per person sharing rides.

SuperShuttle charges $191 for up to two passengers for trips to the Upper Keys; to go farther, you must book an entire 11-person van, which costs $402. For a trip to the airport, place your request 24 hours in advance.

Contacts Greyhound. ☎ *800/231–2222* ⊕ *www.greyhound.com.* **Keys Shuttle.** ✉ *1333 Overseas Hwy., Marathon* ☎ *888/765–9997* ⊕ *www.keysshuttle.com.* **Keys Transportation.** ☎ *305/395–0299* ⊕ *www.keystransportation.com.* **SuperShuttle.** ☎ *800/258–3826* ⊕ *www.supershuttle.com.*

FLIGHTS

American Airlines, Delta, Silver Airways, and United provide service to Key West International Airport. Many other airlines fly to Miami.

Flying time from Miami is 50 minutes, from Orlando just over an hour, and from Atlanta about two hours.

Contacts American Airlines. ☎ *800/433–7300* ⊕ *www.aa.com.* **Delta.** ☎ *800/221–1212 for U.S. reservations, 800/241–4141 for international reservations* ⊕ *www.delta.com.* **Silver Airways.** ☎ *801/401–9100 reservations* ⊕ *www.silverairways.com.* **United.** ☎ *800/864–8331 for U.S. reservations, 800/538–2929 for international reservations* ⊕ *www.united.com.*

▌BOAT AND FERRY TRAVEL

Boaters can travel to and through the Keys either along the Intracoastal Waterway (5-foot draft limitation) through Card, Barnes, and Blackwater sounds and into Florida Bay, or along the deeper Atlantic Ocean route through Hawk Channel, a buoyed passage. Refer to NOAA Nautical Charts Nos. 11451, 11445, and 11441. The Keys are full of marinas that welcome transient visitors, but they don't have enough slips for everyone. Make reservations in advance, and ask about channel and dockage depth—many marinas are quite shallow.

For nonemergency information, contact the Coast Guard Group Key West on VHF-FM Channel 16. Safety and weather information is broadcast at 7 am and 5 pm eastern standard time on VHF-FM Channels 16 and 22A. There are stations in Islamorada and Marathon.

Key West Express operates air-conditioned ferries between the Key West Terminal (Caroline and Grinnell Streets) and Marco Island and Fort Myers Beach. The trip takes at least four hours each way and costs $95 one-way, and from $125 round-trip (a $3 convenience fee is added to all online bookings). Ferries depart from Fort Myers Beach at 8:30 am and from Key West at 6 pm. The Marco Island ferry departs at 8:30 am (the return trip leaves Key West at 5 pm). A photo ID is required for each passenger. Advance reservations are recommended.

Contacts Key West Express. ✉ *100 Grinnell St., Key West* ☎ *239/463–5733* ⊕ *www.keywestexpress.net.*

▮ BUS TRAVEL

The City of Key West Department of Transportation has six color-coded bus routes traversing the island from 6:30 am to 11:30 pm. Stops have signs with the international bus symbol. Schedules are available on buses and at hotels, visitor centers, and shops. The fare is $2 one-way.

The Lower Keys Shuttle bus runs from Marathon to Key West ($4 one-way), with scheduled stops along the way.

Miami Dade Transit provides daily bus service from MM 50 in Marathon to the Florida City Wal-Mart Supercenter on the mainland. The bus stops at major shopping centers as well as on demand anywhere along the route during daily round trips on the hour from 6 am to 10 pm. The cost is $2 one-way, exact change required.

Contacts City of Key West Department of Transportation.

☎ *305/809–3910* ⊕ *www.kwtransit. com.*

▮ CAR TRAVEL

By car from Miami International Airport, follow signs to Coral Gables and Key West, which puts you on LeJeune Road, then Route 836 west. Take the Homestead Extension of Florida's Turnpike south (toll road), which ends at Florida City and connects to the Overseas Highway (U.S. 1). Tolls from the airport run approximately $3. Payment is collected via SunPass, a prepaid toll program, or with Toll-By-Plate, a system that photographs each vehicle's license plate and mails a monthly bill for tolls, plus a $2.50 administrative fee, to the vehicle's registered owner.

Vacationers traveling in their own cars can obtain a mini-SunPass sticker via mail before their trip for $4.99 and receive the cost back in toll credits and discounts. The pass also is available at many major Florida retailers and turnpike service plazas. It works on all Florida toll roads and many bridges. For details on purchasing a mini-SunPass, call or visit the website.

For visitors renting cars in Florida, most major rental companies have programs allowing customers to use the Toll-By-Plate system. Tolls, plus varying service fees, are automatically charged to the credit card used to rent the vehicle (along with a hefty service charge in most cases). For details, including pricing options at participating rental-car agencies, check the program website. Under no circumstances should motorists attempt to stop in high-speed electronic tolling lanes. Travelers can contact Florida's Turnpike Enterprise for more information about the all-electronic tolling on Florida's Turnpike.

The alternative from Florida City is Card Sound Road (Route 905A), which has a (cash-only) bridge toll of $1. SunPass isn't accepted. Continue to the only stop sign and turn right on Route 905, which rejoins the Overseas Highway 31 miles south of Florida City.

Except in Key West, a car is essential for visiting the Keys. The best Keys road map, published by the Homestead–Florida City Chamber of Commerce, can be obtained for $5.50 from the Tropical Everglades Visitor Association.

Avis, Budget, Enterprise, and Hertz serve Marathon Airport. Avis, Alamo, Budget, Dollar, Enterprise, Hertz, National, and Thrifty serve Key West's airport. Enterprise also has an office in Key Largo. ■ TIP→ **Avoid flying into Key West and driving back to Miami; there could be substantial drop-off charges for leaving a Key West car there.**

Contacts Florida's Turnpike Enterprise. ☎ *800/749–7453* ⊕ *www. floridasturnpike.com.* **SunPass.** ☎ *888/865–5352* ⊕ *www.sunpass. com.*

GASOLINE

The deeper you go into the Keys, the higher the pump price goes. Gas stations in Homestead and Florida City have some of the most affordable prices in South Florida, so fill your tank in Miami and top it off in Florida City.

MILE MARKERS

Getting lost in the Keys is almost impossible once you understand the unique address system. Many addresses are simply given as a mile marker (MM) number. The markers are small, green, rectangular signs along the side of the Overseas Highway (U.S. 1). They begin with MM 126, 1 mile south of Florida City, and end with MM 0, in Key West. Keys residents use the abbreviation BS for the bay side of Overseas Highway and OS for the ocean side. From Marathon to Key West, residents may refer to the bay side as the gulf side.

PARKING

The only place in the Keys where parking is a problem is in Old Town in Key West. There are public parking lots that charge by the day (some hotels and B&Bs provide parking or discounts at municipal lots). If you arrive early, you can sometimes find spots on side streets off Duval and Whitehead, where you can park for free—just be sure it's not marked for residential parking only. Your best bet is to bike or take a trolley around town if you don't want to walk. The trolleys allow you to disembark and reboard at will at several different stops. The Conch Tour Train makes only two stops where you can board and disembark.

ROAD CONDITIONS

Most of the Overseas Highway is narrow and crowded (especially on weekends and in high season). Expect delays behind RVs, trucks, cars towing boats, and rubbernecking tourists. The section of highway that travels from the mainland to Key Largo is particularly slow and congested. Occasional passing lanes allow you to get past slow-moving trucks. The quality of local roads in Key West is good, though some side streets are narrow. Traffic in the historic district often becomes congested throughout the day and night.

CAR RENTAL

When you reserve a car, ask about cancellation penalties, taxes, drop-off charges (if you're planning to pick up the car in one city and leave it in another), and surcharges (for being under or over a certain age, for additional drivers, for additional insurance, or for driving across state borders or beyond a specific distance from your point of rental). All these things can add substantially to your costs. Request car seats and extras such as a GPS when you book.

Rates are sometimes—but not always—better if you book in advance or reserve through a rental agency's website. There are other reasons to book ahead, though: for popular destinations, during busy times of the year, or to ensure that you get certain types of cars (vans, SUVs, exotic sports cars).

■TIP➔ Make sure that a confirmed reservation guarantees you a car. Agencies sometimes overbook, particularly for busy weekends and holiday periods.

Unless you fly into Key West and decide to stay in Old Town for your entire vacation—perhaps with a bus trip to another Key or some water-sports excursions—you will need a car. Rentals of all makes and models are available at Miami International Airport, Key West International Airport, and rental agencies throughout the Keys. Reserve your car early during big events such as Homestead-Miami Speedway races (Key Largo is often affected), October's FantasyFest in Key West, and the Christmas and Easter holidays.

▮ TAXI TRAVEL

Serving the Keys from Ocean Reef to Marathon, Luxury Limousine, based in Miami, has luxury Hummers and limos that seat up to eight passengers as well as vans and buses. It'll pick up from any airport in South Florida.

Florida Keys Taxi & Group Transportation operates around the clock in Key West. The fare for two or more from the Key West airport to Old Town is $8 per person. Otherwise, meters register $2.75 for first 1/5 mile, $8 per mile.

Contacts Luxury Limousine.
☎ 855/458–7002 ⊕ www.a1limobus. com.

ESSENTIALS

∎ ACCOMMODATIONS

The most characteristic type of lodging in the Keys is a small, family-owned place, whether it be a guesthouse in Key West or a dive lodge in Key Largo. The islands do have their share of franchised operations and big destination resorts, but intimate lodging is still quite easy to find throughout the Keys. This is particularly true in Key West's Old Town, where many of the historic Victorian homes have been transformed into B&Bs. Most serve only continental breakfast (a restaurant license is required to serve hot food).

Most hotels and other lodgings require you to give your credit-card details before they will confirm your reservation. If you don't feel comfortable emailing this information, ask if you can fax it (some places even prefer faxes). However you book, get confirmation in writing, and have a copy of it handy when you check in.

Be sure you understand the hotel's cancellation policy. Some places allow you to cancel without any kind of penalty—even if you prepaid to secure a discounted rate—if you cancel at least 24 hours in advance. Others require you to cancel a week in advance or penalize you the cost of one night. Small inns and B&Bs are most likely to require you to cancel far in advance. Most hotels allow children under a certain age to stay in their parents' room at no extra charge, but others charge for them as extra adults; find out the cut-off age for discounts. Many of Key West's guesthouses do not allow children under a certain age.

APARTMENT AND HOUSE RENTALS

Although short-term rentals are available throughout the Keys, Key West has the largest inventory, and several rental companies can hook you up. *See Lodging Alternatives in the Key West chapter for local vacation-rental agencies.* National agencies Interhome and Villas International are also good resources for finding a vacation rental in the Keys.

Contacts Interhome. ☎ 954/791–8282, 800/882–6864 ⊕ www.inter-homeusa.com. **Villas International.** ☎ 415/499–9490, 800/221–2260 ⊕ www.villasintl.com.

∎ COMMUNICATIONS

INTERNET

Internet access is the norm in smaller guesthouses, lodges, motels, and resorts. Typically, it's Wi-Fi and often free, although not always available in every room, especially in older concrete-block or tin-roof structures. The larger resorts often charge for the service.

■ EATING OUT

The variety of restaurants in the Keys is vast, but if you were to ask a visitor what is typical, you would probably hear about the colorful seaside fish houses, some with more character than others. Seafood comes so fresh that you'll be spoiled for life. Pay special attention to local catches—especially snapper, mahimahi, grouper, lobster, and stone crab. Florida spiny lobster is local and fresh from August to March, and stone crabs from mid-October to mid-May.

Also keep an eye out for authentic key lime pie. The real McCoy has yellow filling in a graham-cracker crust and tastes pleasantly tart. (If it's green, just say no.) Cuban and Bahamian styles influence local cuisine, so be sure to sample some black beans and rice and conch fritters.

Restaurants may close for a two- to four-week vacation during the slow season—between mid-September and mid-November.

MEALS AND MEALTIMES

Unless otherwise noted, the restaurants listed in this guide are open daily for lunch and dinner.

PAYING

Most restaurants accept major credit cards. Some of the small, family-owned operations do not.

RESERVATIONS AND DRESS

It's a good idea to make a reservation if you can. We only mention them specifically when reservations are essential or not accepted. For popular restaurants, book as far ahead as you can, and reconfirm as

WORD OF MOUTH

Was the service stellar or not up to snuff? Did the food give you shivers of delight or leave you cold? Did the prices and portions make you happy or sad? Rate restaurants and write your own reviews or start a discussion about your favorite places in the Travel Talk Forums on ⊕ www.fodors. com. Your comments might even appear in our books. Yes, you, too, can be a correspondent!

soon as you arrive. (Large parties should always call ahead to check the reservations policy.) Online reservation services make it easy to book a table before you even leave home.

Contacts OpenTable. ⊕ www. opentable.com.

WINE, BEER, AND SPIRITS

If the Keys have a representative tipple, it is the margarita. Several microbreweries have also popped up in recent years.

■ MONEY

ATMs are common throughout the Keys, so there's no need to carry a large amount of money around.

CREDIT CARDS

We cite information about credit cards only if they aren't accepted at a restaurant or a hotel. Otherwise, assume that most major credit cards are acceptable.

Reporting Lost Cards American Express. ☏ 800/528–4800 ⊕ www. americanexpress.com. Diners Club.

☎ 800/234–6377 ⊕ www.dinersclub.
com. **Discover.** ☎ 800/347–2683
⊕ www.discovercard.com. **Master-
Card.** ☎ 800/622–7747 ⊕ www.mas-
tercard.com. **Visa.** ☎ 800/847–2911
⊕ www.visa.com.

▮ TIME

The Florida Keys are in the eastern
time zone. The Dry Tortugas lie in
the central time zone, but the ferries and seaplanes run according
to eastern time. During daylight
saving time, some operations stay
open later.

▮ TIPPING

Tip at restaurants: 15% is suffi-
cient except at the fanciest, most
expensive places, where a larger
tip of around 18% is more common. It's common courtesy to leave
a dollar or two per night for the
housekeeper at your hotel (unless
you are staying at a B&B that's run
by the owners); leave the money
each morning before your room
is cleaned.

▮ VISITOR INFORMATION

There are several separate tourism offices in the Florida Keys, and
you can use Visit Florida's website
(⊕ www.visitflorida.com) for general information and referrals to
local agencies.

**Contacts Big Pine and the Lower
Keys Chamber of Commerce.**
✉ 31020 Overseas Hwy., Big Pine
Key ☎ 305/872–2411, 800/872–
3722 ⊕ www.lowerkeyschamber.
com. **Greater Key West Chamber
of Commerce.** ✉ 510 Greene St.,
1st fl., Key West ☎ 305/294–2587,
800/527–8539 ⊕ www.keywest-
chamber.org. **Greater Marathon
Chamber of Commerce and
Visitor Center.** ✉ MM 53.5 BS,
12222 Overseas Hwy., Marathon
☎ 305/743–5417, 800/262–7284
⊕ www.floridakeysmarathon.com. **Islamorada Chamber of Commerce
& Visitors Center.** ✉ MM 87.1 BS,
87100 Overseas Hwy., Islamorada
☎ 305/664–4503, 800/322–5397
⊕ www.islamoradachamber.com.
Key Largo Chamber of Commerce.
✉ MM 106 BS, 10600 Overseas
Hwy., Key Largo ☎ 305/451–4747,
800/822–1088 ⊕ www.keylargo-
chamber.org.

INDEX

PHOTO CREDITS

Front Cover: Look Die Bildagentur der Fotografen GmbH / Alamy Stock Photo.
[Description: Sunset, Little Palm Island Resort, Florida Keys, USA.] Spine: PHB.cz
(Richard Semik)/Shutterstock. 1, PBorowka/Shutterstock. 2, John Miller / age fotos-
tock. 3 (top), Michael Dwyer / Alamy. 3 (bottom), Todd Taulman/Shutterstock. 4
(top left), Melissa Schalke/ iStockphoto, 4 (top right), George Burba/Shutterstock. 4
(bottom), Fraser Hall / age fotostock. 5, Stephen Frink/TDC/Visit Florida. 6, Robert
J Bennett / age fotostock. 7 (top left), VANILLA FIRE/Shutterstock. 7 (top right),
Dave G. Houser / Alamy. 7 (bottom), Danita Delimont / Alamy. 8 (top left), Marcel
Pepeira / age footstock, 8 (top right), Tim Kiusalaas / age footstock, 8 (bottom),
Angelo Cavalli / age fotostock. 11, Visit Florida. 23, Walter Bibikow / age fotostock.
61, Shackleford Photography/Shutterstock. 79, Johnny Stockshooter / age fotostock.
93, Fotoluminate LLC/Shutterstock. 145, Wilson Araujo/Shutterstock.

About Our Writers: All photos are courtesy of the writers except for the following:
Lynne Helm, courtesy of John Rude.

Fodor's InFocus FLORIDA KEYS

Editorial: Douglas Stallings, *Editorial Director*; Margaret Kelly, Jacinta O'Halloran, *Senior Editors*; Kayla Becker, Alexis Kelly, Amanda Sadlowski, *Editors*; Teddy Minford, *Content Editor*; Rachael Roth, *Content Manager*

Design: Tina Malaney, *Design and Production Director*; Jessica Gonzalez, *Production Designer*

Photography: Jill Krueger, *Senior Photo Editor*

Maps: Rebecca Baer, *Senior Map Editor*; David Lindroth, *Cartographer*

Production: Jennifer DePrima, *Editorial Production Manager*; Carrie Parker, *Senior Production Editor*; Elyse Rozelle, *Production Editor*

Business and Operations: Chuck Hoover, *Chief Marketing Officer*; Robert Ames, *General Manager*; Stephen Horowitz, *Director of Business Development and Revenue Operations*; Tara McCrillis, *Director of Publishing Operations*

Public Relations and Marketing: Joe Ewaskiw, *Manager*; Esther Su, *Marketing Manager*

Writers: Lynne Helm, Jill Martin, Paul Rubio

Editor: Teddy Minford

Production Editor: Carrie Parker

6th edition

ISBN 978-1-64097-194-3

ISSN 1942–7328

Library of Congress Control Number 2018914613

All details in this book are based on information supplied to us at press time. Always confirm information when it matters, especially if you're making a detour to visit a specific place. Fodor's expressly disclaims any liability, loss, or risk, personal or otherwise, that is incurred as a consequence of the use of any of the contents of this book.

SPECIAL SALES

This book is available at special discounts for bulk purchases for sales promotions or premiums. For more information, e-mail SpecialMarkets@fodors.com.

PRINTED IN THE UNITED STATES OF AMERICA

10 9 8 7 6 5 4 3 2 1

ABOUT OUR WRITERS

After being hired sight unseen by a South Florida newspaper, Fort Lauderdale–based freelance travel writer and editor **Lynne Helm** arrived from the Midwest anticipating a few years of palm-fringed fun. More than a quarter century later—after covering the state for several newspapers, consumer magazines, and trade publications—she's still enamored of Florida's sun-drenched charms. Lynne updated the Homestead and Florida City sections of the Gateways to the Keys chapter.

Miami native **Jill Martin** updated the Upper Keys, the Middle Keys, the Lower Keys, and the Key West chapters. As a freelance writer, she has blogged more than 1,000 articles for the state's tourism website, Visit Florida, and also writes for various travel sites and print magazines. She has appeared on numerous TV and radio shows as a Florida travel expert and is the creator of Sunshine Brain Games, a trivia card game all about Florida. She resides full time in Redland and part-time on Sanibel Island.

Paul Rubio 's quest to discover the world has taken him to 110 countries and counting. Paul graduated from Harvard in 2002 with master's degrees in both public administration and economics, but in 2008 he gave into his passion and became a full-time travel writer. He's won over two dozen national awards for his articles and guide-books. The prolific writer is a contributing editor to *Condé Nast Traveler* and the travel editor of *Palm Beach Illustrated* and *Naples Illustrated*. He also regularly contributes to *LUXURY, Robb Report,* and *Private Clubs.*